EVIDENCE-BASED POLICY MAKING IN THE SOCIAL SCIENCES

Methods that matter

Edited by Gerry Stoker and Mark Evans

First published in Great Britain in 2016 by

Policy Press
University of Bristol
1-9 Old Park Hill
Bristol
BS2 8BB
UK
t: +44 (0)117 954 5940
pp-info@bristol.ac.uk
www.policypress.co.uk

North America office:
Policy Press
c/o The University of Chicago Press
1427 East 60th Street
Chicago, IL 60637, USA
t: +1 773 702 7700
f: +1 773-702-9756
sales@press.uchicago.edu
www.press.uchicago.edu

British Library Cataloguing in Publication Data
A catalogue record for this book is available from the British Library

Library of Congress Cataloging-in-Publication Data
A catalog record for this book has been requested

ISBN 978-1-4473-2937-4 paperback
ISBN 978-1-4473-2936-7 hardcover
ISBN 978-1-4473-2939-8 ePub
ISBN 978-1-4473-2940-4 Mobi
ISBN 978-1-4473-2938-1 ePdf

Cover design by Hayes Design
Front cover image: istock
Printed and bound in Great Britain by CMP, Poole
Policy Press uses environmentally responsible print partners

Contents

List of tables, figures and boxes   v
List of abbreviations   vii
Notes on contributors   ix
Acknowledgements   xiii

Introduction   1
Gerry Stoker and Mark Evans

PART ONE: RISING TO THE CHALLENGE

one   Evidence-based policy making and social science   15
    Gerry Stoker and Mark Evans

two   Crafting public policy: choosing the right social science method   29
    Gerry Stoker and Mark Evans

PART TWO: TOOLS FOR SMARTER LEARNING

three   Systematic reviews for policy   43
    David Gough and Janice Tripney

four   Randomised controlled trials   69
    Peter John

five   Qualitative comparative analysis for reviewing evidence and making decisions   83
    Matt Ryan

six   Narrative and storytelling   103
    Vivien Lowndes

seven   Visuals in policy making: 'See what I'm saying'   123
    Leonie J. Pearson and Lain Dare

PART THREE: DEVELOPING DATA MINING

eight   'Big data' and policy learning   143
    Patrick Dunleavy

nine   Cluster analysis in policy studies   169
    Jinjing Li

| ten | Microsimulation modelling and the use of evidence
Robert Tanton and Ben Phillips | 187 |

PART FOUR: BRINGING CITIZENS BACK IN

eleven	Citizen social science and policy making *Liz Richardson*	207
twelve	Deliberative policy analysis *John S. Dryzek*	229
thirteen	Co-design with citizens and stakeholders *Mark Evans and Nina Terrey*	243

| Conclusion: Connecting social science and policy
Gerry Stoker and Mark Evans | 263 |

| References | 271 |
| Index | 305 |

List of tables, figures and boxes

Tables

1.1	Evidence on the non-use of evidence from public officials	17
1.2	Barriers to the use of evidence identified by public officials	18
3.1	Examples of systematic review issues in the four roles of social science in enabling evidence-informed policy and practice	60
5.1	Data matrix	87
5.2	Truth table	89
7.1	Comparing approaches to visual studies	133
7.2	Strengths and challenges of visual methods for policy making	138
8.1	Kitchin's definition of big data	145
8.2	The extended 'tools of government' (or NATOE) framework	147
8.3	Some advantages and disadvantages of using administrative data in a 'big data' mode	150
10.1	Outcome from the 2014–15 budget on couple families with children	200
13.1	Learning tools for co-design	248

Figures

5.1	Fuzzy map of membership in the set of participatory leadership strategy	97
7.1	Q-sort using photographs to determine tourist preferences	129
7.2	Influence diagrams of a respondent who undertook the field trip, showing before (7.2a) and after (7.2b)	131
7.3	Three steps in the use of visual methods in policy making	135
9.1	An example of data points with two clusters	171
9.2	An example of a dendrogram created in a hierarchical cluster analysis	177
10.1	Example of a static tax/transfer microsimulation model	190
10.2	Estimated change in poverty rates from base case to option 1, lone older persons, by SLA, 2008–09	192
13.1	A classic randomised controlled trial	249
13.2	Learning through doing	249
13.3	The International Association for Public Participation spectrum of participation	250
13.4	Learning and co-design	251

Boxes

13.1   Selective list of governmental and non-governmental   245
       organisations devoted to design and innovation
14.1   What would the perfect evidence-based policy system   265
       look like when you have got it?

List of abbreviations

ABS	Australian Bureau of Statistics
ACT	Australian Capital Territory
ADRN	Administrative Data Research Network
AMSTAR	A Measurement Tool to Assess Systematic Reviews
ANPR	Automatic Number Plate Recognition
ANU	Australian National University
API	Application Programming Interface
APPSIM	Australian Population and Policy Simulation Model
ARC	Action Research Collective
ATO	Australian Tax Office
BBC	British Broadcasting Corporation
BIS	Department for Business, Innovation & Skills
BIT	Behavioural Insights Team
BSA	British Social Attitudes (Survey)
CCTV	Closed-circuit Television
CDC	Center for Disease Control
CDCs	Community Development Councils
CDR	Community Driven Reconstruction
CEO	Chief Executive Officer
CGE	Computable General Equilibrium
CSD	Community Services Directorate
CST	Council for Science and Technology
ESRC	Economic and Social Research Council
EU	European Union
FaHCSIA	Department of Families, Housing, Community Services and Indigenous Affairs
FPs	Facilitating Partners
GCHQ	Government Communications Headquarters
GIS	Geographic Information System
GMPAG	Greater Manchester Poverty Action Group
HMCTS	Her Majesty's Courts and Tribunals Service
HMRC	Her Majesty's Revenue and Customs
IAP2	International Association for Public Participation
ICT	Information and Communication Technology
IMA	International Microsimulation Association
ISF	Improving Services with Families
IT	Information Technology
KPMG	Klynveld Peat Marwick Goerdeler
MITTS	Melbourne Institute Tax and Transfer Simulator

MRRD	Ministry of Rural Rehabilitation and Development
NATSEM	National Centre for Social and Economic Modelling
NEF	New Economics Foundation
NGOs	Non-Governmental Organisations
NSP	National Solidarity Programme
NZ	New Zealand
OECD	Organisation for Economic Co-operation and Development
PB	Participatory Budgeting
PhD	Doctor of Philosophy
PRISMA	Preferred Reporting Items for Systematic Reviews and Meta-Analyses
QCA	Qualitative Comparative Analysis
RCT	Randomised Controlled Trial
SAS	Statistical Analysis Software
SF	Score Function
SMEs	Small- and Medium-sized Enterprises
SOCSIM	This is a demographic microsimulation system
SPSS	Statistical Package for the Social Sciences
STEM	Science, Technology, Engineering and Mathematics
UNDP	United Nations Development Programme
UNIDIR	United Nations Institute for Disarmament Research
UK	United Kingdom
US	United States
USA	United States of America
USD	United States dollar

Notes on contributors

Lain Dare is a social researcher with an interest in applied research that delivers real value for study participants and the public. Lain has an interest in designing research that uses a mix of methods to ensure both a robust process and strong stakeholder engagement with the research process and outcomes.

John Dryzek is Australian Research Council Federation Fellow and Centenary Professor in the Centre for Deliberative Democracy and Global Governance, Institute for Governance and Policy Analysis, University of Canberra, Australia. He works mostly in the areas of environmental governance and democratic theory and practice.

Patrick Dunleavy is Professor of Political Science and Public Policy within the Government Department of the London School of Economics (LSE), UK. He is also Co-Director of Democratic Audit and Chair of the LSE Public Policy Group. In addition, Patrick has been appointed to the Institute for Governance and Policy Analysis (IGPA) Centenary Chair at the University of Canberra, Australia.

Mark Evans is Director and Professor of Governance at the Institute for Governance and Policy Analysis at the University of Canberra, Australia. His research focuses on the theory and practice of governance and policy analysis, with a specific emphasis on methods of change governance. Mark has played an international role in supporting good administrative practices in public administration in developed and developing contexts. He has acted as a senior policy advisor, delivered leadership development and managed evaluation projects in 26 countries. Mark is the author, co-author or editor of 24 books in his field and has been the editor of the international journal *Policy Studies* since 2005. He has been awarded honorary positions with the universities of Renmin, York and Hull and is currently a council member of the Institute of Public Administration Australia.

David Gough is Professor of Evidence Informed Policy and Practice and Director of the Social Science Research Unit and its EPPI-Centre, Department of Social Science, University College London. His research is in the development of methods evidence synthesis and in research on the use of research evidence in policy, practice and individual decision making. He is Co-Managing Editor of the journal

Evidence and Policy and an author of the book *Introduction to Systematic Reviews*(1st edition, 2012; 2nd edition, in press).

Peter John is Professor of Political Science and Public Policy in the School of Public Policy, University College London, UK. He is known for his books on public policy: *Analysing public policy* (2nd edn) (2012) and *Making policy work* (2011). He is author, with Keith Dowding, of *Exits, voices and social investment: Citizens' reaction to public services* (2012) and, with Anthony Bertelli, *Public policy investment* (2013). He uses experiments to study civic participation in public policy, with the aim of finding out what governments and other public agencies can do to encourage citizens to carry out acts of collective benefit. This work appeared in *Nudge, nudge, think, think: Using experiments to change civic behaviour* (Gerry Stoker and Liz Richardson were also co-authors), which was published by Bloomsbury Academic in 2011. He is a member of the academic advisory panel of the UK Behavioural Insights Team, and is involved in a number of projects that seek to test out behavioural insights with trials, such as the redesign of tax reminders and encouraging channel shift. He co-edits *The Journal of Public Policy* for Cambridge University Press.

Dr Jinjing Li is currently an Associate Professor at the National Centre For Social And Economic Modelling at the Institute for Governance and Policy Analysis (NATSEM/IGPA), University of Canberra, Australia. His research interests include applied statistical methodology development, microsimulation modelling and labour and health economics. Dr Li has developed a wide range of economic and social simulation models for various government departments and international organisations.

Vivien Lowndes is Professor of Public Policy at the Institute of Local Government Studies, University of Birmingham, UK. She researches institutional change in English local governance, and is currently looking at how different 'traditions' underpin responses to austerity. She is the author (with Mark Roberts) of *Why institutions matter* (Palgrave, 2013).

Leonie J. Pearson is an applied economist at the University of Canberra, Australia, who has provided methodological advice and guidance to students and policymakers over the past two decades. Her interest in using the right method for the job has developed her broad experience in using alternate methods to deliver high policy impact.

Ben Phillips is an Associate Professor at the Australian National University. He has nearly 20 years of experience in economic and public policy analysis work in Australia. Ben's expertise is in the development of microsimulation models for the purpose of analysing tax and transfer systems. Ben also has broad experience in economic modelling, economic statistics and public policy in Australia.

Liz Richardson is Reader in Politics at the University of Manchester, UK. Her work explores how citizens, scientists, practitioners and policymakers can work together for evidence-based social change. She has an interest in methodological innovation, including field experiments and other participatory research approaches to discovering 'what works' in complex policy environments.

Dr Matt Ryan is a Lecturer in Governance and Public Policy at the University of Southampton, UK. His research interests and publications focus on understanding new forms of citizen participation in politics through democratic innovations and the use of methodological innovations in political and social science, including qualitative comparative analysis and field experiments.

Gerry Stoker is Centenary Research Professor at the University of Canberra, Australia, and also Chair in Governance at the University of Southampton, UK. His two most recent books came out in 2015: *The relevance of political science* (edited with Guy Peters and Jon Pierre) and *Nuclear power and energy policy: The limits to governance* (co-authored with Keith Baker).

Robert Tanton is Professor of Economics at the National Centre for Social and Economic Modelling in the Institute for Governance and Policy Analysis at the University of Canberra, Australia. His research interests are in spatial microsimulation, spatial disadvantage and small-area modelling. He has published widely on spatial microsimulation internationally, and spatial disadvantage in Australia.

Nina Terrey is one of ThinkPlace's global executive team and has been at the frontier of applying design in complex contexts within the public sector. Nina is an Adjunct Associate Professor at the Institute of Governance and Policy Analysis, University of Canberra, Australia. Nina is a frequent speaker at international design and innovation conferences.

Janice Tripney is a Lecturer in Social Policy at the Department of Social Science, University College London, UK. Her publications and research interests are relatively broad and eclectic, including systematic review projects in education and international development, and the use of biographical methods to study early 20th-century female social scientists and the roots of modern social policies. She is an editorial board member of the *London Review of Education*.

Acknowledgements

This book emerged out of a conference that took place on Thursday 19 and Friday 20 February 2015 at Old Parliament House, Canberra, Australia. We would like to thank all those who participated in the workshop and especially the policymakers, who provided the first test for the ideas and arguments presented in this book and gave us the confidence to go on. The costs for that conference were generously covered by the University of Canberra, Australia.

Thereafter, we received some very helpful suggestions from colleagues at Policy Press about how to frame the book and present its ideas to the widest possible audience. We are very grateful to all our authors for finding the time in their demanding schedules to offer up a chapter for an edited book, an activity not always approved of by those managers in universities focused on research assessment returns. We would also like to thank the referees for the book, who helped to challenge and thereby tighten up chapters and arguments.

The final production of the book owes a huge amount to Marion Carter, PhD candidate at the Institute for Governance and Policy Analysis, University of Canberra, who showed a great deal of skill and understanding in ensuring that the book was completed.

Above all, our hope is that the book is used. We think that the social sciences have some very exciting and valuable techniques to offer to policymakers and influencers, both in government and outside in civil society. We want to help our university colleagues throughout the world to share their expertise. We do not think that access to good-quality social science techniques will lead automatically to social problems being solved, but we do think that it will help. After using this book, we hope that readers agree.

Gerry Stoker and Mark Evans, April 2016

Introduction

Gerry Stoker and Mark Evans

Social science has a range of methods that can provide evidence-based policy insights. The purpose of this book is to make the case that the social sciences are more relevant than ever in helping solve the problems of public policy. We provide a critical showcase for new forms of discovery drawn from the social sciences that can be applied in policy making, and do so by drawing on the insights of some of the world's leading authorities in public policy analysis. There are many forms of social science discovery that draw from beyond the established or most prominently used tools. They include making more use of randomised controlled trials (RCTs), the analysis of big data, deliberative tools for decision-making, qualitative techniques for comparison using Boolean and fuzzy-set logic, the practice of citizen science, applying design thinking, learning from narratives used by policymakers and citizens, policy visualisation, spatial mapping, simulation modelling, and various forms of statistical analysis (such as cluster analysis). So, the heart of the book is an attempt to expand the awareness of both researchers and policymakers to the contribution that the social sciences can make.

In this introduction, we aim to do some of the ground clearing necessary to make the overall argument of the book more effective. First, we deal with the issue of what the social sciences actually constitute and why we think that they are more relevant today than in the past. Second, we clarify what the core claim of the social sciences can be in respect of solving societal problems. It is not some grand claim to produce a science of society that, if followed, would lead to all societal ills being vanquished; rather, it is a more modest and prosaic set of declarations about how an evidence base provided through rigorous social science can help. Finally, we need to explain our sense that only a limited number of social science techniques are regularly used in policy making and make the case for a wider pluralism and expansion. After these tasks have been undertaken, the introduction concludes with an outline of the remainder of the book.

The rise of the social sciences

The distinctions between different types of academic subjects do not stand up to a great deal of scrutiny. We might think that there are neat lines to be drawn between science-based disciplines, the social sciences and the humanities (these are traditional ways of expressing divides within the university sector), but, in practice, those lines are often blurred. There is an overlap in areas of interest and a sharing in the methods used. When engineers move from the laboratory to the field and propose solutions to deal with water management and distribution in developing countries that involve the establishment of complex human institutional devices, are they doing science or social science? When an RCT looks at behaviour in classrooms in the hands of educational studies researchers (normally classified as social scientists) rather than the trialling of a new medicine by medical researchers (usually classified as scientists), is it any less scientific? The distinctions between types of academic study are not without value but they can lead to a false sense of difference that is neither helpful nor justified.

In particular, we see no great value in making claims that some subjects are 'hard' science – physics, chemistry, mathematics and medicine, for example – while others are 'soft' science, such as the social sciences, which would include economics, sociology, political studies, human geography, social policy and a range of other disciplines (for a full list, see Bastow et al, 2014: 6, Figure 1.2). That the 'hard' sciences deliver useable knowledge and the 'soft' sciences mere informed speculation might be the claim that follows the distinction. However, such a proposition does more harm than good and overlooks a crucial question for the policymaker and, for that matter, a citizen. The issue is not how academia draws up its dividing lines, but rather about which types of research can contribute to the problems we confront: does the research tell us what we need to know? The core concern is not how you know, but what you want to know. If knowledge is going to be useful, it has to be knowledge about something we need to know about.

Our argument is that, if anything, the social sciences have become more relevant because what we as policymakers and citizens need to know more about is how to make human-influenced or human-constructed systems work more effectively. Bastow et al (2014: 20–1) make an argument here that is helpful. They suggest that if we examine technological and developmental trends, it becomes clear that there are relatively fewer purely natural systems and, increasingly, systems are either human-influenced or human-dominated. They suggest that we need to think in terms of purely natural systems as on the decline and human-created systems, such as governments or markets, as on the rise. In addition, there has been an expansion of human-influenced systems, primarily physical environments where human interventions and activity are making a significant difference. The domain of human-dominated systems is that of the social sciences without doubt, but so, too, to a degree, is that of human-influenced systems.

The field for those disciplines that study those natural systems remains, of course, a vast and complex area for discovery. There remains a considerable amount of our physical environment that is untouched by human activity and these purely natural systems are the proper domain of astrophysics or pure mathematics, but they are being squeezed by the extensive impact of humankind on our environment. Even beyond the Earth, worries about the debris created by decaying human-launched satellites led one of the editors of this volume being asked by a natural scientist about social science lessons about the behaviour change being undertaken to encourage compliance down on Earth in the hope that they might apply in orbit (for a discussion of some of those lessons, see John et al, 2011). Human activity plainly stretches into many physical systems.

Human-influenced systems are rightly a focus of attention for policymakers and citizens. These are physical systems where humans have had an impact and we are often concerned to extend, mitigate or ameliorate that impact, which implies understanding the physical environment and how it is changing but also how human behaviour is affecting it and how that, in turn, might be changed. The issues of, for example, climate change, marine management, agriculture and environmental protection all fit into the category where social science research might have to be part of the mix for policymakers and citizens interested in learning from evidence. Human-created or -dominated systems could be seen to encompass all the features of human civilisation – obviously, governments, markets and so on – but other features such as cities or information technology (IT) systems, as well as various cultural products and processes. So, here, social sciences would share the terrain with the humanities and its interest in arts, culture and literature.

The argument is that the social sciences should be seen as at least an equal of the sciences of natural systems, and perhaps, rather, the science with an expanding agenda. Little wonder then that, according to Bastow et al (2014: 29), 'between a third and two fifths of all university research (and much of the wider professional, government and business research) being undertaken in advanced industrial societies takes place in social science subjects'. In the light of the growing importance of either human-influenced or -dominated systems (which are central to our well-being), the issue for policymakers and citizens is whether they are making the most of the social sciences. A lot of research is being done by social scientists about matters that we do need to know about, so should we not be keen to exploit it more?

What does social science offer?

[handwritten margin note: I am not sure people care about big right]

Lack of clarity about what social science research can offer is one stumbling block that could explain why social science might struggle to establish itself. There are other reasons why evidence from social science does not influence policymakers or is ignored in citizen debates. We will look in more detail at the complex issues that limit the impact of social science research (and other research) in the first main chapter of the book. For now, having made an argument about how the problems that our world faces have a strong and growing human dimension to them – making the *prima facia* case for the social sciences – we ask what it is that social science has to offer.

In the 19th century and in several periods in the 20th century, some advocates of social science suggested that what was on offer was either a full-blown or at least embryonic 'science of society'. The prospect of generating general laws – true for all time about human behaviour – has now faded but the sense that social science has somehow failed to live up to that unrealistic promise perhaps explains a sense among policymakers and citizens that social science has not delivered. After all, no less a person than the UK's Queen felt it necessary to ask after the financial crisis of 2007/08, during a visit to the London School of Economics, why economists had not been able to predict the impending fiscal problems (Pierce, 2008). The burden of failing to live up to the demands of creating insights that are true for all time, or all-seeing predictions, asked of social science something that it was not able to deliver. Indeed, research tends to find complexities and variations in behaviour that make the quest for neat and frugal laws of social behaviour a mission impossible (Weiss, 1998). Lindblom, in two important works (Lindblom and Cohen, 1979; Lindblom, 1990), is very clear about the need for social science to be modest about what it can claim to discover. There is no 'science of society' that can guarantee policymakers and citizens the right answers to the challenging issues facing society.

[handwritten margin note: More like Popper's planned social engineered]

[handwritten margin note: Can't answer the big picture]

If boasts of technocratic solution provision have to be abandoned (and we admit that some social scientists are reluctant to forgo that option), we do not think that social science is without a clear-cut answer to its usefulness. What social science can offer is expressed by two strong movements in the development of the discipline (Bastow et al, 2014). The first is the move to support evidence-based policy making by getting better at connecting social science research to policy decisions. Governments, research funders and researchers have taken steps to ensure that research is better shared, communicated and disseminated as part of a wider modernisation of government that came to the fore in many liberal democracies from the 1970s onwards (Bulmer et al, 2007). The second movement could be referred to as 'best practice' research, which deals less with the construction of new research and more with the dissemination of existing research in a way that makes it useable and accessible. Again, there have been institutional developments to advance and promote the capacity to share research. At the most sophisticated end of the spectrum, there is a focus on systematic reviews (see Chapter Three) to provide a rigorous assessment of the available evidence. There are still other valuable good practice guides that provide 'quick and dirty' attempts to assemble what is known, even if the quality of evidence is limited.

Understanding about the use of evidence has become more sophisticated as it has moved from an initial emphasis on 'what works' as being a simple technical matter of designing research tests or pilots of policy measures, to a more subtle recognition that policy influence occurs in a variety of ways. As Nutley et al (2007) show, research can illuminate ways of thinking about an issue, as well as the policy choices available. It can provide empirical evidence but also a conceptual apparatus to challenge and develop existing understandings of issues. Good research may sometimes deliver solutions but it may also often offer a better debate about potential decisions. That contribution can stretch beyond initial conceptualisation of policy options to the processes of implementation. Although we might have evidence that something works at some place and at one time, policy making still needs evidence that it will work in other cases or more particularly in the case in hand. What is required is 'effectiveness' evidence, as Cartwright and Hardie (2012) put it, evidence that some policy measure will work for your organisation, locality or community of interest in addition to knowledge that it has worked elsewhere. In short, we need not only relevant evidence about what works, but also evidence about whether that evidence is relevant to the case in hand. Are the support factors that drove success in place in the new setting? If some are missing, what will be the effect? What could go wrong in implementation? Are there special factors at play in the success of the pilot that would not be in place at roll-out? Above all, research works in an interactive way with policy: 'Research use thus involves two-way rather than unilinear flows of knowledge, in which researchers and research users each bring their own expertise' (Nutley et al, 2007: 305).

The policy process is best supported by continuous acts of exploring, investigating and, yes, research. Social scientists, policymakers and citizens should be working alongside one another in these tasks. Problems are more likely to be tackled, subdued and ameliorated. They may go away in one form, only to reappear in another form at a later time. Learning and discovery are therefore at the heart of good policy making, and they need to be at the heart of the relationship between social science and policy making. Discovery captures the sense of exploration, challenge, checking and rechecking that is required for effective policy making in a complex world. It also engages with the sense that there are many unknowns in any policy decision and that a sense of open investigation is therefore essential.

The case for pluralism in the social sciences

We have shown that knowledge of human behaviour relevant to the human-influenced and human-dominated systems is what makes social science valuable and that social science research delivers not a technocratic fix, but an enhanced capacity to understand policy problems and solutions. So, social science and policy making should be friends not enemies. We need now to make the case for why a key challenge for policy making is to extend awareness of the range and variety of social science techniques and approaches that are available. Our argument breaks into three elements. First, we argue that policymakers, as well as researchers, need to abandon the search for evidence that claims to have discovered 'the truth', which is then used to close down or cut short discussion about a policy option. Some types of social science make that approach easier to sustain but wider appreciation of what social science has to offer makes it unsustainable. Second, we want to get evidence to stretch over the full range of the policy cycle, from policy development, through implementation to evaluation, which, in turn, argues for different techniques and tools to draw on. Finally, we want to argue for the value of diverse ways of knowing, which leads on to the case for celebrating the diversity of the social sciences.

Our starting point is, yet again, Charles Lindblom, the thorn in the side of those social scientists who want to claim that they and they alone have the answer to societal problems: 'No one engaged in social problem solving or in observing the process as ordinary citizen, official, or expert can claim to know, to be able to demonstrate, or to command agreement on how problem solving can best be done' (Lindblom, 1990: x). This statement was both meant to put social science in its place and to emphasise the pluralist mantra that the best policy process is one that allows scope for multiple voices and, indeed, forms of knowledge that stretch from the technical to the local. Curiously, giving up the mantra that 'we know the answer' is a trickier thing to do for policymakers and social scientists in contemporary democracies than it might initially appear given the democratic imperative for valuing many voices. Deciding authoritatively is such a valuable resource in the practice of policy making that it is very tempting to embrace methods that give that veneer of authority. It is clear that some forms of social science are favoured by policymakers because they are more likely to provide that veneer. Cost–benefit analyses or surveys, we will suggest, can give that sense of convincing, solid and irrefutable evidence that clinches a public policy argument. They are valuable tools, we can concede, but they cannot claim a special relationship with 'the truth' since they are built on a web of assumptions and premises that need to be both understood and respected, not venerated or worshipped.

Cost–benefit analysis is a valuable tool, for sure, but its contribution to the policy process can be narrow in focus and can be disputed in practice. It is limited in what it can offer in that it is best at weighing up fully formed policy options rather than creating or developing those options. Second, its judgements are not the product of an unchallengeable technocratic process, but, rather, emerge out of a form of economic and utilitarian reasoning that has strengths but also significant limitations. At first glance, who could object to the idea of weighing up the costs and benefits of contesting programmes by assigning monetary values to the two policies and judging which one delivers the greatest amount of benefit over costs? The problem comes when cost–benefit analysis is touted as a general standard by which to make efficient and wise public policy decisions. There are several flaws that have been identified, which are boldly summarised by Ackerman (2008: 30–1):

> Cost–benefit analysis, widely favored today as a technique for making public policy decisions, is a failure both in theory and in practice. In theory, it cannot comprehend important but priceless values, cannot escape the assumption that everything is for sale and can be traded off against everything else, and cannot accurately reflect the central role of uncertainty and the need for precaution in practice. It persistently tilts toward overstating costs, toward trivializing the future, and toward replacing clear policy debates with obscure technical quarrels.

7

There are those who come to a more positive judgement about cost–benefit analysis (see Adler and Posner, 2001), but even that assessment is not without a strong recognition of its scope and limitations as a technique.

Surveys are another tool strongly favoured by policymakers, but, again, as any good social scientist that uses the technique knows, it is not a method without its challenges and problems (Pastek and Krosnick, 2010). Sampling can be a concern, especially if the survey is aimed at anything other than the most unproblematic representative sample. Question wording or ordering can be an issue and may influence responses. On many issues that they have had no reason to think about or consider, the responses of the public can appear to be unconsidered and even contradictory, appearing to want to capture two incompatible views at the same time. The analysis of the survey may exploit some responses rather than others and more sophisticated forms of multivariate analysis can reveal insights but also need to be judged carefully in terms on the assumptions that are being made. In this light, surveys remain a powerful tool but they need to be treated less as the final word on the issue of policy approval and more as the basis for future discussion.

The use of the social sciences in policy making needs to be less about delivering the killer blow in terms of policy discussion and more about illuminating and expanding knowledge and understanding about the issue of concern. We need to expand our horizons beyond those methods that give a false sense of certainty and authority to the policy process, and instead give greater credence to the scale and diversity of approaches to discovery that are available.

A pluralist set of skills and approaches from the social sciences also makes more sense if the aim is to look at the policy process across time. Some methods may be suited to initiating policy proposals, others may be more effective at enabling choices to be made between options and some may be better at thinking through implementation or evaluating options. The issue of matching social science methods to particular policy issues or challenges is addressed further in Chapter Two.

There is also a more general argument for the value of different ways of knowing. Social sciences can reveal truths in different ways, and there is value in that pluralism. As Nutley et al (2007: 299) comment: 'we see important roles for diverse ways of knowing, with a major challenge for research use being how these various ways are brought together and, if not reconciled, then at least accommodated'. In the range of methods offered in the book, we will see options that draw on more of a positivist understanding of how to know that emphasise

8

the sense that there is a reality to be discovered, for example, RCTs or some of the statistical methods fall into that grouping. Other approaches would fit more comfortably with a constructivist approach, which would be keen to explore the meanings and understandings that people attach to events and policy concerns, such as, for example, approaches that rely on learning from narratives or perhaps working through deliberation. Understanding human-influenced and -dominated systems can be advanced by taking on board approaches from across the social sciences.

That we should use evidence to help us to decide what to do is not disputed. That it is not the only factor at play in policy making is impossible to deny. The argument that this book addresses is that the task of developing better policy is too often being tackled with a very limited number of tools on offer from the social sciences. Hunches, professional judgement, experience and mutual adjustment fill the vacuum left by the failure of the social sciences to engage in a way that helps. They often do a good job but they would do a better job if the richness of social science methods and approaches was more regularly brought into play. As Charles Lindblom (1990: x) argues: 'Society's probe of a social problem is at best open-ended and pursued by a multiplicity of methods'. Lindblom's main point was that social science expertise needs to learn to work alongside other forms of investigating and understanding. We do not disagree with that point, but we want to stress that there is more variety within social science and therefore more scope in what it can offer to the process of policy making than is widely appreciated (and perhaps even Lindblom recognised).

The structure of the book

The argument of the book is divided into four parts. In Part One, we identify two core issues about how to connect social science and evidence-based policy making. The first is dealt with in Chapter One and is about avoiding accusations of naivety about the prospects for social science to influence public policy. Social science and policy making are not natural 'best' friends. Policymakers express frustration that social science often appears to have little of relevance to say and social scientists will regularly complain that policymakers are not interested in using their evidence. Yet, the two groups appear, almost against the will of the participants in them, to be thrown together. Policymakers are told to evidence their policies and social scientists are urged to step up to provide that evidence. The two sides can be locked in a distant, difficult and disobliging relationship. The aim of

Chapter One is to help to improve that situation by identifying some of the main blockages on either side of the social science and policy making fence and see how they can be addressed.

How can policymakers and social scientists better work together to produce more useable knowledge? We take from Lindblom and Cohen (1979) the idea that 'useable knowledge' refers to the production and exchange of knowledge that enables a society to move from one position to another that is more desired. Building a better relationship between social science and policy will require a degree of learning or relearning from each side of the fence. Chapter Two takes into account another key issue: how the choice between social options offers the best prospect for progress in different policy contexts. This chapter aims to give a realistic account of how to select a method, and so provides the reader with a guiding introduction to the methods that follow.

Part Two of the book begins the process of looking at a wider range of social science approaches and groups a range of approaches under the heading of smarter forms of learning. In Chapter Three, David Gough and Janice Tripney argue that learning from existing evidence is a key skill for both researchers and policymakers. But how do you go about doing that? What are the key approaches, how do you make the right choices and what are the common pitfalls? The chapter gives the reader a guide to best practice in systematic reviews.

In Chapter Four, Peter John reflects on the growing use of and acclaim for RCTs as a method of policy discovery. The chapter outlines the social science thinking behind the tool, provides some examples of its use and then discusses its strengths and weaknesses. Chapter Five looks at another technique – qualitative comparative analysis – that has grown in popularity in the social sciences to analyse situations with comparative rigour through access to medium-N. In this, Matt Ryan explores the logic of Boolean and fuzzy-set analysis and then applications to policy learning are identified. The chapter will offer an assessment of the limitations but also the enormous potential of the technique.

In Chapter Six, Vivien Lowndes discusses how policymakers tell stories all the time. Each piece of legislation and policy advice is a narrative in its own right, proposing specific links between ideas, actions and institutions. But what stories do they listen to in formulating policy, and can social scientists influence this process? Chapter Six argues that by constructing stories that 'resonate' with policymakers' everyday experience (based on case studies, action research, appreciative enquiry or ethnography), social scientists are able to facilitate processes of critical reflection and creative thinking.

10

In Chapter Seven, Leonie J. Pearson and Lain Dare look at the technique of visualisation. We see the world and experience it through images, and so policy making can engage citizens through those processes and support a way of learning that does not rely solely on written reports and arguments.

In Part Three of the book, we group a range of methods under the heading of developing data mining. We live in a data-rich world but it is not effectively exploited, so a big opportunity for the social sciences rests in showing that it can access techniques that allow the mass of available information to be tied into policy considerations. In Chapter Eight, Patrick Dunleavy explores how the revolutionary capacity of analysing big data to understand human behaviour is only just beginning to be exploited by social science, and it is opening new opportunities for discovery for policymakers. Again, this chapter will explore its social science foundations, some applications to policy and then address strengths and weaknesses. In Chapter Nine, Jinjing Li explores how cluster analysis could be used to a greater degree by policymakers. The origins of these techniques plus some examples of their practice will be explored, along with a discussion of the scope and limitations of their use. Finally, in Chapter Ten, Robert Tanton and Ben Phillips provide an overview of microsimulation modelling and how it is used to evaluate policy, with an emphasis on tax and government cash benefits. The chapter will provide a brief history and introduction to microsimulation modelling.

In Part Four, we capture a range of techniques that focus on giving a powerful role to citizens in research. In Chapter Eleven, Liz Richardson argues that there is a growing capacity in the social sciences to include people not as subjects, but as active participants in research. This approach has a complex history in the social sciences that needs to be understood but it is emerging in a modern form as a viable technique for discovery, especially among hard-to-reach groups. Examples of citizen science are presented and the strengths and weaknesses of the technique are explored.

In Chapter Twelve, John S. Dryzek shows how open deliberation can enhance the legitimacy of policy making and also, as a science, overcome the bounded rationality of individuals. Chapter Twelve explores the value of deliberation in evaluation, especially in an environment policy context, not as a tool for democracy per se, but as a tool for better policy. The social science background to these claims will be explored and examples are given of the application of deliberation to better policy making. Finally, the strengths and weaknesses of the approach will be explored. In Chapter Thirteen,

Mark Evans and Nina Terrey examine how design thinking, with its commitment to seeing challenges from a user perspective, prototyping and rapid learning, has begun to make headway in the policy world as a technique to review service delivery practices. Chapter Thirteen will review the thinking behind it, connecting design to various social science theories and showing applications of the technique.

PART ONE:
RISING TO THE CHALLENGE

ONE

Evidence-based policy making and social science

Gerry Stoker and Mark Evans

There are good reasons why social science and evidence-based policy making are not always in tune with each other. The aim of this chapter is to help improve and advance the relationship between the two, but, equally, we do not want to fall into the trap of being naive about the inherently challenging character of the relationship. There are features of the way that policy processes operate and social science works that create tensions in the relationship. It is these tensions that we explore in this chapter.

Evidence provided by social science can be misused by political interests, the media can oversimplify complex research findings and, occasionally, the political leaning of the researchers may inappropriately colour the objectivity of the research or at least those parts of the results that are most widely promoted. We can also view as naive an understanding of the policy process as driven by the rational decision-making model. The policy process is not characterised by temporal neatness. The policy process only rarely follows the linear process of conceptualising the problem, designing an intervention, providing solutions and evaluating that intervention. As all the established policy making models tell us, from the multiple streams framework to punctuated-equilibrium models (for a review, see Sabatier, 2007), the policy process involves a complex set of elements that interact over time. Problems, solutions and political opportunities may all become prominent at different times. It is clear that researchers hardly ever find themselves in the position of problem-solving where there is an agreed view of a challenge and a consensus that something should be done about it. Only rarely will the conditions emerge for a pure problem-solving model: a clear and shared definition of the problem, timely and appropriate research answers, political actors willing to listen and the absence of strong opposing forces. Much more often, social scientists, like many other policy players, struggle to find the appropriate window of opportunity in which to make their impact.

Policy making is a political process and we will show how policymakers themselves view constraints on their capacity to take up and use evidence. Evidence is joined by many other factors in determining policy choices, and various system, culture, institutional and environmental factors limit the capacity of policymakers to take evidence on board. These factors can provide external barriers to the impact of evidence. In the second part of the chapter, we explore how social science has several internal barriers to delivering appropriate and valuable evidence to policymakers. Social scientists in universities, in particular, in most Western countries, have professional and career incentives to focus on research that does not have a strong applied dimension. Many academics have doubts about the normative issues thrown up by engaging with power structures and actors through policy making. Historically, social science has developed with a greater focus on providing critical commentary than on offering solutions.

Evidence on the limits to evidence

Drawing on work undertaken by one of us (Evans) derived from a series of executive workshops with senior policy officials held in Australia, the UK and New Zealand (NZ) during 2012–14, we can clearly show that while evidence is viewed as vital to policy thinking and decision-making, it can also be a luxury item used as window dressing rather than as the decisive factor in decision-making. As Table 1.1 indicates, policymakers are clear that evidence is an insufficient criterion for winning the war of ideas in a contested policy environment, and they could identify a range of barriers to evidence-based policy making and the use of high-quality policy advice.

On the issue of whether evidence is a sufficient criterion for winning the war of ideas, strong majorities recognised the importance of evidence as a necessary condition of better policy making, but the vast majority identified an ongoing tension between short-term imperatives of governing and evidence-based policy making, combined with 'ministerial indifference over the facts' as a constraint. Rather than the evidence steering policy, public officials argued that they spent most of their time retrofitting evidence to support decisions that had already been taken – what can be termed 'policy-based evidence-making' (Evans and Edwards, 2011).

There were some differences in attitudes among policy officials. Notably, more respondents who had been in the service for 10 years or more perceived that the use of evidence in policy making was in 'dramatic decline', and women were demonstrably more cynical

Table 1.1: Evidence on the non-use of evidence from public officials

Country	Male	Female
'Evidence is a condition of better policy making' (agree)		
Australia	94	97
UK	97	97
NZ	93	95
% time spent on developing new policy, programmes or interventions through a 'rational process of learning'		
Australia	24	20
UK	27	22
NZ	18	17
% time spent on 'retrofitting evidence to decisions that have already been taken'		
Australia	76	80
UK	73	78
NZ	82	83
% who believe that 'there is an ongoing tension between short-term imperatives and evidence-based policy making'		
Australia	84	85
UK	85	87
NZ	82	84
% who agree that 'there is ministerial indifference over the facts'		
Australia	64	62
UK	59	63
NZ	61	64

than men. The type of department/agency also mattered. The more technical and less politicised the department, the greater the focus on evidence-based policy making. It is also important to note the general perception that austerity, particularly in the UK and NZ, was driving out evidence-based policy making. In both cases, large-scale retrenchment appears to have had short-term impacts on strategic policy capability, such as the loss of specialist expertise and institutional memory. Subsequently, a range of interventions were introduced in both countries to address these issues.

In more detailed deliberations, the policymakers identified a range of barriers to the use of evidence in policy making. We organised these responses (see Table 1.2) around four sets of constraints: 'construction' barriers refer to how evidence-based policy making is perceived and practised; 'environmental' barriers are those barriers that are outside the control of policy officers but impact directly on their work; 'institutional' barriers capture the impact of organisation structures, resources and roles that can block the use of evidence; and 'system'

Table 1.2: Barriers to the use of evidence identified by public officials

Construction barriers	Environmental barriers
• Pathology of the short term • Competing understanding of its merits (political versus bureaucratic) reflected in an anti-evidence culture • Ministerial indifference towards evidence • Culture of risk aversion • Poor commissioning of research	• 24/7 media cycle • Crowded policy spaces (institutional layering) • Public expectations for quick fixes • Prevailing socio-economic conditions • Problems inherent in multi-level governance (less evident in NZ and UK) • Poor strategic alignment across government
Institutional barriers	**System barriers**
• Absence of clear roles and responsibilities for policy officers • Dominant agenda-setting role of special advisors • Poor engagement capacity of policy officers	• Lack of support from politicians • Short-term budgets and planning horizons • Delivery pressures and administrative burdens • Poor rewards and incentives • Capability deficit in political awareness

barriers refer to norms, rules and processes embedded in governance that inhibit evidence-based policy making.

The electoral and 24/7 media cycles have created a strong pathology for fast thinking – 'off the shelf' solutions to policy problems. Evidence-based policy making is associated with slow thinking processes that cannot be immediately integrated into decision-making processes at a time when politicians are looking for quick, high-impact fixes to the problems they are facing. At a bare minimum, there does appear to be some ministerial and political indifference towards evidence (although there are always exceptions to this rule), and where social scientists are deployed in problem-solving processes, their engagement tends to be driven through interpersonal relationships with policymakers. There is also mounting evidence that special political advisors play a key agenda-setting role in Westminster systems, particularly in Australia and the UK, and tend to be champions of 'policy-based evidence-making' (see Eichbaum and Shaw, 2007, 2008, 2011; Tiernan, 2007; Gains and Stoker, 2011; Boston, 2012; Rhodes and Tiernan, 2014). Paradoxically, these perceptions tend to be equated with notions of risk aversion, when the case for evidence-based policy making would appear strongest as the risk of failure is greatest. What is certain is that ministers have a greater range of sources of policy advice than ever before and social scientists (as well as internal policy officers) need to understand that they are engaged in a war of ideas.

The construction barriers are in some ways the greatest stumbling block to the use of evidence, but as Table 1.2 shows, policymakers could also identify a range of environmental, institutional and system barriers to the use of evidence. There are more environmental pressures that push for not using evidence than push for using it. There are institutional factors that limit the capacity to use evidence. The wider system has many constraints set against evidence use. It would appear, then, that there are many obstacles in the policy world that make it less than a hospitable world for academic research findings. As Carol Weiss (1979: 431) remarks:

> There has been much glib rhetoric about the vast benefits that social science can offer if only policymakers paid attention. Perhaps it is time for social scientists to pay attention to the imperatives of policy-making systems and to consider soberly what they can do, not necessarily to increase the use of research, but to improve the contribution that research makes to the wisdom of social policy.

Understanding and challenging the barriers to evidence

It is important to recognise that the barriers to the use of evidence are not driven by the wilful ignorance of policymakers; rather, they are a reflection of their world. The 'listening but not listening policymakers' (that is those that look at evidence but do not use it) phenomena can reflect the desire of politicians just to exercise their own choices regardless of evidence or at the behest of powerful interests, but there are other factors more often at work that reflect less the perversity of politics and more its complexity. The good news is that these factors can be ameliorated to some degree by the way that academics behave. In short, the barriers to the use of evidence cannot be addressed if those reflect a wilful determination to neglect evidence, but if they reflect the complex dynamics of a policy decision, then by understanding those dynamics better, social scientists offering evidence can have a greater impact.

A primary question for the policymaker is: why should I pay attention to this issue rather than many others? When academics enter the policy process, they naturally assume that process started when they entered, but, of course, it did not. As noted earlier, there are only limited windows of opportunity when an issue becomes sufficiently pressing to encourage a focus on it. Understanding the rhythms of policy making around manifestos, big speeches, set-piece agenda-setting opportunities around the Budget or other much more low-key developments can help with getting the timing of the intervention right. Part of the art of having an impact is being in the right place at the right time and then, of course, being able to act when the opportunity presents itself.

Policymakers will sometimes say, and often think, 'bring me solutions not just problems'. As noted later in the chapter, there are factors in the internal construction of social science evidence that can limit its impact. Academic research is often more focused on identifying an issue of concern and its dynamics rather than focusing on potential actions or interventions (they may get mentioned in the last paragraph of a report). Explanation is plainly central to what we do, but academics could perhaps do more to take on the challenge of designing solutions. There still remains an issue in that academics often couch their arguments in terms of the limits of the evidence and policymakers might, in turn, seek a more definitive position. Again, this concern is not insurmountable and one response is for the academic to take the position of 'honest broker', laying out options and choices for the policymaker.

If an intervention is identified that should work, it is still subject to challenge about its administrative, financial and political feasibility. The question for policymakers is not 'Can it be done?', but rather 'Can it be done by *this* government at *this* time?'. Showing that a policy response proposed is right (a solution to the identified problem) is only half that battle, if that. For the policymaker, it is not what works, but what is feasible, that matters. Can the challenges of administration, resourcing and political support and ownership be met? When academics step into the world of policy making, they should be sensitive and as informed as possible about these challenges; avoid giving the appearance of naivety, this is not a strong selling point when trying to persuade. The question for the policymaker is not simply 'Do I support this policy?', but rather 'How much energy and political capital would I have to expend to make the policy win through against opposition from other sources?'. Policymakers know that there are only a limited number of things that they can realistically achieve, and they may have other more pressing priorities. Picking the policymaker both able and willing to run with a policy is by no means easy, but academics need to be aware of this factor in the policy making process and think clearly about how to make the policy appear doable.

Let us say that a cadre of policymakers buy into the idea of doing something but their enthusiasm then gets tested in the wider arena of policy making. They have to show not only that the policy will beat the problem and that it is feasible and doable, but that it can also win in response to the 'opportunity costs' question? The policymaker will be asked: 'If we spend time, money and effort on this proposal what are we not going to be doing that we should have already been doing?'. Policy is a competition for time in a very time-poor environment. There are many issues and so little time; academics know that about their research activities, and so need to remember that it applies with even more force in the world of policy.

Networks matter in research, and they matter in policy making as well. It is not normal for ideas from an unknown source to be easily embraced, and this is true for many areas of life. Politicians and policymakers, in particular, have survived in their careers by being suspicious to some degree. They will always ask, in their heads at least: 'Are you selling me a pup?' Policy making does rely to a large extent on trust in the source and status in the network, so academics need to build both their trust and status if they want to be taken seriously. Years, or decades even, of non-engagement followed by a sudden step on to the policy stage proclaiming solutions is an unlikely formula for success.

In some ways, the point is so obvious that it is amazing how often it gets overlooked: politicians and other policymakers believe in things. They have preferences, philosophical positions (some more coherent than others) and even ideologies about what the world should be and how it should be changed, that is, both ends and means are political choices. Therefore, alongside evidence, values matter in the policy process. The 'what works' rhetoric can imply that choices are entirely technical but nothing could be further from reality in democratic policy making. Choice is about whether a policy matches the chooser's desired means and goals, and understanding that is essential for all academics and democrats. Moreover, academics are not immune from having values, preferences and ideologies, and though we try to guard against their impact on our research, there is no denying that they can, especially on what we choose to research and the manner in which that research is presented.

Nothing is certain and a policy can be killed by the fear of unintended consequences. 'The probabilities suggest ...' – the language of much scientific discourse – may not be strong enough to stop a wave of fear about unintended consequences. Academics rightly want to be clear about the limits of the evidence but they should also be keen to pre-identify and try to undermine spurious objections to their findings. Opponents of any measure tend to frame their arguments along standard lines: 'it will not achieve the desired effect' or, worse, 'it will have perverse effects' or, worse still, 'it will jeopardise much-cherished other gains'. Understanding how interventions are going to be challenged should be something that academics should be aware of when they engage.

However, even all the aforementioned obstacles are overcome and your research does, indeed, lead to a policy intervention, it may be that implementation failures undermine it. The forces of opposition to a policy do not stop once it is adopted. In addition, 'events, dear boy, events' is an alleged explanation that former British Prime Minister Harold Macmillan offered as to why achieving anything in politics is so difficult. The unpredictable, sudden crisis can blow a carefully evidenced and prepared policy process of course. Just as in nature, where we are learning that changes in woods/forests, for example, are driven as much by major events as slow environmental change, so it is in politics that all that appears solid and definite can suddenly melt and become an arena of uncertainty. There are many coping strategies to deal with this phenomenon but they all boil down to: 'if at first you don't succeed, then try and try again'.

Academic incentive structures against engagement

Social scientists may also need to investigate the issues in their own practices and culture that restrict the engagement between social science and policy making. New career scholars know that publishing in good-quality journals is their ticket to a successful career. Making an effort to promote the relevance of their work to policymakers would seem a potentially unproductive waste of time. General theory and groundbreaking work that heads off in novel directions is valued over applied theory. Empirical work is more likely to be assessed according to the virtuosity or novelty of its methodology rather than the relevance of its topic or findings to external observers.

Writing about International Relations, but in an observation that might generally be applied to the social sciences, Walt (2005: 38) argues that '[t]he discipline has tended to valorise highly specialized research (as opposed to teaching or public service) because that is what most members of the field want to do'. There are not many academics that spend much time in the world of government or policy advice and the numbers that have taken up the opportunity in recent years has probably declined. Even in the US, where an extensive system of appointments gives greater scope for scholars to move from academia to government and *vice versa*, the tendency has been for the traffic to diminish. As Nye (2008: 594) comments:

> The United States has a tradition of political appointments that is amenable to 'in and out' circulation between government and academia. While a number of important

American scholars such as Henry Kissinger and Zbigniew Brzezinski have entered high-level foreign policy positions in the past, that path has tended to become a one-way street. Not many top-ranked scholars are currently going into government, and even fewer return to contribute to academic theory.

If you enter the world of government from the academy, the chances are that you will never find your way back.

Another reason why it is so difficult to work across the divide is that academic work is becoming increasingly specialised and it is difficult to keep up to date unless you are a full-time academic. That specialisation has brought some advances, it could be argued, and could, in theory, have better equipped academics to offer policy-relevant work given the enhanced intensity and focus of their expertise. However, in practice, it has tended to widen the gap between policy and academics as the latter has become more specialised and less accessible in their knowledge production. The resultant growth and specialisation of knowledge means that no one − least of all time-poor policymakers − can keep up with the subfields of social science.

Specialisation has also taken a hold on the very process of transferring knowledge from outside government to the inside. Think tanks, the media, public intellectuals, professional associations, non-governmental organisations and other bodies now play a stronger role in linking to policymakers than universities or academics more generally. Universities are no longer at the fore in the transmission of ideas to the world of policy. They have been crowded out and outcompeted. It may be that in teaching and in preparing the policymakers of the future, academics do shape core ideas among policymakers (Stoker et al, 2015). However, the evidence suggests that the world of policy advice has become crowded with actors that have the communication skills, a commitment to provide immediate expertise at a moment's notice and a zeal for engagement that is not observable in the academic world.

Doubts about the intellectual case for engaging with policy

In a broad sense, all social scientists have something to say about the societies they live in. Moreover, what constitutes relevance is not fixed. It can vary according to time, circumstance and, indeed, the standpoint of the observer (Gerring, 2001). Expressed in this way, it seems difficult to see how any academics could object to the idea of relevance or deny that they might be relevant (Stoker et al, 2015).

The challenge becomes greater when the discussion moves on to the question of what to do next. Describing and explaining an issue, event or context may offer relatively comfortable territory for most academics. Even a more specific diagnosis of a problem or policy challenge might be acceptable terrain for many. However, queasiness can begin to set in when it comes to the next stages in the potential exchange between academics and the world of policy making.

One proffered objection is that when social scientists have pursued relevance, they have often ended up putting their research into the hands of established power-holders and simply acted to provide so-called expert judgement to underwrite partisan policy making (Norton, 2004; Piven, 2004). There is likely to be a kernel of a truth in this observation, as our earlier analysis of how policymakers approach evidence indicates. The social scientist in pursuit of relevance, however, does not need to be a technician of the state working for power and against the powerless. There are some cases where social scientists have sided with power and some where they have not (see Stoker et al, 2015).

The uneasy relationship between 'facts and values' comes more sharply into focus as social science enters the world of prediction, prescription and evaluation (Stoker, 2010a, 2010b). There are at least three types of objection that come to the fore. The first is to claim that the empirical and the normative need to be kept separate for effective science and any blurring of the boundaries in pursuit of relevance is undesirable. A second line of attack accepts that empirical and normative theorising are intertwined to such an extent that they cannot be separated, so that when social scientists move into the world of relevance, they should not seek any special status borne out of their expertise. At most, they can claim that their knowledge is only a particular organised form of opinion, being as valid – but no more so – as others that might stem from direct experience, craft practice and so on. The third objection is that any guiding value or framework that academics might use to steer their predictions, prescriptions and evaluations to move them beyond the status of simply being their opinion is likely to be vacuous and untenable. For these and other reasons, including the 'quietism, resignation, and intellectual conservatism' (Farr et al, 2006: 586) of the profession, any vision of a social science community committed to a science of society has failed to muster much support in recent decades.

There are other doubts that have been raised about the intellectual case for making social science relevant. The evidence may not be clear enough to allow for clear and workable solutions to be identified.

Claims to be able to establish causality, which could, in turn, guide a claim to provide solutions, should be treated with scepticism. Those who are inclined to see political science as an attempt to develop causal statements about general features of society may nevertheless hold the view that these statements, at best, can come in probabilistic form. As Walt (2005: 37) notes:

> a scholar might be delighted by a theory predicting that, on average, a 20% increase in X would produce a 25% decrease in Y, but a policymaker will ask whether the problem now occupying his inbox is an outlier or an exception to this general tendency.

One response might be to develop more contextual, middle-range theory (George, 1993). Although this approach can have advantages for the policymaker in that it is sensitive to his or her situation, it can also lead to a highly contingent form of advice: 'if you do X, then Y will occur, assuming conditions a, b, c, and q all hold, and assuming you do X in just the right way' (Walt, 2005: 36). Some policymakers might wonder about the value of such circumscribed advice. Advice might be easier to give in stable settings but it is more often asked for in situations of uncertainty and change, where making claims about the special knowledge of political science might be more problematic. Some social scientists, of course, hold that the pursuit of scientific-style knowledge is meaningless. Piven (2004) argues that attempts to identify linear cause-and-effect dynamics when examining a problem lead to the attempt to build policy on fictitious grounds as realities are always more complex than any simple model can capture.

Most social scientists are comfortable with the idea that their work could inform and enlighten; they are less comfortable when their role is pushed towards prediction, prescription and evaluation. They appear hesitant about how to manage the relationship between normative and empirical theorising – indeed, a common response is an ostrich-like refusal to confront the issue – and unclear about the quality and capacity of their theories and evidence to carry the burden of solution-seeking rather than, at best, diagnosis. Dealing with the interface of normative and empirical theorising is not made easier by the gap in the discipline between those that deal with normative theories who seek to argue about how political and social arrangements should be, and those that deal with empirical theory who try to account for how society works in practice (Shapiro, 2003). The two sides of the discipline are often uninformed about each other's positions and the result is doubly unfortunate 'because speculation about what ought to be is likely to be more useful when informed by relevant knowledge and ... because explanatory theory too easily becomes banal and method-driven when isolated from the pressing normative concerns' (Shapiro, 2003: 2). One response has been to call for social science to move to a problem-oriented focus in order to unify and share insights from various parts of the discipline, not least normative and empirical theorists (Shapiro, 2007). The argument is that there should be a relationship between the world of social analysis and the world of practice. Many social scientists could accept, at a general level, the virtues of a more problem-oriented approach. A strong case could be made that a great deal of social science has a lot to say about the problems of our social systems, if properly communicated and synthesised.

Yet, even if that intellectual battle was won, there remains much more doubt about the capacity of the profession to deliver solutions. Many could be moved to answer the question 'What is wrong?', but many fewer appear able to successfully grapple in depth – with institutional clarity and a clear sense of how to achieve delivery – with the question of 'What should be done?'. Even if the bar is lowered to identify appropriate trade-offs and options, social science fails to offer much in the way of solutions to some of the most pressing problems faced by our policymakers (Peters et al, 2010). This failure to address and score highly on the solution-oriented side of the relevant challenge is a reflection of the lack of design thinking within the discipline of social science (Stoker, 2012; Stoker and Taylor-Gooby, 2013). Chapter Thirteen develops the idea of a design orientation, and its thinking could be applied more generally in the social sciences.

Conclusions

Policy making is heavily constrained by the immediacy of current priorities, by the exigencies of political support and now, in many countries, by all the pressures of the financial crisis. If changes are to take place in the relationship between academics and policymakers, they are most likely to occur on the academic side: in the way academics think about policy issues and offer options to policymakers. There are a wider range of methods that could be helpful to policy making than are regularly used. The battle to get them adopted will not be straightforward, but a greater awareness of the pluralism of the potential approaches on offer from the social sciences could help to heighten interest and allow policymakers to understand in more depth

26

how evidence-based social science comes in a variety of forms, some of which may be exactly what they need in the tough policy contexts they find themselves in. If this extension and opening is going to take off, then what is also required is 'self-conscious attention to the practical issues of policy design, and a move towards a more synthetic and goal-centred approach' (Stoker and Taylor-Gooby, 2013: 247). Our aim is to help ensure that the policy making community gives the contribution of social science the attention it merits. However, that value is partly demonstrated through the way that research is presented by social science and partly through a greater awareness of the depth and variety of the social science offer.

- SS can be wrong - skepticism
→ wards its value

- Heuristics - dumsy thru gut

TWO

Crafting public policy: choosing the right social science method

Gerry Stoker and Mark Evans

The classic adage is that the selection of a research method depends on the research question that is the focus of attention. Thus, if you are trying to find out what the result of a national election might be in terms of voting preferences, you would need a method that could deliver a representative sample of voters and ask about their intentions in order to have the best chance of finding an answer. So, the method chosen would be an opinion poll, although, as the failure of polls to correctly predict the outcome of some elections (notably, the 2015 general election in the UK) suggests, the chosen method might not always deliver a successful outcome. Yet, the advice that you should let your question determine your choice of method remains generally good counsel; however, in the world we are interested in – connecting social science to public policy – we would argue that the selection of a method requires the consideration of a range of other issues. Above all, the issue of choosing a method depends not only on your question at stake, but also on the state of play you face in policy making.

In particular, it is important to recognise at the very least that the character of policy making is influenced by time constraints, by the preferences or needs of relevant interests, and by the limits of available resources to deal with an issue. These are all points raised in Chapter One and they explain, of course, why evidence is not the sole criterion for making policy choices. In addition, there are times when policy options are more open and times when they are more closed. The policy context, as a result, directs the choice of research method that might be appropriate. The general argument is well presented by Bardach and Patashnik (2016: 14), in their classic, if not unproblematic, book providing advice to policymakers, which is in its fifth edition as of 2016: 'Thinking and collecting data are complementary activities: you can be a much more efficient collector of data if you think, and keep on thinking, about what you do and don't need (or want) to know, and why'. There are several elements of a policy context that will need to be considered, and in this chapter, we examine several policy set-ups or scenarios and give a sense of how a policymaker might select a method to match. By way of an introduction, some of the general issues in policy design and construction are briefly considered.

Meeting the policy challenge

We think that policy making is a craft that can be supported by social science. We agree with Bardach and Patashnik (2016: xvi) that 'policy analysis is more art than science' but disagree with their assumption that, as a consequence, policy analysis has to draw 'on intuition as much as on method'. It may be that, in practice, policy making reflects hunch, interests and even prejudices – as noted in Chapter One – but we would argue that, if a wider array of social science tools could be brought into play, there is more scope for evidence-based policy making than some allow for. In contrast, Bardach and Patashnik (2016: 47) are rather dismissive of the role of social science, noting that policy analysis 'uses social science to the degree that it can' but that it appears to be very little in practice. They fear that the standards of knowledge production of social science are too exacting for policy analysis and tend towards a narrow focus on one element of an issue rather than the broader understanding of a complex system of relationships that is likely to be in play in the context of a policy choice. However, their thinking reflects a rather narrow understanding of social science and its methods. It appears that they have a particular type of model-building, quantitative version of social science in mind, and our point and the argument of this book is that, although there is much of value in that type of social science, it represents only a small part of a much more diverse and pluralist universe of social science. There are multiple methods that social science can offer that still enable the policy analyst to move beyond informed guesswork towards a more rigorous evidence-based policy making.

Related to the argument about the unexploited richness of social science is an argument about the complex nature of evidence required for policy making (Nutley et al, 2007). First, evidence comes in a variety of forms but is always both contextual to a degree and contingent to a certain extent, and always partial and limited. There are few universal laws generated by the social sciences, but, rather, a complex array of insights. Evidence-based policy making needs to get better at exploiting that multifaceted knowledge and understanding, combining the empirical and theoretical insights produced by social science with practice and local-based knowledge.

Second, the range of questions and challenges that need to be met if an effective policy measure is going to be put in place makes the case for embracing the breadth of the social sciences: as different challenges are confronted, so different types of social science method may come more to the fore. Ekblom (2010) offers a '5i' framework for thinking through the challenge of undertaking successful policy. There is a need to know about what the problem is and how it can be explained, that is, the challenging of *intelligence*. There is a need to work out what works in the sense of what policy options could meet the problems identified, that is, the task of designing an *intervention*. There is then the issue of know-how, of how to turn a general policy idea into an effective practice on the ground, that is, the *implementation* issue. Next, there is the challenge of working out who is going to take action and carry the policy forward, that is, the question of *involvement*. Finally, of course, it would be good to have some way of knowing that the policy was working or how it could be tweaked to improve its performance, that is, the process of understanding and assessing *impact*.

In short, good policy design stretches over formulation and on to implementation (Howlett, 2011) and will generally involve the mixing of a complex range of governance tools. Again, trends in public policy led to the need for a greater and more pluralistic contribution of social science in that complex process of constructing. Policy making is a process that is messy, long-run and multifaceted, and will involve a range of actors interacting with one another over quite a long period of time. Howlett (2011: 145) states that 'Understanding who these actors are and why and how they act the way they do is a critical aspect of all policy making activity, including policy instrument selection and in policy design'. A pluralist social science can help do what is required in today's complex world: expand the menu of government choice about what to do and extend the understanding of the context-dependent nature of the tools of intervention, thereby enhancing, but not guaranteeing, the chances of success.

Social science can, in this sense, contribute to a new policy process of policy design which recognises that as public policy extends into more subtle and interactive fields of human behaviour, it requires more and different types of evidence. In the main, this is because the terms of trade of what is likely to be an effective intervention have changed. Problems have become wicked in the sense that they are multi-causal in nature, and 'squishy' in the sense that there are 'system effects' which mean that a gain in one place can lead to a loss or step back in another. In this light, the future of public policy is more likely to be based around practices of co-production than in its past. The term 'co-production' has been used in a variety of ways but its essence rests on the understanding that successful outcomes in public policy usually involve a contribution from both expert professionals and thinking and engaged members of the public (Bovaird, 2007). For example, environmental action is likely to require behaviour change from citizens and actions by government. As Durose and Richardson (2016: 49) argue, this challenge implies a rather different form of policy development based less on a hierarchical control model and more on engagement with a range of partners and with recognition of the value of different forms of knowledge and insight. From the narrow perspective of the argument we are making, the emergence of co-production makes the case for a contribution from a wider base of social science stronger. Cost–benefit analysis or surveys alone are unlikely to be able to cut it in this complex interactive world; we need policy making to embrace a much wider range of social science methods.

Exploring policy set-ups

We have argued that the nature of policy making is changing and that those developments call for a range of social science tools to be brought into play – but how does the analyst choose a method? The choice is neither straightforward nor always the same; it is context-dependent. Some methods will suit some policy contexts better than others, and in this second part of the chapter, we explore a variety of policy set-ups or vignettes to support a process of thinking through the selection of methods that are fit for purpose.

Is there a lot of evidence already in play?

Policymakers need to ask whether there is already a lot known about an issue, or perhaps given the novelty of the policy concern or the newness of innovations in the field, whether there is relatively little experience to draw on. So, the first choice for the policymaker is whether the need is to have a research tool for knowledge refinement or knowledge development.

Some research tools are of more use when you know more and some are of more use when you know less. If the policymaker is aware that there is an extensive body of knowledge that is directly relevant to the policy choice that has to be made, then it would seem that a systematic review is the obvious option. Why spend money on new research if research results can be assessed and used to provide an answer? There may still remain the question: will it work here (Cartwright and

Hardie, 2012)? That is, although the systematic review shows the likely impact of an intervention, there may remain doubt about whether it will work in a particular setting. Here, a randomised controlled trial (RCT) could be designed in the light of known evidence to test whether the particular intervention works in the context that the policymaker is focused on.

Of course, a systematic review depends on there being in place a high-quality range of evidence. Several of the techniques we examine are suited to those occasions when you may know less. Qualitative comparative analysis (QCA), for example, is particularly useful where there are a small or medium number of cases to drive decision-making. As Ryan explains in Chapter Five, the techniques associated with QCA have their own logic but were originally designed by the initial creator Charles Ragin as a way for researchers to be able to make more systematic comparisons when there are only a limited number of cases available to examine a set of relationships. Cluster analysis, too, is at its best when the analyst is searching for patterns in the data and very uncertain about what they might find. If the policymaker senses that they first need to understand the range and grouping of factors at play in a policy arena, then it might be a valuable tool. Design tools or visioning techniques could also provide a way of developing a more exploratory approach to policy learning and development.

Are there latent data available?

Closely related to the issue of the available evidence base are the extent, quality and organisation of the accessible data about the policy topic under consideration that have not yet been brought into play. The second choice facing the policymaker is whether there is a mountain of unexploited data that could aid policy making if it was turned into useable insights.

In their everyday interactions with the public, governments generate a lot of information about their needs, requirements and the way that processes work. Learning about these realities could make a big difference to the design of public services or programmes. Could this latent data be exploited by some research methods? If you are data-rich but much of that data is not yet consolidated into useable knowledge, then the techniques of big data analysis would seem highly relevant. Again, cluster analysis can help in the exploration of large mounds of data.

There may be other ways in which data can be unearthed as well. The techniques of visualising could help respondents bring into their minds issues and concerns that perhaps a straightforward interview question would not elicit. The use of design techniques where a service provider is put metaphorically in the shoes of the client (or even vice versa) can help a policymaker to understand the world from the citizen's perspective, and, in that sense, can release data and understandings not previously available. Listening to and then making sense of the stories that stakeholders tell about their experiences in respect of a policy issue can also help to reveal hidden data.

Are the ideas of policymakers relatively fixed about what action to take or are there opportunities for or interest in an open search?

As Bardach and Patashnik (2016: xvii) comment in many policy making settings, 'some steps are already determined'. There may be a clear preference for a particular definition of the problem or even a particular solution. The third choice facing policymakers is whether they are engaged in evaluating a preferred policy option or whether they are searching for a yet unknown solution. There are times when policymakers are reasonably certain about the solution and other times when it is far from clear what to do, for example, in the context of a wicked issue that you or anyone else are unclear about.

Some techniques work well when you know what to do, in the sense that you know that something will work. In that context, a cost–benefit analysis makes sense as you are trying to judge the benefits or otherwise of the intervention. There are also, as Chapter Ten points out, a range of statistical modelling techniques that can be used to calculate the distributional consequences of different actions. If policymakers are determined to go down this path, then one thing that social science research can do in that policy context is let them understand the potential consequences of their action.

There is always a range of issues to consider beyond the important distributional issue of who will be the gainers or losers under a policy. There is, some argue, the potential threat of creating moral hazards whereby the policy insulates people from the consequences of their actions. If governments, for example, paid out for the repair every time you had an accident in your vehicle, it would weaken your commit to get proper insurance, which might be considered a policy mistake. If those that pollute our air, water or the environment are not made to pay for the costs of their actions, a moral hazard might, again, be created. Another common ethical concern is whether a policy solution will create rent-seeking opportunities, where organised interests can simply use the policy and the resources associated with it to get themselves a bonus but deliver little in terms of the broader policy goals of collective benefit. Employers, for example, could be given incentives to take on young people as workers but are then under no pressure to deliver effective training for those young people; the policy, in effect, delivers free labour not a developmental experience for the young person as a result. Some research techniques might help tease out some of these issues: the use of deliberative investigation.

Beyond the ethical dilemmas created by policy, there is often a range of unintended consequences behind policies. There is a wide literature on the move from government to governance in modern-day policy making (Chhotray and Stoker, 2009). Governments do more through other organisations, interests and individuals as the scope and depth of what they attempt to do become more complex. Building roads and creating an army are tasks that are more straightforward than trying to resolve issues of traffic congestion, climate change or security against terrorist attack. Working with and through others is an increasingly common challenge for government, and with those interactions come greater power interdependencies between the various actors, and then a greater possibility of unintended consequences. Although collaboration may be fruitful and effective, it can deteriorate into blame avoidance and an unwillingness to take responsibility. Again, social science techniques may be able to help reveal the unintended and potentially undesirable consequences of an agreed-upon course of action. Indeed, if you consult Google Scholar, you will see that academics have quite an industry in publishing articles that capture the unintended consequences of numerous government policies. However, there are also several of the techniques presented in this book that might enable policymakers to explore unintended consequences with stakeholders: deliberation, citizen science or learning through storytelling might help to enable a proposed policy to be judged more effectively in terms of consequences that would not otherwise be understood or predicted.

Of course, on other occasions, the policymaker is required to think up new solutions. As Bardach and Patashnik (2016: 19) comment: 'It's good to brainstorm'. We would simply add that social science techniques can provide a good supporting dynamic for that activity among policymakers. Exploration capacity can be delivered in spades by design approaches, visualising techniques and deliberative approaches. They all open up the policy process to research that enables solutions to be discovered. If the first policy challenge is to think creatively, then these techniques should be among the first to be looked at by policymakers.

Is passing the technical or legitimacy challenge more important to policy approval?

In any developed and effective setting, two questions will always be asked, though perhaps in different ways. These questions are: 'Will the policy work?' and 'Will it be feasible?'. Some research techniques lend themselves to providing insight on the former question and some on the latter. Policy choice is about not only what could be done to achieve an end, but also what is politically acceptable, so some research approaches might be better at delivering that crucial information in a timely and powerful way. Will the policy be able to pass the technical challenge (that it will work)? In addition, will the policy be able to pass the legitimacy challenge (that it will be supported)?

The first question captures a range of technical concerns. Is the analysis of cause and effect correct and so will the intervention achieve its purpose? Will it be cost-effective: can we be clear that the costs will not outweigh the benefits? These issues of technical success can be to the fore in all policy choices. A systematic review might deliver a good sense of the connections between cause and effect in a policy area, so would a well-designed and executed RCT. As Peter John explains in Chapter Four, RCTs can and are increasingly being developed as part of a process of policy advance. When it comes to judging the costs and benefits of proposals, there is, of course, cost–benefit analysis but there are so many more options. There are extended forms of cost–benefit analysis that take into account environmental or other factors. There is also the work on microsimulation, as suggested in Chapter Ten.

However, in those policy arenas with a higher public profile or impact, the second question – about policy legitimacy – becomes more important. Think of policy dealing with issues of high political salience around defence and security, the economy, immigration, health care, housing, and so on. Here, again, a range of issues are likely to matter. Is it likely to have more supporters and opponents? Will there be powerful and well-resourced interests stacked up against it? Is the policy politically feasible? Is it managerially viable? Will service providers – those who are going to have to buy into it in order to deliver it – believe that it is a workable option? Finally, we might expect policymakers to consider the sustainability of policy intervention: will the policy have a capacity to survive the rough world of implementation and stick around to have an effect in the longer run?

Again, when it comes to enabling policymakers to explore the legitimacy of their policy options, social science offers a range of techniques. Deliberative policy analysis can provide insights on these issues, of course, alongside the more commonly adopted option of a public opinion survey, and has the advantage that you can get a more considered set of reflections from citizens rather than the more knee-jerk responses that can be elicited by survey work. Citizen science might also provide powerful insights, and so could other techniques that bring citizens back in, including co-design approaches.

Is the target of the policy intervention the general public or a more specific group?

If the policy measure is aimed at the whole population, then most methods would seem applicable; all those covered in the book could provide insights, as well as the established and widely used approaches of cost–benefit analysis and a representative sample survey. The latter is, of course, designed to provide understanding of how a general population responds by means of careful sampling in order to get a fair cross-section of society, and the follow-up use of various forms of statistical analysis can yield valuable perspectives on how factors across the population interplay and relate to one another. Conducting surveys in a cost-effective way has led to a greater reliance on Web-based respondents, which can, in turn, lead to questions about the representativeness of the samples, a factor helping to explain why, as noted at the beginning of this chapter, surveys appear to get results that are contradicted by later behaviour, as in the 2015 UK general election (BBC News, 2016). Often, these biases and limitations can be addressed in the analysis that follows the data collection, so surveys remain a very valuable tool.

However, what about a situation where the target of the research is a particular group, or perhaps even a hard-to-reach group? The reasons why a group might be difficult to capture insights from could be multiple. It may be that the group is very dispersed or thinly spread in the general population; perhaps they have distinctive circumstances or concerns. It may be that groups have reasons for being wary of officialdom and are concerned about responding to enquiries when they are not clear what the point of them is going to be, or perhaps are unsure of the benefit to them. Some of the research methods identified in this book might be helpful.

It is worth highlighting the potential role of citizen social science in reaching target groups that might be more difficult to reach with other methods. Citizen science aims to potentially get citizens involved in all aspect of scientific work, from the formulation of research questions, through the collection of data, and then the analysis and presentation of results. If citizens engage, then they can approach their peers in a way that might be more difficult for government or higher education-based researchers to do. In short, they may be able to reach groups that standard methods cannot connect to so easily. Having citizens directly involved might also improve the focus of research questions and encourage a more attentive and interested audience for any findings that emerge. The way in which these advantages might lead to more effective evidence collecting and result in better policy decisions, aimed at, for example, homeless people, is an option that policymakers need to be open to in their selection of methods.

Some of the other methods outlined in the book – the use of deliberation, learning through storytelling, visualisation and design techniques – could also reveal insights into more target groups for policy making. By working directly with the relevant groups, these methods could yield understandings of what would make for more effective public policy. A well-designed RCT could also work for particular groups to test the impact of interventions, and big data analysis is easily able to offer the tools that enable a better understanding of the behaviour, attitudes or preferences of segments of the general population, often in a very cost-effective way.

Is the policy issue 'wicked' in its construction such that it demands a co-production solution?

The issue raised by this policy set-up has already been touched on earlier in the chapter and concerns the idea that much policy today is not about government acting on its own, but instead about government acting alongside stakeholders, partners and, indeed, citizens. Tackling issues as diverse as climate change, unwanted teenage pregnancy or anti-terrorist security concerns may require government action, but they will plainly require a range of actions from a mix of other actors in order to address the complex range of factors that might be driving the policy problem. In this light, an approach to policy analysis might be required that is less top-down and more bottom-up. The challenge for researchers in this context is about being prepared to join with others in the search for knowledge and insight that might improve the effectiveness of policy. As Durose and Richardson (2016: 205) argue:

> [c]ollaborating with policymakers, practitioners and activists outside of the academy does have fundamental implications for our research practice. It does not mean abandoning our role or expertise as researchers. Instead, co-production of

research means respecting and valuing different forms of expertise in the research process. Co-production of research also allows the authority, resources and status of the academy to contribute as part of an advocacy coalition for social and economic change.

The researcher remains committed to rigour and the careful construction of research findings in this new world of policy but does so in a way that shows engagement with others and a concern with the challenges of achieving positive change.

The construction of policy success in the world of co-production is a complex task, in part, because constructing effective policy and practice in this world is a considerable balancing act (Ostrom, 1996). Trust needs to be developed among participants and that trust needs to be maintained through the process of policy implementation. In this light, it may be worth noting how some of the methods in this book might offer greater opportunities to develop a participative approach to policy development through research. Deliberative policy analysis, citizen science and design methods are methods specifically identified to bring citizens back in, and would appear to be at the top of this list. So, if co-production is a core component of a policy response, then it would seem wise to think about choosing research methods to match.

What are the time constraints surrounding the policy decision? Are policymakers working to a very short timescale or is a longer-time horizon possible?

There are times when a policy response has to be quick. Some research methods tend to take a degree of time to deliver results. The construction of an RCT or the unfolding of deliberative policy analysis has a need for time to pass as largely integral to the method in order for results to be delivered. However, that does not imply that all that is left to policymakers is the practice of 'policy making by Google', as identified in Chapter One. There are a number of methods discussed in this book that can deliver rapid results. If a systematic review is available, then it can provide the policymaker with access to years of previous research work and policy development in as much time as it takes to read through the relevant document. Other techniques, such as those of big data analysis explained in Chapter Eight or the QCA described in Chapter Five, can also provide very rigorous but also very rapid results. If the demand is for speed, there are still research methods available that can help in the delivery of more effective policy.

Is developing a theory of change a core policy objective or is the causal process largely held to be a given one?

The final issue to be addressed in this chapter is one that could again lead to a criterion for choosing some research methods rather the others. There are some policy areas where it is perhaps felt that the underlying theory of change – what explains how the policy interventions will work – is very widely understood or not necessary to know. For example, reducing the speed limit of moving vehicles in built-up areas is a mechanism that would deliver a relatively predictable outcome and the underlying causal dynamics are probably fairly well understood. Travelling at low speed in the vehicle means that accidents are less likely, and when they do occur, are going to be less damaging or traumatic for those involved. In this case, research might explore how to best ensure that speed limits are observed or it might examine how to make an effective cost–benefit judgement about whether to put in place a new speed limit, but the underlying theory of change is not the issue at stake.

In less well-worn policy arenas, however, policymakers might be much keener to use research to help them explore how to achieve effective interventions. The standout method in terms of recent practice in this respect is the RCT, as analysed in Chapter Four. Repeated RCTs, carefully constructed to explore different dimensions of an issue, can help policymakers explore what is driving change. There are other methods that can also deliver this exploratory quality as well. The design approach is a good example of a practice developed to enable learning through prototyping solutions and then developing them through testing and readjustment. Other methods could be vital in ensuring that forgotten or buried factors affect the process of change. Cluster analysis has the capacity to reveal unexpected connections, as does, from a very different tradition, the process of narrative and storytelling.

Concluding note

The underlying message of this chapter is that different methods can deliver a range of valued insights. We cannot claim to have exhaustively covered all policy contexts, but we have worked through enough scenarios to show how choices about social science methods could be determined. Understanding what you need to find out and, in particular, therefore, identifying the policy context will enable policymakers to connect their questions to the wider range of research methods that are covered in more detail in the remainder of the book.

PART TWO:
TOOLS FOR SMARTER LEARNING

THREE

Systematic reviews for policy

David Gough and Janice Tripney

Research to inform policy

Social science is concerned with the study of society and the individuals within it. Policy is the articulation of aims and principles for action, and is used particularly for organisations with remits to undertake action, such as local and central governments. As policies are often concerned with societal and individual issues, social science may provide insights and research results to inform such policies. This chapter is concerned with systematic methods for bringing together in a rigorous and transparent way (systematic reviews) the findings of that research to inform policy and practice decision-making.

Over the last 20 years, there has been an increasing concern, both in the UK and internationally, to ensure that research evidence is used to improve the design and outcomes of public services. This has led to the rapid growth of systematic reviews in many areas of public policy. The systematic identification, mapping and synthesis of research not only tells us what we know from existing research, but also focuses our minds on what we do not know and what more we might want to know from research. Systematic reviews of research are therefore a crucial component of the knowledge-to-action cycle (Graham et al, 2006; Best and Holmes, 2010).

The core of this chapter introduces the common principles and overarching approach of systematic reviews, including what they involve in practice. The purpose is to briefly outline the methods rather than to provide detailed explanations of procedures, which are elaborated elsewhere (eg Gough et al, 2017). In the final section, consideration is given to the multiple overlapping and interrelated roles of social science in understanding and enabling the use of research evidence in decision-making, roles in which systematic reviews are central.

The need for systematic reviews

Research is an industry providing careers for many research staff. It is challenging for researchers to keep abreast of all the research in an area, and thus even more difficult for others who are less likely to have the skills, experience or background knowledge to access, appraise and contextualise research evidence. So, how do policymakers and other non-academic users of research access research knowledge? One approach is simply using research that the policymaker happens to know about. Academic researchers are increasingly expected to market and achieve impact from their research, and so their findings may be reported in the media or be presented directly to policymakers or their staff. In addition, there may be many other incidental ways that people may become aware of particular research studies. The problem, of course, is that such routes of access to research may not result in the most relevant or most reliable studies being known. More fundamentally, any individual or group of studies may not represent all the relevant studies that could be considered. Publication and other forms of selection bias may occur from particular types of studies being more likely to be known and referred to than others, and these may not necessarily be the best or most representative studies. There may be features of the studies that make them more or less likely to be known, such as being associated with particular fashions, individuals or vested interests that misrepresent the totality of research that exists on any given topic.

One solution to this problem is the use of experts who know about a research field and can provide policymakers with access to that knowledge. There are many advantages of this model in using existing expertise to provide a timely and efficient overview of all relevant studies. There are, however, dangers. First, one needs to be clear that the area of expertise is appropriate. This might seem like a simple issue of ensuring that the topic specialism is correct, but there are, for example, cases of practice and research skills being confused, for instance, where a professor of clinical practice is asked about research data as an expert witness in court. Second, even if the topic specialism is appropriate, the breadth and depth of expertise may be unknown. The expert may know some things in more depth than others and this may bias their account of the literature. Third, and related to this, the expert may have good skills in conducting and appraising research but they may not be so skilled in bringing together and synthesising that knowledge in the way requested by the potential user of that research. Fourth, the expert may have some hidden biases based on particular theories or their own research work and hypotheses that they are studying. In sum, the expert may be able to provide a very quick and efficient, and very accurate, portrayal of the research literature; the difficulty is in ascertaining whether this is the case.

Another solution to enabling policymakers' access to research evidence is the literature review, providing a summary of the research studies undertaken to date. In many ways, this is similar to expert accounts of the literature, except that it is written and therefore potentially a more public account of the literature. The potential weaknesses of a literature review are also similar to expert accounts in the potential for hidden biases. There is, however, a way to minimise this weakness by providing an account of how the review was undertaken. This is essentially what a systematic review is: a literature review with an explicit, accountable methodology (Gough et al, 2017).

Nature of systematic reviews

Research uses rigorous methods so that the results of such research are trustworthy. These methods also need to be explicit and transparent so that the methods are open to question and thus accountable. Systematic reviews are pieces of research. They are literature reviews with explicit and rigorous methods in order to examine what is known from already-existing studies. Primary research applies research methods directly to the society we live in. Systematic reviews are similar, but instead of applying these methods to study phenomena directly, they apply them to the findings of primary research. Systematic reviews are thus more of a level of analysis – the analysis of secondary data – than a totally different methodology of research.

Research is question-led; a question is posed and the methods of research aim to explore and answer that question. Some literature reviews are very broad and ask questions about what is known about a topic rather than addressing a specific research question. Systematic reviews, informed more by the thinking of primary research, tend to be question-driven rather than only topic-driven. In one topic area, therefore, you may find many different systematic reviews, with different questions, different data being considered and therefore also different answers. Across all technical, medical and social sciences, there is a vast array of disciplines, topics and questions. All of the research questions that can be addressed at the primary level can also be addressed at the review level.

Systematic reviews and primary research on the same question are likely to be very similar in two main ways. First, and rather obviously, reviews answering a particular question are likely to include the studies that are addressing that question in primary research. Second, the methodology of that review is likely to share the research paradigm and approach of those primary studies. If, on the one hand, you are undertaking a primary qualitative study exploring and developing ways of understanding a particular phenomenon, then a review of such studies is also likely to be exploratory and conceptual. On the other hand, if you are undertaking an experimental controlled quantitative evaluation of a policy initiative, then a review of such studies is likely be informed by the thinking of such experimental controlled evaluations.

The distinction between what is often called qualitative and quantitative research is an important one in research as it effects so much of the thinking and practical approaches used by these two main research paradigms. The terms 'qualitative' and 'quantitative' are, however, rather vague beyond the fact of whether the studies do or do not use numbers. Many qualitative studies make quantitative statements and vice versa. We prefer to use the terms 'configuration' and 'aggregation', which refer to the extent that the analysis stage of a study is either concerned with arranging (configuring) and rearranging data into patterns to develop conceptual understandings, or concerned with adding up (aggregating) data within such conceptual understandings (Sandelowski et al, 2012).

A qualitative primary study and a review asking similar research questions (and thus including such studies) are likely to be predominantly configuring in approach. They are likely to take an iterative exploratory approach, with the detailed methods developing as the study proceeds and more interest in exceptional cases than aiming to be representative of a sample or a situation. There may, however, be some aspects of aggregation, for example, with statements of the degree or extent that things happen in different circumstances. One form of qualitative configuring research is ethnography; one form of systematic review of such studies is meta-ethnography. Ethnography studies small samples in detail and develops concepts to understand the processes being examined. Meta-ethnography is a form of review that examines and configures the concepts in those primary studies to develop overarching (meta-)explanatory concepts that cover the insights of the individual primary studies (Noblit and Hare, 1988).

Quantitative primary studies and reviews asking similar research questions (and thus including such studies) are, in contrast, likely to be predominantly aggregative in approach. They are likely to take an a priori approach to specifying their method and be anxious of iteration or any aspect of the research method that might lead to any bias. Instead of developing theory, the approach collects data within a particular theory to describe the world or to test or make predictions about empirical outcomes. Experimental controlled trials are one form of aggregative quantitative study testing the hypothesis that a certain intervention has a particular outcome, often that the intervention has the desired outcome and 'works'. Statistical analysis is used to test the extent of any experimental effect of the intervention. A review asking the same question brings together the statistics of the individual studies into a statistical meta-analysis. Together, all of the studies have a greater sample size and thus much more power than an individual study. Although the approach is predominantly a priori and aggregative, there may be configuring iterative aspects. One example is a post hoc regression analysis of how some of the independent and dependent variables relate to each other. This is an iterative exploratory hypothesis-generating process rather than the main aggregative a priori hypothesis testing.

Practice of systematic reviews

The logic of systematic reviews is quite straightforward. They involve the use of explicit, rigorous research methods to bring together what is already known to answer different research questions. They are a level of analysis (secondary rather than primary research) and they answer the research questions by interrogating existing research studies. This all sounds rather abstract without some discussion of what such reviews involve in practice.

Although there are many types of research question on different topics and involving many different research paradigms and research methods, there are some basic stages of the review process common to many reviews. These are outlined next and then briefly discussed in turn:

1. Developing the initial question.
2. Clarifying which studies are relevant.
3. Identifying studies.
4. Checking that the studies found meet the selection criteria.
5. Mapping.
6. Further coding of studies for synthesis.
7. Quality and relevance appraisal.
8. Synthesis.
9. Communication.
10. Recommendations and guidance.

Developing the initial question

All research is driven by a question that people want answered. Even within the same topic area, different people will be interested in different issues and will have different perspectives about the priority issues and the ideological and theoretical assumptions that frame the question. This is not an issue of questions being correct or wrong, or good or bad; it is an issue of purposes and the methods to achieve those purposes. It should not be surprising that an academic coming from a particular research tradition would have different priorities and ways of understanding an issue to a policymaker, a professional practitioner or a user of a service. The development of concern for public engagement in research (Oliver et al, 2015), or more public processes for identifying research priorities in health research,[1] arises from a realisation both of these differences in perspective and of the waste that can occur without the prioritisation of research (Chalmers and Glasziou, 2016).

There are three important implications of this for systematic reviews (and also for primary research). First, the perspectives and the assumptions underlying a research question determine the way that the research is conceptualised and undertaken, as well as the resultant findings and conclusions. Second, in order to operationalise the research question in a way that enables the research to be coherent, consistent and transparent, we need to be very careful about making these assumptions explicit. The execution of all stages of the research and the findings achieved will depend upon how the initial research question is framed. Third, we should expect research questions that seem similar but differ in perspective to result in different research findings and conclusions. Fourth, debates about research findings are often a complex integration of perspectives and research results created and framed by those perspectives. These debates may be about disagreements about the perspectives and/or about the coherence of the process by which results were produced and interpreted within these perspectives.

All of this means that the development of the research question in a systematic review is crucial. It will determine all stages of the review. Several weeks may therefore need to be taken to unpack the purposes of the review and the assumptions underlying the review question. Practical processes to enable this can include developing the review question with various stakeholders, such as those that the review hopes to serve, in other words, the users of the review. It might also involve checking the question with those coming from different academic or broader societal perspectives. A review may not be useful for everyone, but engaging with the views of others may help surface hidden ideological and theoretical assumptions underlying a research question.

Other more detailed practical approaches involve defining every concept in a research question. A question on, for example, the effects of homework on children would need to be clear about what was meant by homework and children. For some research questions, there are standardised lists of questions to ask of research questions. If, for example, the research is on the effects of an intervention on people, then the research question may need to specify the population (P), the experimental intervention (I), the control group intervention (C) and the outcomes measured (O), summarised as PICO. There are a range of such acronyms to assist research question development.

Clarifying which studies are relevant

The review question leads to a consideration of the types of primary research studies that would help answer that question. Clear specification of the criteria as to which studies to include in the review assists the practice of finding such studies and the reporting of the review, and avoids misunderstanding about what the review was really about. In aggregative reviews, taking an a priori stance, specification and consistent application of the inclusion and exclusion criteria help reduce bias as to which studies are included in the review. These criteria are similar to the specification of a sample in a primary study. In primary research, the sample may be made up of human participants; in a review, the sample may be made up of such primary studies.

Common inclusion criteria in a review relate to the topic being considered and the methods used to study the phenomena in the primary research. If the review question is about prevalence, then primary prevalence studies are likely to be specified; if the review question is about the impact of an intervention, then experimental intervention studies are likely to be specified. Another common inclusion criterion is the year of publication, with restrictions on how far back in time the review will go. Sometimes, such date limits can be justified due to changes in historical contexts, but they are often also used as a pragmatic way to limit the studies being considered by a review (which is not a good basis for such a decision).

Identifying studies

Once there is clarity about the studies to be included in a review, then such studies need to be found. In an a priori-type review, the aim will be to identify all relevant studies. If only a subset of studies meeting the inclusion criteria are found, then these may be a particular type of study with a particular type of findings, and so may misrepresent the total population of such studies. In more iterative reviews, for example, to synthesise the different ways a social issue has been conceptualised, the search for studies may be more exploratory and the aim may be to identify at least one example of each type of study (saturation) rather than to find multiple examples of very similar studies.

The nature of the strategy for identifying studies will depend upon the review question and where relevant studies are most likely to be found. In some areas of research, government or other websites may be most fruitful; in other areas of research, the studies may be found mostly in books. In many reviews, there is great reliance on bibliographic databases of published journal papers. This may be very appropriate for some systematic reviews but there still needs to be thought given as to which databases to use and how to operationalise the search in practice (Schucan Bird and Tripney, 2011). In all cases, the need is for a search strategy that can be reported and justified in terms of the needs of the specific review question. It is not a simple technical process of a quick search of a few databases; it is a thought-through strategy.

Many reviews rely on bibliographic databases for identifying studies. This can be very efficient in that the technology helps to find studies meeting the inclusion criteria. It can also be inefficient in that it is often very imprecise and many non-relevant studies are identified in the search. The studies may have been coded by the bibliographic databases but this will be in broad categories. The databases can also be searched using free text searching for words specified by the searcher but the papers may not be very clear in their use of language and in specifying their topic and methods (particularly in their titles and abstracts). In addition, to avoid bias from missing studies, the search is over-inclusive. The result is that many thousands of mostly not relevant studies may be identified in the search.

Checking that the studies found meet the selection criteria

Once potential studies have been identified, they need to be checked (screened) to ensure that they really do meet the inclusion criteria. This can be a very time-consuming exercise if a large number of studies has been identified through the search strategy. As many of the identified studies may be totally irrelevant, it is common for there to be a two-stage screening process, with the first stage just examining the titles and abstracts of identified studies and excluding those that are clearly not relevant. In the second stage, the full text of the studies is sought in order to have a more detailed examination of these remaining 'potential include' studies.

As the study identification and screening process can be so inefficient, attempts are being made to use text mining to automate aspects of this process. If humans screen some of the studies, software can learn from these judgements and apply them to the rest of the list of identified studies. There are, of course, anxieties about the accuracy of text mining in making these judgements but studies of this process are finding that the machines can be more accurate than humans, particularly when topic specification is built into the process (O'Mara-Eves et al, 2015). The use of technology in these processes is also part of broader developments that integrate bibliographic information about research with the research production and use processes.

Mapping

The studies identified as relevant in the screening process are the studies included in the review. Some information about these studies will be required, such as authors and titles, simply to manage them through the review process. However, it is also possible to record much more descriptive information and to use this to create a 'map' of the literature specified by the research question. The variables on which this research literature is described will depend upon the interests of the reviewers, funders and other stakeholders. It might include country of study, sub-topic, the conceptualisation of issues and the research methods of the primary studies. Research maps do not typically include research results as these will not have been checked for quality and relevance (see later).

The map can be useful in many ways. First, it describes the research field. It is important to note that the nature of this 'field' will be determined by the review question and the resultant inclusion criteria. It may therefore cut across and not fit with traditional academic boundaries of research fields, particularly if non-academic views were involved in the question formulation. Maps may be useful in clarifying what has been studied and how it has been studied.

Second, maps have the potential to identify gaps in what has been studied. It may, for example, be that there are many new developments in policy and practice and (due to the vagaries of the research production process) only specific subsets of this real-world activity has been studied, and so the research may provide an incomplete account of important issues. As maps can be so useful, they are sometimes undertaken as reviews on their own and do not proceed to synthesis.

Third, for reviews that do proceed to synthesis, the next stage is clarification of that synthesis. This may have all been specified at the start of the review, but the mapping stage allows this to be reconsidered. It may, for example, be decided to only undertake a synthesis on part, not all, of the map. In effect, this is a narrowing of the review at the synthesis stage: a broad map with a narrower synthesis. Such narrowing can be useful when, for example, the map results suggest that a synthesis on the whole question is not useful or is problematic in some way. For example, it may be that the studies are too heterogeneous for the synthesis to be meaningful or achievable. Also, if the plan is to undertake a series of synthesis reviews on a particular topic, then it may be more efficient and helpful to undertake one broad map and then undertake a series of syntheses on sub-questions from that map.

A fourth benefit of a map is that when the synthesis question is narrowed, the broader description of the field provided by the map provides the context for understanding and interpreting that synthesis. This broader perspective provided by the map may be concerned with the topic of study, but it may also concern the methods used in the primary research. In evaluations of the effectiveness of interventions, there may be a very broad range of studies that might be relevant to a broad map with which to understand the research field, yet there may be a much narrower group of studies with the power to make clear conclusions about effectiveness. However, only studying the narrow, technically powerful studies may misrepresent the research field and its potential to provide other sorts of insights and information about the interventions under study. Another way of looking at this is that being aware that review questions can be narrowed down when moving from the map to synthesis means that you can start with a broader (and thus potentially more relevant) review question, knowing that the map stage allows a narrowing down to a more manageable synthesis question.

Further coding of studies for synthesis

There are three main reasons to code information about studies in a systematic review. First, there is the mapping process already described. Second, information is obtained about the quality and relevance of the studies for inclusion in the synthesis. Third, information is also collected about the results of the studies as this is required for the synthesis. A strategy is needed as to what information is needed (needs to be coded) for all of these three different purposes.

In terms of the practicalities of undertaking a review, it may be more efficient in some cases to code information for all three coding purposes at one point in time. This is less likely to be efficient if only a small proportion of studies in the map proceed to the synthesis stage and if the review is very iterative when the nature of information required later in the review may not be known until that stage is reached.

Quality and relevance appraisal

In order for the results of research studies to be included in the synthesis, there needs to be consideration of the quality and relevance of these studies. There are many different scales and systems for making such critical appraisals and these consider all or some of three conceptual components (Gough, 2007). The first is that the studies were well executed within the expectations of the research methods employed. The second is the extent to which the research methods are relevant to the review question being asked. In some cases, the research approach in the primary study may not be ideal, but if the study was well executed, then there may be more reliance on its findings than a more appropriate but poorly executed method. The third dimension is the relevance of the study to the review question. The inclusion criteria have the role of only allowing relevant studies into the review, but even studies meeting the criteria may be judged at this later stage as being less relevant than other included studies. Reasons might be such things as the context in which the study was undertaken, the way in which any interventions or outcomes were operationalised, or issues such as the ethics of the studies.

The first component about the execution of method is a generic appraisal issue; it would apply whatever review was being undertaken. The other two components are 'review-specific' as they depend on the review question being asked. A poor score on these two components is thus not necessarily a criticism of the study being considered. Taking the three components together provides an overall view of the quality and relevance of the study to the review question and the weight that should be given to an individual study's results in the synthesis. In practice, this is often a decision to include or exclude the study, though in iterative reviews using qualitative data, the critical appraisal may just be used as a way to describe the studies and to inform the reader as to the nature of each study.

Often, the many scales for critical appraisal do not explicitly distinguish the three components described here. This is often because the scales are developed for specific research questions and methods, and so focus on the first component of the quality of execution of that method. In the quality appraisal in 'what works' reviews, the main research method is randomised controlled trials, and so the quality appraisal checklists assess the extent to which such a method has been applied and the measures taken to avoid any selection bias influencing the study results.

Although the quality and relevance appraisal of studies included in a review is an issue prior to synthesis, it is something that occurs throughout a review, from specifying inclusion criteria through to the process of synthesis. In addition, the overarching quality and relevance question persists at the review level in terms of whether the review itself is of the appropriate quality and relevance (in terms of how it was undertaken, the quality and relevance of included studies, the nature and extent of the evidence identified, and the resultant 'work done' by a review in addressing a research question). The appraisal of individual studies within the review is just part of this wider process (for a more detailed discussion, see Liabo et al, 2017).

Synthesis

Synthesis is the process of bringing together the results of the included primary studies to answer the review question. The approach to synthesis will depend upon the nature of the question and is likely to mirror the approach taken to answer the review question at the primary level of research. The two extreme examples of synthesis have already been referred to. At one end of the continuum are hypothesis-testing questions, such as 'what works', which are commonly addressed using a priori bias-avoiding research strategies. The primary studies in such reviews provide quantitative measures of the 'effect size' of the impact of an intervention. The reviews bring together these individual effect sizes (adjusting for study sample size) to provide an overall effect size. At the other end of the spectrum are more exploratory concept-developing questions, which are commonly addressed by reviews that produce a synthesis of existing conceptual studies. A well-known example is meta-ethnography, which interprets the concepts in individual ethnographies (or similar qualitative studies) to produce new overarching meta-conceptual distinctions.

Communication

As with all research, reporting is an important stage of the research. As previously mentioned, this involves explicit accountable reporting of the methods used as a requirement of research accountability. Other aspects of communication, though, depend on the audience for the work. The requirements for academic publication are different from communication to policymakers and practitioners to inform policy and practice decisions. These users of research are likely to require much shorter, less technical, accounts of the research, without academic jargon and forms of communication, though full details of the review may be important in some cases to enable the interpretation and implementation of findings. Non-academic users will also need the potential of access to full technical reports for reasons of accountability, though some of this is probably achieved indirectly through the branding as a systematic review and the credibility of the author or other indications of the source of the review. Some reviewers grouped together by common methods (as in realist synthesis) or topic interest (as in the Cochrane and Campbell collaborations) have developed branding and standards for different types of reviews. Although this concern for quality is an important step, it is also important to be aware of the dimensions of differences of reviews that are more fundamental than current groupings of review types.

Another way of making review-level evidence available is to provide Web-based toolkits, which provide user-friendly ratings of research evidence on different issues, with the ability to link through to the detailed reviews underpinning these overviews. One example is the Education Endowment Foundation's Teaching and Learning Toolkit,[2] which provides summary evidence from systematic reviews of the effectiveness (and strength of such evidence) of different educational interventions. Another example is the Crime Reduction Toolkit provided by the What Works Centre for Crime Reduction.[3] This also provides information on the mechanisms underlying different interventions, which is very helpful for policy users in considering how the results of generalised research findings may be applied to their own contexts.

Recommendations and guidance

Research results may suggest courses of action but do not in themselves specify action (Davies et al, 2008). In addition to communication and other forms of engagement with research, the research needs to be interpreted before it can be applied. Just as there are formal processes for conducting research (including systematic reviews), there are also now formal processes for moving from research to recommendations from that research. One such approach in health – GRADE[4] – combines an evaluation of the strength and trustworthiness of research on the efficacy of health interventions with the acceptability of the interventions to users of health services. A particular health treatment may, for example, be very effective and yet cause great discomfort or other unhappiness for the patient, potentially limiting the intervention's use.

Another formal system is used for health resource allocation and health and social care service guidance by the National Institute for Health and Care Excellence. This includes the involvement of interested stakeholders, such as service providers and users of such services, in defining practice issues that can be informed by systematic reviews of research evidence, which are then interpreted by such stakeholders to determine guidance and standards for English health and care services.

Dimensions of difference and developments in systematic reviews

The discussion so far has emphasised that review questions and reviews vary but the focus has been on the variations in the research paradigm (of a priori deductive aggregative and iterative inductive configuring approaches). Reviews, like primary research, can also vary extensively in terms of other dimensions, including the type of question, the breadth of question, the depth of analysis and the resultant 'work done' by the review (Gough et al, 2012, 2017).

How much work should be done by a review? Many people advocate rapid reviews on the grounds that they are cheaper and quicker, and therefore probably more timely, than more substantial reviews. This is the same as in primary research, where there will be different types of questions and different time and other resource constraints that lead researchers to undertake studies of different sizes and scope. There is always a balance between the different pressures. The main issue is to be aware that it is a balance. Rapid reviews may be fit for purpose in a range of circumstances but the 'work done' by them will be less, either in scope or in thoroughness, than in larger reviews.

Reviews do not have to be at one or other end of these dimensions of difference of approach, question, method or work done (Gough et al, 2012, 2017); they can vary in degree along these continua.

Thematic synthesis, for example, is similar to meta-ethnography in taking an iterative approach to examining thematic components within primary research studies but with less sociological theory involved in the process of synthesis (Thomas and Harden, 2008). Framework synthesis is similar to thematic synthesis but uses some a priori structures to guide the coding of data from the primary studies and thus also the synthesis of those results (Oliver et al, 2008). Framework synthesis is thus slightly more a priori and slightly less iterative in approach compared to thematic synthesis.

The mixing of dimensions of difference in reviews can be further developed with mixed-methods reviews through mixing several review components in one review. One approach to mixed-methods and components reviews is to ask a broad question and then employ two sub-reviews to examine two aspects of the question. A common approach is to ask a sub-question and sub-review on the impact of some social intervention, as well as a sub-question and sub-review on people's views or understandings of issues related to the intervention. The combination of these aggregative theory-testing and configuring theory development sub-reviews allows for a much richer and broader analysis than is available from one sub-review alone (Harden and Thomas, 2010).

Even where there are not specific sub-reviews, reviews of the impact of interventions are becoming more complex through greater specification of theories of change being tested in the review. In the past, many reviews took a 'black box' approach that tested the hypothesis that some intervention has a positive impact with little attention to the reasons as to why this might or might not be the case. The simple 'black box' question is appropriate in some circumstances where the answer of efficacy (or of negative impact) is crucial, but for many social policy interventions, it is important to learn more about causal processes for at least two important reasons. First, without any understanding of cause, increasing the efficacy of an intervention is going to be trial and error. Second, in order to apply the intervention in different circumstances and contexts, an understanding of the causal process can inform as to how such adaptations can be made. Increasingly, systematic reviews of impact evaluations test more complex logic models and search for the active ingredients of interventions using process data and techniques such as qualitative comparative analysis (Thomas et al, 2014, 2017).

The concern for theory-informed evaluation is widespread but has been particularly championed by realist evaluation and synthesis (Pawson, 2006). Realist approaches, however, have particular mixes of configuring and aggregative strategies. In realist synthesis, middle-level theories are often tested across a number of different policy domains. The first stage of the review is a configurative synthesis that unpacks the theory under review into its assumptions of causal processes and necessary conditions. This is followed by the empirical testing of each of these processes and conditions. Realist reviews tend to be richer than other reviews in the theory clarification process but the more unique feature is that the empirical testing stage is iterative and investigative rather than the more a priori approach of many other theory-driven evaluation systematic reviews (Gough, 2013).

Another important issue in impact evaluation reviews is the current emphasis on randomised controlled trials. These are highly valued because of the way that they control the effect of other potential intervening variables. Observational studies are seen as more open to bias due to the lack of control of variables. An example would be that differences in employment outcomes after the initiation of a new social policy might be different to the policy or to other changes that confound the interpretation of the non–controlled outcome data. More recently, a broader range of evidence has begun to be included in effectiveness reviews. There is considerable potential from the inclusion of data from very large cohort or other longitudinal data sets to both provide context and also indicate causal effects as there is the possibility of internal control over many variables. Similarly, routinely collected administrative data mean that you can carry out simple randomised controlled trials by making adjustments in policy to some clients and then waiting until the routine data are available. In this way, there is a greater linkage being achieved between experimental studies and observational data.

Another development is the concept of living reviews, where a review is never finished but is updated when new research data meeting the inclusion criteria are produced. This is more than just a more frequent and regular update of a review as it subtly changes the way that we think about reviews. Traditionally, the main concern has been on primary research, and reviews help us to bring their findings together. However it is now increasingly recognised that the starting point should be 'what do we already know from reviews and living reviews?', and only then, 'what more do we need to know from primary research?'. Living reviews make this even more explicit. If you are planning a study on an impact evaluation of a question covered by a living review, issues such as the statistical power required by the review will not be limited to study-specific issues (such as the necessary effect to show a difference with the selected outcome measures) (Elliott et al,

2014). Instead, the concern becomes the statistical power necessary in order to make a difference to the conclusions of the systematic review. So, although reviews are primary research, the emphasis should first be on secondary research. First, what do we know from secondary research, and then what more primary research do we need to further this knowledge?

Systematic reviews and the social science of research production and use

The chapter has so far considered the mapping and synthesis of research as a logical step in the research production process that enables the direct, rational use of research to inform decision-making. Although this might be seen by some as an ideal form of production leading to use, the situation is rather more complex in the way that research production and use are linked together. While systematic reviews are often designed with instrumental notions of research use in mind, they also have the potential for a broader enlightenment function, wherein they change the ways that problems are conceptualised and understood, which feeds back to influence future research (Weiss, 1979). Research production and research use are in dynamic interplay with each other and are increasingly characterised using a systems approach, rather than as a one-way linear or even two-way interaction (Best and Holmes, 2010). Social science has a number of different roles in that process. In this final section, we therefore consider the issue of how systematic reviews can be located within a wider picture of the multiple overlapping and interrelated ways in which social science enables the use of research evidence in policy and practice. Together, these roles encompass the theory and practice of policy making, the nature and foundations of research, and relations between the two. In the following, we consider four of these roles, which we briefly discuss in turn and provide examples of relevant systematic reviews in Table 3.1.

A key role for social science, and the focus of this chapter so far, is the development of the social science knowledge base. Social science is a broad area of inquiry covering a variety of topic and disciplinary approaches, each with many different, often competing, ways of understanding the world. Even within a particular topic or discipline, social science may be attempting to answer many different types of question and may use many different methods of research. Studies may, for example, be theoretical, descriptive, diagnostic or evaluative. They may provide conceptual understandings of social issues that can

Table 3.1: Examples of systematic review issues in the four roles of social science in enabling evidence-informed policy and practice

Social science role	Systematic review examples
1. Developing the knowledge base about social issues	There are now many hundreds of thousands of systematic reviews on substantive topics of potential interest to policymakers, practitioners and other users of research. For example: • Meta-narrative review of the conceptualisation of community (Jamal et al, 2013) • Systematic review evaluating different truancy interventions, seeking to improve school attendance of chronic truant students (Maynard et al, 2013)
2. Developing the technical and methodological aspects of studying social issues	Advances in systematic review methodology: • Use of text mining to assist in screening potentially relevant studies (Brunton et al, 2017), including a systematic review of current approaches relating to the use of this technology (O'Mara-Eves et al, 2015)
3. Building understanding about the demand side of the equation – the nature of policy and practice	This is a relatively new area for systematic review and there are only small numbers of such analyses. For example: • Systematic review examining a body of public health policy literature to identify whether theories of the policy process have been used to analyse why policy decisions have occurred (Cullerton et al, 2015) • Systematic review focusing on the complex interface between politics, policy and the use of evidence (Liverani et al, 2013)

4. Building understanding of how research, including systematic reviews, interacts with policy and practice	Sub-areas:
	(i) Measuring research use and wider research impact:
	  • Although there are increasing numbers of primary studies assessing the use and wider impacts of research, this body of literature has not yet been subject to systematic review
	  • Overview of reviews to identify the most common approaches to research impact assessment (Banzi et al, 2011)
	(ii) Capturing processes by which use/impact occurs:
	  • Systematic review of barriers and facilitators related to the use of evidence by policymakers (Oliver et al, 2014)
	  • Narrative review of conceptual models (Milat et al, 2015)
	(iii) Studying strategies to improve the use of research in decision-making:
	  • Systematic review of research on strategies to increase research use in decision-making (Langer et al, 2016)
	  • Systematic review of the quality and types of instruments used to assess the implementation and impact of such strategies (Van Eerd et al, 2011)
	(iv) Studying how to achieve evidence-informed behaviour change (implementation science):
	  • Systematic review of the use of theory in the design of guideline dissemination and implementation strategies (Davies et al, 2010)
	  • Systematic review of barriers and facilitators related to the implementation of surgical safety checklists (Bergs et al, 2015)

then inform what sorts of policies would be appropriate. They may also provide data on both the extent and causes of a phenomenon that a social policy is being developed to respond to. Research may also provide information on the effects of existing social policies or the likely effect of any new policy intervention. As such, social science provides an evidence base for informing policy in all stages of the policy cycle: in defining issues and shaping agendas; in identifying options; in making choices of action; in delivering them; and then in monitoring and evaluating their impact (Pollard and Court, 2005).

Different types of systematic reviews can inform each of these different parts of the policy process (Lavis, 2009). At the agenda-setting stage, for example, reviews can enable policy actors to be aware of the nature and importance of an issue. Reviews of qualitative studies can help to identify alternative framings of the problem, whereas reviews of prevalence and other observational studies can help to establish the magnitude of the problem or the factors that contribute to it. At the policy formulation stage, when decision-makers are involved in determining the policy options and then selecting the preferred option, reviews of impact evaluations can help to characterise the benefits and harms of each option being considered. At the implementation stage, reviews of observational studies could be used to identify potential barriers to implementing a preferred option.

Policymakers and other stakeholders can find increasing numbers of all of these types of reviews. However, as the vast majority of research investment is in primary research, the knowledge base contribution of systematic reviews is still relatively small, with the exception of some very specific areas, such as clinical medicine. Also, although the number of reviews is growing, there is still poor coordination between those undertaking reviews on similar issues and a lack of clarity about where reviews can be found beyond a few well-known databases and review collaboration websites.

A second role for social science relates to the technical and methodological aspects of studying social issues. Social science has developed a whole range of approaches to studying these issues at the primary research level and is now (belatedly) doing the same in systematic reviews of that research. Systematic reviews are a relatively new level and form of analysis, and technical development in the methods is developing quickly. As methodologies for systematic reviewing have matured, so there has grown increasing consensus over what makes a good systematic review (Gough et al, 2017), though, just as in primary research, methods of review vary considerably depending upon the type of research questions being asked. Detailed guidance on the process of preparing and maintaining different systematic reviews is increasingly available, as in, for example, the Cochrane handbook on undertaking systematic reviews on the effects of health-care interventions (Higgins and Green, 2011). Guidance is also available for reporting systematic reviews. The PRISMA statement, which provides reporting standards for impact reviews that focus largely on randomised controlled trials (Moher et al, 2009), has recently been extended to studies with a focus on health inequity (Welch et al, 2012). Readers of such reviews can be guided by the AMSTAR systematic review appraisal tool to assess their methodological quality (Shea et al, 2007). Publication standards have also been developed for meta-narrative reviews and realist reviews (Wong et al, 2014). Despite these developments, systematic reviews still have many methodological challenges to overcome. In addition, there are many technical, theoretical and value-related issues relevant to the production of recommendations and guidance that are derived from reviews of research and other forms of evidence. A core issue is the extent to which the social science methods of systematic reviews enable 'work to be done' in progressing our social science content knowledge.

Third, social science helps develop and support evidence-informed policy and practice by building understanding about the demand side of the equation, through the systematic study of the policy making process. Policy studies and political science are well-established areas of social science, and since the 1950s, have developed many theories to explain the various factors that influence the decision-making process, including ideas, knowledge, interests, power and institutions. Systematic review authors have taken an interest in this, examining the policy literature to investigate how widespread the use of policy theories from the field of political science is in analysing the process (Gilson and Raphaely, 2008). Political scientists and others are also increasingly influenced by the idea that research impact cannot be separable from the policy process as a whole. Often building on the pioneering work of Lasswell (1951) and Merton (1949), recent work emphasises the significance of different conceptions of policy making, including the stages model and the advocacy coalition framework, for our understanding of the relationship between research and policy/ practice (Sabatier and Jenkins-Smith, 1993; Burton, 2006; Cairney, 2016). A key message from such work is that the use of policy theories allows a greater understanding of the complexities of the policy making process and why particular policy decisions were made, which can help advocates (including advocates of evidence-informed policy and practice) to identify key actors and leverage points for power and influence in the process (Culleron et al, 2015). The study of professional practice is also a well-developed field being similarly influenced by research use/impact interests.

As the study of policy making increasingly examines the role of research evidence, it begins to overlap with the fourth and final role for social science considered in this chapter. This relates to the vital role played by social science is developing a better understanding of how research, including systematic reviews, interacts with policy and practice, through systematic study of the 'research production to use' process. Although there is a long tradition of using research in policy making, and the relationship between social science and policy making has, in a general sense, been the subject of debate for many years, this is a fairly new and as yet underdeveloped field of study. Prompted by the recent resurgence of enthusiasm for evidence-informed policy making in the UK, there is interest shown by key research funding agencies, such as the English Economic and Social Science Research Council (ESRC) and others. Concerned specifically with the relationship between research, policy and practice, this broad and growing field – what we refer to as the 'social science of research production and use' – has a fundamental part to play in addressing recurring questions about the scale, standing and public value of the social sciences (Brewer, 2013). As Davies et al (2000), among others, have observed, it is something of an irony that the new policy focus on evidence-informed policy does not have a strong evidence base underpinning it. There remains wide variation in the uptake of research evidence, whether single studies, reviews of research or even whole programmes of work. Although systematic reviews provide an explicit and rigorous way of informing policy and practice users of research, users may face a whole array of obstacles when attempting to utilise this, or any other type of, evidence (Oliver et al, 2014). It is therefore important that research in this area progresses.

Such research may include a broad range of research questions. We will briefly refer to four sub-areas of research activity connected with this developing field of study. Further examples can be found in *Evidence and Policy*, a specialist academic journal focused on research use in policy and practice.

First, there is a growing number of output-oriented studies concerned with the measurement of research use and wider research impact. In an early example, Carol Weiss (1979) examined the way in which research was used selectively to support decisions made for reasons other than research evidence, finding that the enlightenment impact of research in informing how decision-makers thought about policy issues was greater than any instrumental effect from research findings. More recently, Wooding et al (2007) examined how the ESRC's Future of Work research programme influenced policy and professional practice.

A second sub-area of research activity consists of process-oriented studies. Here, attention is focused on capturing *how* policy and practice decisions and actions are influenced by research, including identifying the barriers and facilitators to such use (eg Oliver et al, 2014). Some studies are particularly concerned with user communities themselves (eg Gabbay and Le May, 2004; Kyratsis et al, 2012). Other studies offer conceptual frameworks for thinking about the concept of moving knowledge into action. Much-used and -cited examples include models developed by Knott and Wildavsky (1980) and Graham et al (2006).

The third sub-area of research activity is concerned with strategies to enhance and support the use of research evidence in decision-making. In recent years, many different initiatives have been developed to improve the communication, interpretation and uptake of research, with the aim of helping decision-makers of different types make better use of research. Systematic reviews and resultant user guidance have emerged as important tools in many areas of public policy, helping strengthen the bridge from knowing to doing. Other ways of trying to narrow the gap between research production and use include communication and marketing strategies and the use of specialist knowledge brokerage services. Social science is fundamental to both the design and evaluation of these strategies. There is now a considerable body of research, including systematic reviews, evaluating the impact of strategies designed to help decision-makers of different types make better use of research (Langer et al, 2016). The results of a recent review of reviews in this area have shown that many strategies are not effective when used in isolation. We need to examine the mechanisms of evidence use in order to better understand and more efficiently study which combination of strategies are most effective (Langer et al, 2016). In essence, we need more theoretical work to help understand these processes, and then to use this to inform the implementation and delivery of such strategies.

Finally, there is a considerable body of research activity concerned with how evidence-informed interventions are put into practice (or not) in real-world settings. The focus of this emerging area of social science – the field of implementation science – is less on facilitating the use of systematic reviews and other sources of evidence in policy development and decision-making, and more on achieving the changes that the research recommends. In other words, the overall goal is on helping accelerate the spread of evidence-based practice, programmes and policies. Often, those implementing these will have some knowledge of the research underlying the recommended actions, but this is not always necessary. The intent is mainly to change behaviour in line with what the research-based guidance advises. As the aim is often to investigate and address major bottlenecks (eg social, behavioural and economic) that impede effective implementation, understanding the behaviour of professionals and other stakeholders is central. To that end, implementation science draws upon the theories and techniques of behaviour change research, for example, the examination of (and intervention in) the capacity, opportunity and motivation for behaviour to change (Michie et al, 2014).

Conclusion: the many roles of social science in research production and use

This chapter has focused on the role of systematic reviews as a resource for policy making. In doing so, it has argued that policy is often about social science issues and so social science should be able to inform policy making. Although simple in principle, finding relevant, reliable research can be difficult in practice, even for researchers. Systematic reviews have an important role in providing a formal explicit method for mapping, synthesising and enabling wider access to existing research, thereby increasing potential for its use. They can be applied to all research questions and to all areas of research. As a secondary (or meta-level) method of research analysis, reviews employ a range of methods depending on the research question being asked (just as with variations in question and method in primary research). Although reviews are often designed with instrumental notions of research use in mind, it is acknowledged that they also have potential for a broader function within the complex, interactive process between research production and use, changing the ways that problems are conceptualised and understood. A further important consideration is that the current 'impact agenda' seems to focus more on impact alone (policy initiatives to encourage all academics to have impact with all of their research) rather than a concern for the quality and consistency of the evidence base informing that impact. Systematic reviews are useful here in providing a broader understanding than can be provided by any given individual or an unrepresentative sample of studies.

All of these issues can be understood within a wider view of how social science relates to research production and use. The chapter identified some of the overlapping and interrelated ways in which social science enables the use of research evidence in policy and practice: in initial policy discussions; in the policy choices that flow from these; and in the resultant practical implications of the decisions taken. These roles relate to:

1. the development of the knowledge base about social issues;
2. the technical and methodological aspects of studying social issues;
3. building understanding about the demand side of the equation – the nature of policy and practice; and
4. building understanding of how research, including systematic reviews, interacts with policy and practice, with the intention of enabling such interactions to become more frequent and useful, for example: (i) measuring research use and wider research impact; (ii) capturing the processes by which use/impact occurs; (iii) studying strategies to improve the use of research in decision-making; and (iv) studying how to achieve evidence-informed behaviour change (implementation science).

In mapping research activity and in synthesising research results, systematic reviews can be located within each of these four roles. The results of these reviews (telling us what has been studied and what these studies have found out) also feed back to inform future research and so influence the nature of social science and social science methods. In addition, research production and use are driven by policies and practices that are themselves open to research study.

In sum, systematic reviews have a central and a dynamic interactive role in mapping and synthesising research as part of the research production and use process, but they also have a dynamic and interactive role in mapping and synthesising evidence on each of the stages of the research production–to-use system.

Further reading
A key guide is provided by Gough et al (2017). To get a sense of what systematic reviews deliver, visit the Education Endowment Foundation's Teaching and Learning Toolkit (available at: https://educationendowmentfoundation.org.uk/evidence/teaching-learning-toolkit/), which provides summary evidence from systematic reviews of the effectiveness (and strength of such evidence) of different educational interventions. Another example is the Crime Reduction Toolkit provided by the What Works Centre for Crime Reduction

(available at: http://whatworks.college.police.uk/toolkit/Pages/Toolkit.aspx).

Notes

[1] See, for example, the work of the James Lind Alliance, available at: http://www.jla.nihr.ac.uk/

[2] See: https://educationendowmentfoundation.org.uk/evidence/teaching-learning-toolkit/

[3] See: http://whatworks.college.police.uk/toolkit/Pages/Toolkit.aspx

[4] See: http://gradeworkinggroup.org/index.htm

who is this for? the social scientist to become more relevant?

FOUR

Randomised controlled trials

Peter John

Randomised control trials (RCTs) – sometimes just called 'trials' – have recently come into their own as a preferred method of evaluating public policies. Policymakers around the world now use them much more regularly than they used to, evaluating a range of policies with RCTs, such as development aid, educational practice innovations and measures to promote the growth of firms, just to name a few of the applications currently in play. These examples join established trials of health interventions, such as on exercise, smoking cessation and attendance at medical clinics, and follow on from long-running programmes of randomised evaluations in welfare and employment that go back to the 1960s. There has been a gradual maturation in the skills of using the method and policymakers have gained more experience in designing and implementing trials (see Torgerson and Torgerson, 2008). The growth of official interest in trials has run in parallel with their diffusion across the academy. Whereas RCTs used to be restricted to a few areas of academic study, like health, many disciplines, such as political science (see Druckman, 2011), have seen a growth in the use of trials to answer important questions that were hitherto hard to appraise with observational data, such as the effect of canvassing on voter turnout (Green et al, 2013). The other main driver has been the recent interest in behavioural public policy: using ideas from the behavioural sciences and behavioural economics to redesign the tools of government (Oliver, 2013). Nudges and other forms of behavioural redesign, especially when directed at government communications, are particularly amenable to testing by RCTs, whereby each nudge is evaluated in a treatment arm (John et al, 2011).

RCTs have the benefit of simplicity, at least on first inspection, particularly where there is only one intervention to evaluate compared to a control group (see John, 2016). The idea rests on creating a fair comparison between something that a public agency or researcher does and a different state of affairs, which might be no intervention at all or where the recipient group just gets a normal package of services or a comparable intervention. The units under study are randomised into groups and when one group gets an intervention and the other does not, it is possible to compare average outcomes across the groups. Not only can the researcher or policymaker say that an intervention worked or not, but they can also tell by how much and thereby include such calculations in their assessment of the costs and benefits of policy choices. In short, trials work by creating two groups that are equivalent to each other, subjecting one but not the other to a policy measure, and then measuring the difference that the policy measure made to the group that received it compared to the one that did not. Any difference in outcomes can confidently be put down to the policy intervention.

Of course, trials can get complicated very quickly when there are multiple arms and stages. There are a number of features of the outside world that impinge on their design, such as attrition or loss of subjects, and where only some respondents or areas select into the treatment or intervention. These situations can create some complex issues when running the analysis. It is important to realise that a good knowledge of statistics is essential when designing a trial. Trials require careful planning and coordination; they require the handling of large amounts of data; and it is usually essential to implement trials in cooperation with a range of partners (see John, 2016). However, the conclusion to draw is that even with the challenges and complexity in delivering trials, they are very much worth doing because they provide what other methods find very hard, if not impossible, to achieve: a causal inference. With the data at hand, the policymaker or researcher can ascertain whether, in fact, there is a relationship between a policy and an outcome, such as a job training programme and the numbers of people in employment.

Assessing causation is an important goal of social science, but one that has proved surprisingly elusive with many methods, such as case studies, surveys of stakeholders, regression methods and even time-series analysis. These techniques can identity whether an intervention is associated with outcomes of interest, but they cannot usually prove the relationship, largely because they cannot generate a counterfactual from which to compare the intervention. Random allocation between a control and treatment group creates that counterfactual because only one factor distinguishes each group, which is the intervention, as the control group presents what would have happened had the intervention not taken place. This is exactly what policymakers want to know – or at least should want to know. They can find out if what they decided worked or not and whether they should adopt or abandon it.

The University of Chicago Press

REVIEW COPY

Evidence-based Policy Making in the Social Sciences
Methods that Matter
Edited by Gerry Stoker and Mark Evans

Published by Policy Press at the Univ of Bristol
Distributed by the University of Chicago Press

Publication Date: November 15, 2016

Paper $45.95 ISBN: 978-1-4473-2937-4

For more information, please contact Nicholas Lilly by phone at (773)702-7490, by fax at (773)702-9756, or by e-mail at nlilly@uchicago.edu

Please send a PDF of your published review to: **publicity@press.uchicago.edu**
Or, by mail to: **Publicity Director, THE UNIVERSITY OF CHICAGO PRESS**
1427 E. 60th Street, Chicago, Illinois 60637, U.S.A. Telephone 773-702-7740

ORDERING INFORMATION

Orders from the U.S.A., Canada, Mexico, Central and South America, East and Southeast Asia, and South Asia, and China:
The University of Chicago Press
Chicago Distribution Center
11030 S. Langley Avenue
Chicago, IL 60628
U.S.A.
Tel: 1-800-621-2736; (773) 702-7000
Fax: 1-800-621-8476; (773) 702-7212
PUBNET @ 202-5280

Orders from the United Kingdom, Europe, Middle East, Africa, and West and South Asia:
The University of Chicago Press
c/o John Wiley & Sons Ltd. Distribution Centre
1 Oldlands Way
Bognor Regis, West Sussex PO22 9SA
UNITED KINGDOM
Tel: (0) 1243 779777
Fax: (0) 1243 820250
Email: cs-books@wiley.co.uk

Orders from Japan can be placed with the Chicago Distribution Center or:
United Publishers Services Ltd.
1-32-5 Higashi-shinjshima
Shinagawa-ku
Tokyo 140-0002
JAPAN
Tel: 81-3-5479-7251
Fax: 81-3-5479-7307
Email: info@ups.co.jp

Orders from Australia and New Zealand:
Footprint Books Pty Ltd
1/6A Prosperity Parade
Warriewood NSW 2102
AUSTRALIA
Tel: (+61) 02 9997-3973
Fax: (+61) 02 9997-3185
Email: info@footprint.com.au
http://www.footprint.com.au

For Information:
International Sales Manager
The University of Chicago Press
1427 E. 60th Street
Chicago, IL 60637
U.S.A.
Tel: (773) 702-7898
Fax: (773) 702-9756
Email: sales@press.uchicago.edu

Other methods can also appraise the causal relationship, such as when there is a natural experiment when differences between areas or people happen 'as if random' (Dunning, 2012); but these situations are hard to identify. Quasi-experimental methods, such as matching or difference-in-differences, can also offer a lot of leverage, but, in practice, these suffer from limitations as it is not possible to rule out whether unobserved differences between people or places have affected the outcome of interest. RCTs offer something to policymakers that no other method can provide.

Basics of the method

RCTs involve introducing random allocation to treated and non-treated subjects, and then comparing the average outcomes between the groups after the intervention. There are different elements to the process. The first is the identification of the sample of interest, whether it is individuals in a policy programme or communities affected, so there needs to be attention to what the unit of measurement is as it determines how randomisation takes place. The researcher needs to decide on the treatments and whether to have a control group or not. The treatment tests what the policy intervention or other is seeking to evaluate, which may be easy to think of, but interventions are usually complex and can take different forms depending on the client or context. A treatment arm can only really test one thing at a time, which is uniformly applied to all in the group. If the treatment varies according to who gets it, it is hard to ascertain what it is about the intervention that is working or not working. The solution is to increase the number of treatment groups but this can put pressure on the sample size and the statistical power of the experiment. A related aim is to work out what happens in the control condition, which seems an easy task to do and can be thought about as an experimental condition without the treatment. However, in the policy world, where everyone is getting treated to a degree, it is hard to work out what the 'policy off' or control condition might be.

The researcher needs to estimate the total sample size for the experiment and for each treatment arm. This is where a good understanding of the statistical foundations of trials is needed because there is a relationship between the anticipated effect size, the variance (standard deviation) in each treatment arm and the sample size needed in each group. It is possible to use software, whether customised or online, to make the calculations; however, it is important not to just plug in the numbers without some understanding of what is going on. Moreover, even though the software looks simple, it often prompts users to make choices, such as between one-sided and two-sided tests, whether there are repeat measures or not, whether to analyse proportions or means, to supply the standard deviation, and to say what level of statistical power is acceptable. The designer of experiments needs to understand these concepts, though, of course, the real world often intrudes during the experiment to blow these calculations off course, and even the sample size calculation itself relies on making assumptions before the experiment that can often only be known afterwards.

Randomisation is crucial and it is the aspect of an RCT that sets it apart from other methods. It means applying a random number to a set of data points and then dividing the sample into control and treatment conditions. These numbers can be entered into a spreadsheet and, with clear instructions about who is to get the treatment and control conditions, can then be passed on to the administrator or research team who will implement the experiment. It sounds simple, but it needs careful control and the researcher needs to be very sure that the random allocation is respected throughout the course of the experiment as real life or pressures on the bureaucracy can blow random allocation off course. There are also more complex kinds of randomisation, such as randomisation in blocks or pairs, which are harder to implement but have their uses in improving the balance of the experiment between treatment and control arms.

Designers of RCTs need to pay a lot of attention to the collection and management of data, which need to be planned in advance. There is the collection of information about the sample and who or what qualifies to be in it, as well as a need to calculate what levels of attrition might occur during the trial and how many people or areas are likely to take the treatment. The outcome variable or variables should to be carefully thought about: what these are and how effectively and accurately they can be collected. In particular, these data need to be matched to the control and treated conditions through identifiers in official or other records, such as surveys. Other variables are useful, such as covariates on the personal characteristics of the sample or indicators of the characteristics of the areas, which can be used to check if the randomisation is balanced. These variables can be used to find out whether the treatment effect varies across the sample. These analyses need to be planned, however, as it is possible to find these subgroup effects by chance if enough interactions are analysed. There is always at least a one in 20 chance that a relationship is going to be statistically significant, and the researcher may be tempted to retrofit his or her theoretical model on the basis of one of these invalid findings. Increasingly, researchers in the social sciences are following their colleagues in the medical sciences by registering their research designs in advance in an official registry.[1] This makes explicit the aims of the research and guards researchers against 'fishing' their results for statistically significant findings.

The final stage is the analysis and writing up of experiments, which has the features of apparent simplicity and underlying complexity alluded to earlier. It is simple in that averages or proportions of the outcome variable are measured across the treatment and control arms, which can be represented as means or percentages, either as numbers or as figures, such as in bar charts, which can be attractive to present to practitioners. The statistics that can be used to determine whether these differences – if they exist – are more than by chance are also fairly straightforward to apply. For averages, t-statistics can be reported and whether these are statistically significant or not; for proportions, it is possible to use the z-score or even a chi-squared statistic. These figures can convey whether the trial has worked or not, as well as by how much, which is often all the policymakers need to know. Sometimes, policymakers are also interested in the effect of the treatment on different kinds of people, which can be calculated by comparing averages or proportions in the treatment and control groups within each subgroup. Regression analysis is comprehensible to most people involved with evaluation. RCTs place the outcome as the dependent variable and the treatments as independent terms. It is also possible to include other covariates into the statistical model and then to interpret the coefficients and standard errors just like observational research. Even some of the statistical tests for the balance of the sample between the treatment and control groups are quite straightforward, being nothing more than a comparison of means or proportions. There is an array of textbooks to hand (see the further reading section at the end of this chapter) for the more complex issues that might arise, such as attrition, and an increasing number of experts working in government (eg the UK Cross-Government Trial Advice Panel) or in the academy (University of York Trials Unit) who are prepared to help.

Examples of the use of randomised controlled trials

There are numerous examples of RCTs, as the opening paragraphs of this chapter indicate. The first example here comes from policies to help the growth of small firms, and is taken from the UK. Growth vouchers were a UK policy to offer free training and advice to small businesses.[2] They were introduced in January 2014 and ended in March 2015 (BIS 2015), and were targeted at 20,000 small businesses. There was an online marketplace managed by Enterprise Nation, and the programme allocated growth vouchers to small businesses. The idea is to test whether the advice and vouchers actually lead to the better performance of these small businesses. It is a research project and the idea is to inform future government policy. However, it is very much like the policy itself as real firms got benefits. The trial design was incorporated into the policy as part of the stages that a firm needs to go through to get a voucher. At stage one, businesses applied to the programme and were assessed for their eligibility. Then, in stage two, businesses were randomly allocated to either an online or a personal assessment to determine their business needs. In stage three – and this was not random – businesses were offered advice in one of five fields: raising finance and managing cash flow; recruiting and developing staff; improving leadership and management skills; marketing and attracting/keeping customers; and making the most of digital technology areas. What was random at this stage was that they got allocated a growth voucher, with a 75% chance of getting a voucher. At stage four, businesses selected a supplier of training from a set of approved trainers. At stage five, businesses arranged to receive their advice, arranging a price of up to a maximum of £2,000. At stage six, they claimed their subsidy.

With this design, it is possible to evaluate the impact of the two kinds of intervention (online advice and growth vouchers) on policy outcomes, which are data relating to firm survival and profitability measured over a five-year period. The trial also allows a test of how the interventions combine, whether getting face-to-face advice helps the impact of the growth voucher. With 20,000 firms, the trial does not suffer the familiar problems of low statistical power, and, indeed, the government did statistical power calculations before deciding to carry out the trial. There are number of complex features of this trial that make it interesting, as well as being one of the first of this kind of business support. One is the classic problem of determining the causal mechanism exactly: what is it about the voucher that might or might not have an effect? To that end, the ministry commissioned a substantial qualitative element to the study to run alongside the measurements needed for the trial in order to try to get at this effect, and the evaluation was hence mixed-method. It is also hard to work out with the trial design which of the streams worked. As firms selected into these activities, it is not possible by a trial (or any other method) to work out which one was more useful for the firms. The final issue is that the trial is likely to suffer from attrition because firms may drop out if they do not get a voucher and it may be hard to find the data. Firms that do not get a voucher are less likely to complete the surveys that are part of the evaluation, or even be a part of the qualitative evaluation. This is called one-sided attrition and is a common experience with voucher schemes (see Angrist et al, 2006). Economists have devised complex re-weighting schemes to replace the missing data to the degree to which researchers can have confidence that the loss is not damaging. The research is ongoing so it will be interesting to see if the policy worked or not.

The second example comes from the development field and is the evaluation of a programme to introduce community development in East Congo, called Tuungane (see Humphries et al, 2012), which has been in operation since 2007. Agencies concerned with funding development have introduced policies to involve those affected, the citizens in the communities concerned, in the delivery of the programme, in particular, so that they can make decisions about the allocation of funds within communities, something the community and its leaders decide. The idea, which is common in advocacy and intellectual circles, is that direct participation can improve the performance of communities by encouraging the ownership and commitment of those affected in the programme (Fung, 2006). It tries to counter the passivity that poorer communities feel when receiving aid. It can be associated with measures to improve the governance of small communities in terms of representation and engagement. In development, this is called community-driven reconstruction (CDR) and is directed to communities that have experienced conflict and war.

The programme in East Congo is vast given the size of the territory and the about 1.7 million people living there. Tuungane I got £29,685,253 (US$46,309,000); a second phase of the project (Tuungane II) has a value of £60,986,977 (US$95,139,684). The element of the programme that was evaluated with an RCT was an unconditional cash transfer programme for 560 villages in treatment and control areas, which got block grants of US$1,000. The treatment condition for 280 villages got the Tuungane programme. The control just got the financial benefits allocated in a more standard way, so that both treatment and control had equal amounts of financial benefits. The project collected data on about 200 outcome measures to evaluate the effect of the programme. Overall, the researchers found no effect of the programme on most outcomes. There was no impact of the community participation compared to the villages that did not get the treatment.

There are various issues that emerge from this RCT. The first is the scale of the operation and the vast effort needed to implement this well-administered trial. Measuring the outcomes themselves was a large operation, requiring the assistance of researchers who travelled from village to village, often in areas torn by conflict. In one case, a researcher was captured and the researchers had to negotiate for his release. The second is the negative effects themselves and what they mean. Do they show that participation elements of the policy do not have an impact? It is hard to say. The evaluation has received a lot of resistance from the countries concerned and workers in the field. Was it just the one programme that did not work because it was implemented at a point of time in a particular way, or does it show that not all citizen involvement programmes work? This cuts into the external validity of experiments and drawing conclusions from them. In spite of the negative results, the RCT was very provocative in stimulating debate in the development policy field.

The third example comes from the behavioural agenda alluded to at the start of the chapter, where policymakers have used the insights from behavioural economics to encourage better performance from public agencies, being pioneered by the UK Behavioural Insights Team (BIT) (Halpern, 2015). The example was a project with Her Majesty Courts and Tribunals Service (HMCTS) using SMS text messages to encourage those who owe court fines to settle their debts. In the UK, unpaid fines amount to more than £500 million. Managing non-compliant accounts and dispatching bailiffs to collect fines in person is costly. BIT and HMCTS designed a large RCT designed to test the effectiveness of mobile phone text messaging as an alternative method of inducing people to pay their outstanding fines (Haynes et al, 2013). An adaptive trial design was used (stopping randomisation when significant findings were detected), first to test the effectiveness of text messaging against no treatment, and then to test the relative effectiveness of alternative messages. Text messages, which are relatively inexpensive, were found to increase significantly the average payment of fines. The research found that text messages were especially effective when they addressed the recipient by name.

The fourth example is different from the large-scale evaluations just described, which need a large amount of resources and involvement of government agencies. Experiments can be done by small groups of researchers or people in communities using their own resources and do not need large numbers if well designed. The example here is the use of a social or community event to increase voter turnout (Addonizio et al, 2007). The researchers wanted to see whether having an outdoor party with entertainment and food would encourage people to go to the polls, whether making voting fun would overcome voter apathy and help recreate the positive social experiences of voting of previous decades, when voting was associated with discussion with friends and was itself a social event for the community. In 2005 and 2006, they carried out these experiments in 14 selected suitable areas (what are called 'place-based' experiments), where precincts were randomised to treatment and control conditions (in effect, this is 14 separate experiments). On election day in these places, often on the front lawns of public schools, the researchers held parties, offering food and non-alcoholic drinks, and played games. There was a large tent and signs alerting passers-by about the event. The event was also advertised in advance. By comparing turnout in the treatment and control conditions, the events were found to increase voter turnout by 6.5 percentage points. It shows that community engagement matters for turnout and is a nice complement to trials mainly based on voter mobilisation. Such experiments cannot be done everywhere. Often, election law forbids the giving of any benefit near a polling station, so this experiment cannot be replicated where this is the case.

When to use the method

RCTs cannot be applied to evaluate all aspects of public policy, though, with some imagination, they can be used to cover a lot of policy issues and extend to many more than they do currently. In fact, opponents of RCTs often like to restrict their usage and say that complex policy interventions cannot be effectively evaluated by RCTs that have such a narrow range of applications (see Pawson and Tilly, 1997; Cartwright and Hardie, 2012). Such criticisms have some validity in that RCTs are good for particular things, such as where there is a precise element of policy that needs to be tested that has application to a large number of subjects. However, overall, the critics are too pessimistic as trials can be used more generally to evaluate government actions and to suggest the feasibility of new policy options. A lot depends on the ingenuity of the experiment to introduce elements of randomness, even in complex programmes, such as through a stepped-wedge design, where implementing areas are all gradually randomly allocated to a policy.

Of course, the critics are right that RCTs work well when there is a feature of a programme that can be varied, such as a new training opportunity for employees or a new teaching provision, for example, using teaching assistants in the classroom. There needs to be large numbers of units (eg employees or classrooms) in order to have sufficient statistical power to detect an effect with certainty, and the intervention needs to be delivered uniformly to all in the treatment group. There needs to be a control group that does not get the intervention or a comparison group that gets a normal package of interventions. Treatment and control groups cannot make contact, or, if they can, there needs to be variation in the extent to which they make contact to estimate the contamination. There needs to be ways to ensure that attrition is not a problem by investing in resources to trace lost subjects and to get data from them (which could help with the growth vouchers trial discussed earlier).

Large numbers are not always available, of course. It might only be possible to try out a new policy on a few communities rather than the hundreds that were available in the Tuungane project. It might not be possible to deliver an intervention uniformly if there are particular needs to be met. Politicians and others might not want to approve a project that denies services to some groups, even if they can promise to provide those services later when the trial is over. These are usually political constraints and do not say that a trial cannot be carried out, merely that the policymakers have not tried hard enough to find the units and to deal with the potential issues. Trialists need to persuade policymakers and overcome these constraints by finding more sample areas and arguing that lotteries occur anyway. Rather than pilots, where it is hard to find out whether an intervention works, RCTs allow governments to find out whether something works before it is rolled out everywhere, thereby saving much needed public resources and concentrating them where they are known to have a positive effect.

Many of the challenges of doing trials have to do with the lack of familiarity with policymakers and officials; once they get used to them, they find them much easier to do. They can roll them out easily and to many new fields as there is less consideration needed to commission each one. Many public authorities do not know how to randomise easily and then to match the randomly allocated data to the treatment conditions. With more experience, it gets easier to perform these tasks, which is just how the private sector operates, such as Google or large supermarket chains. These companies have internal systems to roll out trials in what is called A/B testing, which can be done without much difficulty and in real time: information is fed back to decision-makers quickly so that they can adjust their strategies. More integration of official information, as envisaged in an age of 'big data' (see Chapter Eight), might make it easier to access the data for trials. It is also possible to imagine public authorities designing the roll-out of policies that have randomness embedded in them. In fact, where there is the political will, it is relative easy to get trials done because bureaucracies implement interventions when instructed, and evaluators can use official data to measure outcomes that they have access to. As politicians authorise trials, it is usually not thought necessary to have an external body approving the ethical conduct of the trial (as would be the case in a university, where there is a formal ethical approval process requiring extensive preparation). Recently, there has been more official attention to ethical guidelines, and agencies are increasingly introducing some ethical oversight or referring projects done in partnership with academics to ethical review committees.

It may be hard to generalise from a trial that an intervention will work elsewhere, when conditions are different, which is the classic external validity problem often attributed to RCTs (but, of course, often applies to all other methods of evaluation). The solution is to do many trials to replicate the findings so as to have enough to carry out a meta-analysis, that is, to analyse many trials in order to generalise the findings. Sometimes, government or other agencies may not have the resources or time to do many interventions, but where doing trials becomes routine, such as at Her Majesty's Revenue and Customs (HMRC), the UK tax collection agency, it may be possible to replicate trials over a long period of time.

Trials are also thought not to deliver understanding of the causal mechanisms, so the researcher or policymaker only knows that it works, but not why. It is often thought that qualitative methods have greater traction on this problem. This criticism is not entirely correct because qualitative methods also find it hard to get at the causal mechanism because they will approach a small number of people or other units that have selected into talking to them, and so are not typical of the treated and non-treated groups. The small numbers mean that it is hard to generalise from these studies. Qualitative studies also rely on self-reports, such as people saying to an interviewer why they acted, which can be unreliable. Despite this common criticism of RCTs, other methods also do not address causation, even though they may offer greater understanding. In fact, the way to get more traction on the causal mechanism is to carry out another trial with more treatment arms that summarise the expectations from a model. For example, if it is found that personalisation increases compliance, it is possible to address the causal mechanism by varying the kind of personalisation or its extent in a later trial.

Trials are often thought to be of more use down the implementation chain, which is because they are better at ascertaining the exact processes that deliver a policy rather than coming up with options in the planning process. In fact, one area of the expansion of trials is on settled processes of implementation, such as collecting taxes and fines and tweaking the debt recovery process so as to make best use of existing procedures and resources (eg Haynes et al, 2013). Trials are also good ways to evaluate tweaks or modifications to existing programmes as they are being implemented, especially if the agency introduces the possibility of randomness in standard operating procedures. Here, new ideas may be introduced to make a policy intervention work more effectively, such as better advice in job centres in a job-training programme. However, there is no reason why trials cannot be part of the policy formulation process, particularly as, in practice, policy formulation and implementation are very closely linked and can be treated as similar activities by the peak decision-making agency. So, the growth vouchers trial looks like policy implementation as a policy is being rolled out on the ground; but it is, in fact, about policy formulation. The ministry wants to know whether this kind of policy can work. With this knowledge, it can then formulate business assistance policy in a future iteration. Trials can become an essential tool to help make policy, and perform much better than pilots in influencing these choices. Of course, there are limitations to their use, and it is not possible to use a trial to solve some fundamental problems in public policy and politics, such as whether to have an independent central bank or to withdraw from the European Union. However, most problems in public policy are more humdrum, being about the delivery and improvement of public services or ensuring that citizens act in ways that help respond to public problems. This is where trials are so useful in making the machinery of government work much better and in rolling out policies more in tune with citizen expectations. RCTs allow policymakers to try things out, which is what they often like to do, and then to retry ideas based on the feedback they get from trials. It is possible to envisage the emergence of the experimental public authority, one that is committed to randomness and to continual evaluation, ever sceptical about what can be claimed, and willing to stop doing things if trials do not show positive effects.

Conclusion

For anyone involved with evaluation, RCTs have always been – at least since the 1920s – known about as a superior means to generate knowledge. They are the so-called gold standard because they can attribute a causal relationship, which other methods find hard to do. For example, the UK government handbook of evaluation, *The Magenta Book* (Treasury, 2011), placed trials at top of the hierarchy of available methods. However, until recently, they would have been regarded as a rarity by most agencies and government organisations. They were not done frequently and were restricted to particular fields, mainly health-related interventions, and also welfare and employment policies, even in the US, where trials have had much more of a pedigree. They were widely believed to be complicated to do, and official knowledge has been burdened by some histories of poor implementation (the famous one being the negative income tax experiment in the US; see Ross, 1970). As the social science research programme started in employment and welfare, where experiments were used to study complex interventions that change over time, it is possible that policymakers thought them harder to do than they really are.

Today, experiments are much more readily embraced as a form of evaluation that any policymaker would wish to consider. This change has happened because policy experiments are much more the norm. As shown by the work of BIT, they have been carried out in a straightforward and timely manner, and show considerable savings of resources at a time of fiscal austerity (see John, 2014). These developments parallel the growth of RCTs in developing-country contexts and across the social sciences more generally. They can assist policymakers to develop and refine most kinds of policies, so long as there are sufficient numbers of units to work with. As policymakers and evaluators get more experienced in using RCTs, randomness can be embedded in standard bureaucratic procedures so that they are much less effort to carry out. Access to big data can provide more information on who to randomise, more covariates and swifter and more accurate outcomes that vary over time, which will make trials more timely and easier to do. There is every reason to think that in the future, every public agency will have its own trials unit monitoring performance and quickly feeding evaluation back to the core policymakers.

Further reading
There are numerous books on RCTs, which make different assumptions about the prior knowledge of the reader. The most straightforward is by Torgerson and Torgerson (2008). It is particularly useful for policymakers because of the many applied examples that

the authors provide. Another general book, which has particular application to the development field and also does not make strong assumptions about prior knowledge, is Glennerster and Takavarasha (2013). More advanced is Gerber and Green (2012), which is probably the best textbook around, especially for those designing and analysing trials. For those who want more guidance on the practical side of delivering a trial, John (2017) reviews the steps that researchers need to follow.

Notes

[1] See, for example: http://egap.org/content/registration

[2] For details see: https://www.gov.uk/apply-growth-vouchers

FIVE

Qualitative comparative analysis for reviewing evidence and making decisions

Matt Ryan

This chapter makes the case that the tools of qualitative comparative analysis (QCA) can help policymakers make better decisions. I show that QCA is an accessible method. It takes everyday logic that many people already use when making decisions based on competing evidence, uses simple tools to extend the available evidence base and allows us to draw more systematic conclusions about the effects of action in different contexts.

QCA is a method of reviewing and comparing evidence whose influence has grown steadily in the academy over the last 30 years. Despite previous advocacy and proof of concept (see Rihoux et al, 2011; Blackman, 2013; Blackman et al, 2013), QCA's potential for policy making is yet to be realised. Most academic introductions to QCA of which I am aware start with a consideration of its approach to examining the social world and try to differentiate it from 'mainstream' or 'traditional' methods and assumptions by introducing a whole new set of nomenclature. Instead, I am going to start by providing a practical how-to guide that follows a very basic example of QCA from my own research. My hope is that this will help orientate the reader and convince them to read on. I then consider some of the challenges that regularly face practical policy decisions, and explain how they may suffer from certain biases in the collection and analysis of relevant information, and where QCA can help. I discuss some of the known limitations of the method and how they can be addressed before offering some concluding thoughts on how QCA ought to contribute to information-gathering and decision-making as an important part of a broader complementary toolkit.

How to dance qualitative comparative analysis – the basic steps

In this section, I want to use an example to run through a rough-and-ready QCA. Methodology-wonks reading this might wince at the thought of describing a 'rough-and-ready' version of a method that is supposed to trade on sophistication and nuance. QCA enthusiasts might feel especially sensitive as the method has come under increasing (and, in my view, very welcome) scrutiny as its influence has grown. However, my experience is that the usual preface of methodological affray that accompanies academic introductions to QCA can confuse and alienate newcomers, and references are provided in the further reading section at the end of this chapter for readers who would like to explore the issues in greater depth.

The example I use here is a slightly simplified version of previously published research, extracting and comparing six out of 18 cases compared in a study of participatory budgeting (PB) programmes (Ryan, 2014). The substantive focus of my example is on trying to understand in what contexts citizen-participants are able to have meaningful control over budgetary decisions and in what contexts they are not. I also want to invite the reader to imagine and mimic these steps with a policy issue of their own in mind. My purpose here is to show that the method is actually quite accessible and simply extends the logic with which many human-being-decision-makers already approach evidence. In many cases, the best practices I describe, especially the early steps, are not unique to QCA and apply across many research approaches. I want to argue that like all good research methods, QCA is a tool that harnesses the innate intuitions of human information-seekers, as well as the received wisdom of experience (what is sometimes called common sense), but also provides some useful systematic checks on bias and other common errors of logic.

Step 1: Select an outcome that you want to explain

The outcome could be a policy problem that is present in a few different locations but not in others (eg low tax compliance, high rates of drug abuse, absence of safe cycling, etc). With such an outcome in mind, we can think about what is common to the contexts in which the problem is absent compared to what is common where it is present. This information helps us to think about what factors we might need to introduce or remove in a given context to mitigate the problem. Alternatively, we might first think of a proposed solution that has worked well in some cases but not in others. Again, comparison allows us to look at the factors that might be driving success and failure (For example, why do harsh penalties increase tax compliance in some contexts and not in others?).

The basic unit of analysis to compare could be cities, countries, schools, health programmes and so on, and the scope of this unit should be flexible but eventually definite. In my research example, I wanted to explain when and why PB programmes, a potential solution to the problem of democratic deficits, succeeded and failed across different cities worldwide. Here, democratic deficits refer to the increasing sense that governors and the governed operate in different worlds to the extent that the latter group feels that they have little chance to influence the former group. These deficits have become a key concern for governors across the democratic world, who are conscious of the threat that democratic deficits pose to the perceived legitimacy and acceptance of political decisions.

The outcome – what regression analysts often call the dependent variable – has some basic prerequisites. First, if you are intending to carry out comparative analysis, it needs to have occurred in more than one case of which you are aware. This might all seem very straightforward but there are issues to be mindful of here. The pressure of public outcry and the proximity of a policymaker's situational expertise can make it easy to see a particular problem as unique and wicked. The temptation here is myopia. Moreover, policymakers often have incentives to market a problem as unique or a solution as innovative in the hope of drawing attention and funding to it. However, usually, the more cases that you can compare – especially if they are diverse – the better. I cannot claim that this is a particularly original or nuanced observation and I cannot here discuss best practices in the sampling of cases at length. What matters is that QCA is an approach that incentivises the accumulation of cases that may appear at first glance difficult to compare. Cases that appear unrelated or irrelevant can often be quite informative if we stop even for just a short moment to assess their comparability.

Second, the outcome should vary across cases, in particular, if you want to explain both the presence of an outcome and its negation. When comparing across cases where the outcome is a constant (ever-present or ever-absent across cases), it is still possible to identify as irrelevant supposedly important explanatory conditions. Doing this is quite useful – allowing perhaps for the elimination of a cost that does not contribute to solving a problem. However, maximising variance on the outcome further increases the possibilities for analysis. In my example here, I compare three instances where citizens achieved control over meaningful budgetary decision-making, at least for a short time (Porto Alegre, Poitou-Charentes education budget, Rome districts), and three where they did not (Berlin-Lichtenberg, Morsang-Sur-Orge, Rio Claro).

It is worth noting that early discussions of QCA eschewed the language of variables in order to distinguish the propositional logic based on the Boolean algebra underpinning QCA from the correlational logic based on the linear algebra underpinning regression analysis (sometimes called variable-oriented methods). Here, I use the terms 'independent variable' and 'influencing condition' interchangeably because I think the costs to understanding for the novel reader do not outweigh the benefits. Thiem et al (2015) provide a sophisticated update on where differences in approaches are likely to lead to misunderstandings.

Step 2: With a selected policy problem/solution in mind, identify the three or four most important influencing conditions (independent variables) that are likely to explain success or failure

Again, there is nothing too novel about this for those trained in, or even with some notion of, scientific/rational decision-making. To explain citizen control of budget decisions, I assess: A) whether or not the political leadership is committed to participation; B) whether or not there is active civil society demand for participatory innovation; and C) whether or not the municipality/region/association is in a relatively healthy financial state and thereby able to commit money to projects.

Step 3: Select cases and create a regular data matrix summarising measures of presence and absence of conditions

For simplicity, I take six cases for this example and look at the presence/absence of three influencing conditions related to the outcome in these cases. However, despite what you may read or hear elsewhere, there is no ideal number or even range of cases for QCA. The key advantage of QCA in this regard is that it provides a stepwise systematic approach to visualising and analysing data, and a test for necessary and sufficient conditions for an outcome.

Also for simplicity, I present binary data. Data matrices like the one in Table 5.1 may be made up of qualitative or quantitative data using any level of measurement. Readers used to looking at data matrices

Table 5.1: Data matrix

Case ID	A. Participatory leadership? (IV)	B. Civil society demand for participation? (IV)	C. Financial basis to spend? (IV)	Citizen control of budget decisions? (DV)
Buenos Aires	0	0	0	0
Porto Alegre	1	1	1	1
Rio Claro	0	0	1	0
Poitou-Charentes	1	0	1	1
Rome	1	1	0	1
Santo Andre	1	1	0	0

Notes: 1 = present; 0 = absent. IV = Independent Variable; DV = Dependent Variable

might note that the one presented here assumes full information on each case, and has no missing values. One of the limitations of QCA is that, up to now, instruments to deal with missing values remain blunt.

Step 4: Analyse variation in your data

All good comparative research training should advocate the use of visualisation tools to check for skew in data before mathematical algorithms can be used to check for relationship patterns. An important question to ask at this juncture is: are there any constants in the data matrix? If you have variation in an outcome and a supposed influencing condition is or approaches a constant, it suggests that the condition may actually be trivial.

Such a finding can be incredibly useful for assessing policy programmes – it is not uncommon for scientists and policymakers to believe that some condition is a crucial part of any strategy to solve a policy problem, and to be too immersed in routine management approaches to realise that investment for change could be better directed elsewhere in a particular context. As an example, I once worked with a colleague who wanted to understand what conditions led certain sub-national regions to constantly push for greater devolved powers. After speaking at length to a bunch of constitutional experts, he became convinced that the presence of constitutional provisions for devolution was a profoundly important necessary condition that enabled demand for devolution and explained variation in the outcome. The implication would be that those who wanted to make changes in the area ought to concentrate a lot of time on lobbying for constitutional change. However, following much trawling through constitutions, on close inspection, although each case of strong demands for devolution could be linked to the presence of a constitutional provision for such, these provisions were equally present in all the negative cases. In other words, very few constitutions looked at explicitly prohibited devolution short of secession. Beware here, however, if your intuition is that this condition should present as a variable, finding a constant can also point to problems with the interpretations employed in the coding process. That is, it may be that your threshold for calculating the presence/absence of the condition is too low or high to pick up relevant variance. In the previous example, devolution is perhaps defined too loosely or it is, in fact, something approaching secession that interests the researcher but s/he is yet to see the wood for the trees. This careful systematic approach when taken in a stepwise fashion is not overly time-consuming, but provides sensible channels for iteration between hunches and evidence.

A second important check is for multicollinearity. In the six cases that I have selected for this example, conditions A and B co-vary to an extent and have similar values, and one might want to investigate the not-unreasonable possibility that there is an uncontrolled confounder that is behind demand for participatory politics both within civil society and within government.

Step 5: Derive a truth table from the data matrix and code the presence or absence of conditions

This step is where QCA begins to distinguish itself. One of the key tools introduced by the QCA literature is that of the truth table. Truth tables 'do exactly what they say on the tin'. A truth table is a table that maps out the combinations of properties that known and observed cases do take on to those combinations that they *could* logically take. When making policy decisions, the key question is 'What will work?' and the best tools to answer that question are evidence about what has happened before (also known as empirical data) and informed assumptions about other things that could be important within the scope and context of the impending action (also known as theories). A truth table holds empirical and theoretical information together in an accessible and intuitive way when it is too difficult to hold it together in one (average) person's head.

To derive a truth table from a data matrix, you will have to code the information in your matrix (which is not necessary in our example as we already have binary data in Table 5.1) and add what are called logical remainders to your matrix. To do this, you will need to identify:

1. cases that are logically equivalent (ie they have the exact same key properties of presence or absence of a given condition – in my example, there is one pair in the shape of Rome and Santo Andre);

2. the potential combinations of conditions that are logically possible but for which you do not know of any real-world examples (these are the logical remainders) – with six cases and three influencing conditions, a truth table is bound to contain at least two logical remainders. For each k number of conditions, a truth table will have 2^k rows, that is, when analysing four conditions, the truth table will have 16 rows, five conditions will have 32 rows and so on, as the number of logically possible combinations of presence/absence of these conditions in combination increases.

With this information, you should be able to construct a truth table that looks something like the one in Table 5.2. A truth table must have one row each corresponding to the potential combinations of presence and absence of the influencing conditions. With three independent variables, the truth table will have eight rows only. In Table 5.2, where we do not know the outcome (where you have logical remainders), I put a '?' in that column. Where the outcome is unclear because two cases with the same properties disagree on the outcome, I have written 'contradiction'.

Table 5.2: Truth table

Row #	A. Participatory leadership? (IV)	B. Civil society demand for participation? (IV)	C. Financial basis to spend? (IV)	Citizen control of budget decision? (DV)	Cases
1	1	1	1	Yes	Porto Alegre
2	1	0	1	Yes	Poitou-Charentes
3	0	1	1	?	No cases
4	1	1	0	Contradiction	Rome, Santo Andre
5	0	0	1	No	Rio Claro
6	0	1	0	?	No cases
7	1	0	0	?	No cases
8	0	0	0	No	Buenos Aires

Note: IV = Independent Variable; DV = Dependent Variable

Step 6: Assess the truth table – what can it tell you?

The beauty of the truth table is that with a small number of key explanatory conditions and a relatively small number of truth table rows, it becomes a very useful visual tool to enable the assessment of how cases behave and where they logically converge and differ across the population. So, here are the questions that I ask every time I see a truth table, which you can try for yourself:

1. Look at the logical remainders (rows without any cases). It is interesting to think about why we do not have these cases in our sample. Ask yourself the question: do you know of a case that could fill this row or is it unlikely to find such a case (eg that such a case is logically impossible)? It might be that you are ignoring certain types of cases as evidence that could be useful to you. In my previous example, I have no empirical cases where participatory leadership is absent and civil society demand for participation is present. I should ask myself whether my sample is impaired because I have biases that lead me to consider such processes as cases of some different class of things to those that I am trying to understand (some kind of movement-based politics perhaps), when, in fact, they are quite comparable. In this way, the QCA approach can guard against unnecessary myopia. Alternatively, remainders might help to quickly suggest what kinds of actions in particular contexts are more likely to occur.

2. If you have any, look at rows for which you have more than one case. Should these cases go together based on what you know about them? If they contradict on the outcome, it means that there is likely something important missing that explains this variation. Are you overlooking an important condition that explains policy success/ failure? Think about whether it is a good idea to add another condition that can explain this variation and what that condition might be. If cases are similar in a way that you had not anticipated, this may signal avenues for policy learning and information sharing.

3. Finally, look at the rows that have single cases (or relatively low numbers if comparing a larger number of cases). Should these cases really be on their own? Did you really think they were that different to other cases of the same policy phenomenon? What have you learned about how conditions manifest together in different cases?

Step 7: Boolean minimisation and a parsimonious solution

In two separate stages, you will want to explain the outcome and the negation or absence of the outcome. One of the useful assumptions of our approach here is that explanations of outcomes can be asymmetrical and conjunctural. That is another way of saying that because it is always the mix of contexts and conditions that matters, removing one or many of the conditions that in combination are sufficient for, say, a failure will not necessarily lead to a success, and vice versa. For example, we might find that where governments have successfully shifted from centralised care models to community care, a combination of political will (on behalf of the government and Parliament), bureaucratic will (on behalf of providers and managers) and revenue streams to cover switching costs were, in combination, sufficient conditions for positive change. However, when looking at failed attempts in this regard, we might find that even when political will for change is high and funding is available, this can actually contribute to failure where bureaucrats do not immediately buy in as entrenchment occurs and politicians focus revenue streams on other projects. Therefore, we explain the success/failure, or presence/absence, of a condition separately because the explanations are assumed to be distinct. Readers might suggest that this is another way of saying that we should test for interaction effects in the way that is common in many forms of regression analysis. As explained by Schneider and Wagemann (2012) and Thiem et al (2015), the algebra undergirding QCA and the propositional logic on which it is based is not easily reconciled with that of regression-analytic methods and tests different qualities of relationships among variables.

How to engage in Boolean reduction

Identify all the rows that correspond to your outcome and write them out in the following notation, where presence of a condition is defined by upper case and absence by lower case. So, in my example, if I want to explain citizen control of budget decisions, I would take the first and second row (where the outcome is present) and write as follows:

Row 1: ABC
Row 2: AbC

If the terms differ on one variable, only you can eliminate it. If not, you will have to combine rows for a more complex solution. Taking only these two rows, I derive the solution:

AC → citizen control of budget decisions

In plain English, this says that whenever we see the presence of participatory leadership combined with the presence of financial spending capacity in PB programmes, citizens are able to gain meaningful control of important decisions. Civil society demand is irrelevant (at least to explaining the outcomes in these two cases). The same can be done for the negation of the outcome:

Row 5: abC
Row 8: abc
ab → absence of citizen control of budget decisions

Step 8: Interpreting your findings and taking action

So, on the basis of this evidence (again remembering that it is simplified from the original research for purposes of demonstration), those wanting to implement effective citizen participation procedures would be advised to concentrate their efforts on increasing political will or, where it is already present, increasing financial capacities.

So that, approximately, is what a basic QCA looks like. Following this taster, I now go on to answer the question as to what QCA's real added value is for making new discoveries and implementing better policy.

Responding to biases in the evidence–policy paradigm: outliers, risk aversion and policy science

Globally, political/social scientists have recently spent much more time reacting to threats to their worth brought on by accusations of irrelevance. There has been a resulting clamour to justify or claim respect by showcasing impact. For many academics, this has served to highlight their lack of impact, and (for most) frustration that despite good answers to important research questions, uptake of evidence and advice among policymakers or others who influence governance is unpredictable. Evidence presented in the academy must answer to peer review, which judges wisdom, method and robustness. When evidence meets policy making, the necessity of swift judgement in response to crises and more proximate fiscal and human responsibilities account for a different kind of pressure. For policy decisions, time is scarcer, yet risks are greater and the scope of impact is broader (at least in the short term). Simply put, it is different when you *have to* make a decision. Of course, translating research findings into impact is an art, and there are others better placed than I to impart it (see Stoker et al, 2015). However, I would like to argue that the QCA approach holds promise for overcoming at least one barrier on the route from robust research to impact.

At least some of the frustrations of scientists whose research findings are ignored or, often worse in their eyes, misrepresented in policy making stem from misunderstandings of the complex compound that is conceived when evidence meets interests in political decision-making. There are many famous examples of collective decisions that are thwarted by the risk-averse tendencies endemic in policy making and policy debate (climate change, vaccinations, fluoridation, etc). In these cases, what might be called an outlier – that is, some small contradictory evidence that deviates significantly from the average – is usually presented, and publics and their representatives whose interests are placed at risk tend to overvalue the probability of the event occurring by some factor of what damage it could cause to their interests if it did occur. Any politician/policymaker will be forgiven for being cautious not to act where they have knowledge of any case for which the intervention is correlated with a bad outcome and where such outcomes seriously threaten their interests and those of their constituents with which they are bound. Scientists can be exasperated when despite overwhelming evidence in favour of a certain action, policymakers use outliers to justify opposite actions or inaction.

Some years ago, I worked with a policymaker who was attempting to solve a long-term energy cost crisis in his constituency and others nearby by enabling planning for a particular type of large-scale fuel-production plant. This would bring much-needed jobs to the district while lowering the cost of fuel across the state. However, constituents were alerted to two relatively recent explosions in similar plants elsewhere, which resulted in tragic losses of life. I observed as representatives changed tack in response to the groundswell. Many who were initially supportive of building continue to support indefinite moratoriums on the production of this fuel despite the ever-increasing success of this type of production worldwide. Fuel poverty remains a severe problem in that area. Was this a victory for the precautionary principle? Certainly, it is very difficult to argue that human lives are worth risking when alternatives are available. However, an approach that is sensitive to explaining cases in context might have resulted in a very different debate. In this case, the public and their representatives' sample of cases was not adequately diverse;

it was biased by the proximity of cases that resulted in human tragedy. Also, it later emerged that explanations of the tragedies had very little to do with the fuel itself, but were a result of safety conditions observed by builders and workers in the context of the particular surrounding environments in which the plants were built.

Of course, all decisions suffer from some bounds in which rational decision-making can occur (Simon, 1991). Moreover, for all working in governance, making judgements over competing evidence is the name of the game. QCA can, I argue, provide some gains here because of the way it deals with so-called 'outliers'. In the QCA approach, outliers are allowed the kind of attention that they might not get from regression analysts, whose focus on measures of central tendency incentivise attempts to 'explain them away' (Ragin, 2000). Instead, these cases are 'explained' in conjunction with other evidence in order to investigate when multiple similar conjunctions of explanatory conditions can lead to different outcomes. QCA probably cannot eliminate the important values, interests, fears and entrenchment that all contribute to politics and the policy outcomes described earlier. However, for policy formulators, they can provide explanations of diverse cases and contexts upstream that can anticipate future problems.

Policies are complex. Their interactions with contexts increase their complexity. Policy making, by its nature, requires situational knowledge and innovation with sensitivity to context. Moreover, in the contemporary era of governance, pressures on being shown to be 'innovative' grow and grow as claims to ingenuity have become a key selling point for policies. There may be an intuitive tension between innovating and evidence-based diffusion. Pressure on innovation incentivises the conceptualisation of cases as relatively unique and leads to 'too many variables, not enough cases for comparison'-type thinking. QCA allows comparative analysis of all the possible compounds created by the combinations of the key characteristics of a policy in context – treating them as complex wholes rather than collections of elements. QCA asks what conditions are necessary and, in combination, sufficient for a given policy outcome.

The policy sciences, wrote Harold Laswell (1971), must be sensitive to context, problem-oriented and employ diverse methods. The opening chapters of this volume cogently confirm the case that evidence-based policy making can benefit from more plural approaches to methodologies and methods. I argue that QCA, as a complementary tool in a broader toolkit, improves the sensitivity to context and the problem orientation of the policy sciences.

Limitations and possibilities

Here, I will try to briefly present some of the key discussions surrounding the appropriate use of QCA, both old and new, and discuss responses in a way that is accessible to newcomers. The discussions draw out both exacting critiques and responses that can lead to exciting possibilities. As with *all* methods, the limitations of QCA are various. Recent critical engagements from social scientists with expertise that cuts across a range of methodologies have helped expose failings in the method as it has been practised (Hug, 2013; Lucas and Szatrowski, 2014; Paine, 2015). In some cases, these critiques introduce new challenges, and in others, they clarify and expound on hunches and doubts that had been voiced for a while. Importantly, they have engendered more apt clarifications of the approach and its merits from QCA researchers. As is the Achilles heel with many methodological debates, some contributors are rather hasty to recommend throwing the baby out with the bathwater while others seem a bit too keen on the dirty bathwater. I try to be neither.

The fuzzy truth

An early refrain heard when students are introduced to QCA in the manner presented earlier is something along the lines of 'well that would be all well and good if the world was made up of only ones and zeros'. Of course, the important factors we want to analyse and understand are not just 'there' or 'not there'; they are present to a matter of degree. The fuzzy-set variety of QCA (fsQCA) accounts for this. With fuzzy sets, cases can be ascribed fuzzy membership between 0 and 1 in the set that denotes presence/absence of a condition. Here, fuzzy should not be confused with vague. Fuzzy membership is a relatively precise measure of the degree to which a condition is present/absent in a case.

'Crisp' dichotomies directly correspond to fuzzy-set memberships and allow the same type of analysis as described earlier (see Ragin, 2009: 94–103). Fuzzy sets are a simple expansion of the crisp dichotomies. Each case will still display a membership score either side of the 'crossover point' (0.5) that is closest to its crisp-set membership of 1 or 0. Therefore, nothing of QCA's commitment to conceptual clarity is lost. If, for example, a policymaker wants to assess a common intervention to promote recycling in the context of wealthy/not wealthy neighbourhoods using fsQCA, s/he would still need to decide what makes a neighbourhood more in the set of wealthy neighbourhoods (fuzzy membership > 0.5) or more out (membership score < 0.5). This disciplined conceptualisation is a key strength of QCA because it helps us understand better what it is we think cases are examples of, and how they can usefully be compared. The main advance of fuzzy sets, then, is to provide for more nuanced judgements because they allow more fine-grained appreciation of the degree of regularity across cases.

A second claimed advantage is that fuzzy sets provide a relatively good bridge between formal and verbal logic (Ragin, 2000), ascribing membership scores to complex verbal statements. The claim that fuzzy sets reflect natural language is disputed by Lakoff (2014), and debates around this characterisation of fuzzy sets as better reflecting understandings of the world than common statistical levels of measurement continue. Interesting as these debates are, they distract from the key possibilities of the method. Fuzzy sets do not have any innate advantage over other ways of connecting words and numbers. The real advantage of fuzzy sets is that they create a dialogue between theories and case evidence in a distinctively useful way. Constructing fuzzy sets can be a very fruitful procedure when undertaken collaboratively and transparently by policymaker-researchers, who necessarily work in networks drawing together experiences and evidence. It can allow different understandings of conditions to be made commensurate as definitions of what constitutes a case being fully in, fully out, more in than out or more out than in are reformulated. In my work, I was able to map out my definitions of different set memberships and the coding of cases before presenting them to caseworkers in a way that was easy for them to interpret (see Figure 5.1). In this way, we could engage in the input, iteration and specification of understandings in an open and robust manner. Of course, there are always trade-offs in how long one can spend perfecting measures, but these tools provide options to undertake the process in a manner that is relatively systematic and transparent, allowing some replicability and adaptation for future reanalysis.

Debates about Ns

Answers as to when QCA is the best method have been previously associated with the number of cases. It is important to understand why. QCA was originally introduced to the social sciences as a way of harnessing the holistic approach of 'small-N' comparative methods beyond a handful of cases (Ragin, 1987). Here, N stands for the number of cases. Medium-N is usually crudely defined (if at all) as

Figure 5.1: Fuzzy map of membership in the set of participatory leadership strategy

Participatory leadership strategy

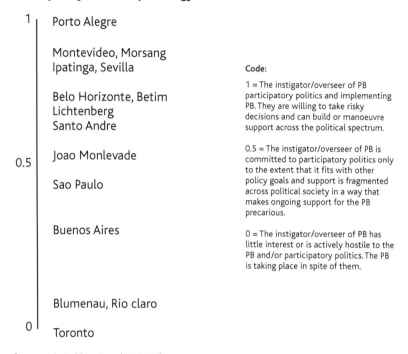

Code:

1 = The instigator/overseer of PB participatory politics and implementing PB. They are willing to take risky decisions and can build or manoeuvre support across the political spectrum.

0.5 = The instigator/overseer of PB is committed to participatory politics only to the extent that it fits with other policy goals and support is fragmented across political society in a way that makes ongoing support for the PB precarious.

0 = The instigator/overseer of PB has little interest or is actively hostile to the PB and/or participatory politics. The PB is taking place in spite of them.

Source: Adapted from Ryan (2014: 130).

more than a handful of cases and less than enough to make robust generalisation relying on probability theorems from a sample of cases to a population from which it is drawn. Ragin (2000: 25) does show clearly that there is a paucity of analyses in the social sciences that tackle such a medium-N of cases. This suggests that researchers in the academy and in policy circles alike are biased towards answering questions that lend themselves to a higher or lower caseload. We rarely try to accumulate evidence beyond a handful of cases unless we can increase the sample of cases very rapidly. That probably does have something to do with the tools that we are trained to use in analysing the world. Enthusiasts have continued to argue that QCA is a particularly useful method for reasoning within this overlooked middle range of cases (Berg-Schlosser and Cronqvist, 2005). These arguments should be of interest to policymakers. Perfect policy making might require full implementation and exact measures of abstract concepts, but good-enough policy making that takes place in the real world of time-sensitive responses to multiple crises is probably a good fit with a compromise between the depth and breadth of information.

However, is QCA really a medium-N cure-all? More recently, critiques based on randomly generated data modelling and simulations (eg Hug, 2013; Lucas and Szatrowski, 2014) have provided food for thought for QCA researchers by demonstrating the unreliable inferences drawn from QCA. Here, the basis of the approach is to simulate a world where the true causal story is known and test whether and how often performing QCA analysis can arrive at that correct outcome. QCA tends to be presented as performing quite badly in relation to more established regression methods, particularly in regard to its sensitivity to predicting different outcomes when different cases are sampled for analysis, or when the same cases are measured slightly differently (ie simulating errors). Particularly galling for some, critics have argued that evidence of QCA's advance on the ability over other methods to predict or diagnose outcomes is not convincing, especially when using a medium-N of cases. High-level debates continue to rage as to whether these simulations are fair tests or whether they force QCA to jump through hoops that it was not designed for (see the further reading section at the end of this chapter).

I argue that these critiques are important but far from disastrous for QCA. Some of the misunderstandings stem from over-exuberance on behalf of those using a medium-N to make universalising assumptions, and others stem from a tendency among critics to undervalue the logic of purposive case selection when working pragmatically with imperfect, real-world data. It is true that estimating correlations using large-N regression analysis has become one of the key evidence-analytical techniques used in policy making. Due to its dominance, this statistical method has benefited perhaps more than any other from the experience, critique and innovation of a community of dedicated practitioners and scholars. Therefore, much of the regression analysis we execute will perform well on a number of important criteria relative to other methods that do not have such an advantage. Nevertheless, regression methods have weaknesses and lacunae, and cannot answer all questions of interest to policymakers. Regression methods work best with large numbers in the units of analysis in order to be able to take advantage of partial correlations. This feature sometimes makes them prone towards favouring data on individual behaviour or proxy variables that can be very far abstracted from the concepts that they seek to measure. The dominance of this method, then, introduces biases in the types and kinds of questions that policymakers ask and the way in which problems are framed. The value of QCA approaches and tools is that they incentivise more comparison using intuitive comparative logic across more dimensions of comparability than researchers and decision-makers are currently making use of. As explained in the steps presented earlier, in practice, QCA incentivises the accumulation of cases beyond a handful, and purposive selection of diverse cases, which can leverage interesting findings.

Mechanisms, correlations and necessary and sufficient conditions

QCA has also been criticised by case-study researchers for its inability to investigate mechanisms of causation, despite a penchant for QCA researchers to draw on sequential explanations of the conjunctions they uncover. QCA is a quite static method of comparison and it is generally accepted that if users are interested in the sequence of events that produce an outcome, process-tracing methods are more appropriate – of course, these methods can be fruitfully combined (Schneider and Rohlfing, 2013). As I have suggested earlier, although the number and nature of cases in a sample always matters, the question as to whether QCA is a better or worse approach depends not on the numbers of cases, but on the intentions of the policy analysis and the nature of the problem at hand. QCA is a method for mapping necessary and sufficient conditions and negotiating parsimony and complexity in explanations (Rihoux and Lobe, 2009: 238; Thiem et al, 2015). It works best when users are interested in identifying overly parsimonious explanations of outcomes (underdetermination) and overly complex explanations of outcomes (overdetermination). With the former, we can think about eliminating superfluous inputs; with the latter, we have a clue about what might be missing from the mix in a policy solution.

As the contributors to this volume make clear, policymakers need a large toolbox of methods to understand the world in ways that lead to intelligent policy making. Imagine that a group of policymakers are interested in making changes to drug treatment policy to both improve health and reduce costs. QCA is not a good method for understanding whether more funding of community care at the expense of more funding for large drug-rehabilitation centres will lead to better health-care outcomes on average. Regression methods will better answer that question. QCA is a relatively good method for trying to understand whether a lump investment in both community care and a trauma centre is required or not for better health outcomes in the context of an epidemic. Again, QCA is a relatively poor method for understanding whether, in a particular case of interest, community care became more cost-effective over time because the costs of the physical upkeep of a centre became prohibitive, or whether new evidence promoting community care as a best practice found its way to key decision-makers, who then re-evaluated the cost-effectiveness of a centre and advocated community care. The latter case might benefit from process-tracing or narrative analysis. An appreciation of appropriate methods and their ability to complement one another with different types of information can be key to effective policy making in a world of bounded rationality.

Conclusion

seems to miss the richness of most small n-explanations

In this chapter, I have introduced QCA – a novel and important method for the systematic comparison of evidence. I have provided a brief overview of the logical foundations of the analytic method and provided an outline of how it might be used by practitioners. I have outlined the method's limitations and highlighted the ongoing critique that is a necessary complement to any good method of analysis. Following Laswell (1951: 5), the policy sciences are 'advanced whenever the methods are sharpened by which authentic information and responsible interpretations can be integrated with judgement'. While lessons drawn from applying different measures can help us to think critically as to the standards to which others are held, different types of questions will continue to require different methods of analysis. A greater awareness of the method's possibilities as it is practised and understood by those at the coalface of policy formulation, implementation and evaluation should help to improve policy making and, in turn, the method itself. QCA, I argue, should become an important part of the arsenal of policy analysts and decision-makers, and I implore them to share their experiences with it.

Further reading

QCA's introduction and promotion in the social sciences owes much to Charles Ragin, and his 1987 book, *The comparative method*, is still an excellent introduction to the thinking that undergirds the approach. Slightly more recently, Schneider and Wagemann's (2012) *Set-theoretic methods in the social sciences* can be used as both textbook and reference book, as well as making many erudite contributions to the development of the method. It introduces readers to fuzzy membership at an early stage. The QCA user community is very supportive and the best window in is the www.compasss.org website – it provides links to electronic mailing lists and discussion forums, has a well-maintained bibliography of papers using QCA, and reviews the variety of software available. When it comes to software packages, beginners who are used to Windows interfaces will probably want to start with Ragin and Davey's (2014) *fs/QCA 2.5* (available for free download at http://www.socsci.uci.edu/~cragin/fsQCA/software.shtml). For readers more comfortable with programming languages, I recommend Thiem and Dusa's (2013a) *R package, QCA 1-1.4*. The authors of the package have also written a short guidebook – *Qualitative comparative analysis with R: A user's guide* (Thiem and Dusa, 2013b) – which will aid, in particular, those unfamiliar with the *R* environment. Finally, all good methods have challengers. For radical critique (some of which is highly sceptical of the method), interested readers comfortable with more abstract methodological debates may consult *Sociological Methodology (Special Issue)* 44(1), as well as contributions to the section on 'Exchanges: QCA and set theory', *Qualitative and Multi-Method Research* 12(2).

Glossary

Constant – Refers to invariance. A constant connotes a value that does not change across cases.

Data matrix – An ordered arrangement of data that provides the inputs for further computational analysis. It is usually presented with rows representing data records (cases) and columns representing variables.

Multicollinearity – Refers to an occasion when two or often more independent variables are highly correlated, which suggests that they might not be all that independent after all.

Skew – Refers to how asymmetrical a distribution of values is. The more symmetry, the lower the skew.

Acknowledgements

The author would like to thank Tessa Brannan, Catherine Durose, Ian Fitzgerald, Liz Richardson and Gerry Stoker, as well as all the participants at the Canberra Symposium on 'Methods that Matter', for their very helpful comments on earlier drafts of this chapter.

SIX

Narrative and storytelling

Vivien Lowndes

Introduction

Stories are important. Every new piece of legislation, every piece of policy advice or guidance, is a narrative in its own right, which links together beliefs, actions and institutions in a distinctive manner (Bevir and Rhodes, 2006: 4). However, policy analysis is dominated by 'decisionism' (Majone, 1989: 19). The emphasis is on finding technical fixes to policy puzzles, with the task of social scientists defined in terms of the generation and utilisation of 'evidence'. This chapter asks whether policy analysis pays enough attention to the role of policy narratives, which deal with 'why' as well as 'how' questions.

'Evidence-based policy making' has become the dominant paradigm (Davies et al, 2000). However, policymakers quip cynically that 'policy-based evidence-making' is more common, with what counts as 'evidence' being manipulated to fit predetermined policy preferences. Some feel that the search for neutral evidence is misplaced anyhow, arguing that policy making should be explicitly a value-led process. At a workshop for policymakers at our university, one participant argued that 'We don't want *evidence*-based policy making. We want *political* policy-making', and another put in a plea for 'stories not spreadsheets'. Paying more attention to the role of storytelling and narrative can be a way of putting the politics back in to policy making, and blowing the cover on claims for value-free evidence. It offers new forms of discovery for policymakers, and new opportunities for social scientists to support better policy making. A well-connected US political scientist, reflecting on his experience of engaging with policymakers, recently remarked to me that 'They don't want our research findings, they want a model of the mind'. Supporting policymakers in decision-making can be as much to do with cognitive mapping as with the supply of detailed data. Exploring actual and potential policy narratives provides an opportunity to map and re-map the connections between actors, ideas and institutions. Narratives offer a way to 'stabilise ...

assumptions about political dilemmas and come to conclusions about what to do'; they can be defined as a 'chronological account that helps actors to make sense of and argue about policy issues (Boswell, J., 2013a: 621–2). To this extent, stories are prior to evidence. We only know what kind of evidence we need, and how to evaluate it, when we are clear about the policy narrative.

The chapter starts by looking at social science insights regarding the role of narrative in public policy. I consider why narrative is important and how it can be understood, distinguishing between narrative as knowledge, meaning and metaphor (building on Dodge et al, 2005). These understandings are mapped on to three forms of intervention in the policy making process: mobilising narratives, generating narratives and contesting narratives. I discuss such interventions in action, focusing on social scientists' work with policymakers in city governance. The chapter finishes with a consideration of the future potential of these techniques and a discussion of their limitations.

The ubiquity, and utility, of narrative within the policy process

We can define narrative as 'a sequence of events, experiences, or actions with a plot that ties together different parts into a meaningful whole' (Feldman et al, 2004). Narrative is explicitly referred to in the political world. Politicians are assessed in the media and by pollsters as to whether they have 'control of the story' or are able to establish new narratives. As McBeth et al (2007: 88) put it: 'Narratives are the lifeblood of politics'. Traditionally, in policy analysis, there has been a dismissal or distaste for the role of narratives and stories in policy making, and a desire to maximise the distance between policy analysis and storytelling. Deborah Stone (writing initially in 1988) observes that the 'new field of policy science, supposedly devoted to improving governance, was based on a profound disgust for the ambiguities and paradoxes of politics' (Stone, 2011: x). Should we leave narrative to the politicians then? To do so is to replicate the traditional attempt to separate politics and administration. This attempt casts politicians as storytellers, engaged with values and visions, and policymakers as technicians, concerned only with 'evidence'. Stone (2011: x) claims that this is both incorrect and undesirable. On the first point, she argues that 'we need to render more visible the political claims underlying what is usually passed off as scientific method' (Stone, 2011: x). On the second, she reminds us that politics is actually a source of creativity; value-laden narratives provide us with a way to 'help each other see from different perspectives' (Stone, 2011: x).

Such an approach does not imply a rejection of the role of evidence in policy making, or of social scientists in generating and communicating evidence. Rather, a narrative approach puts evidence in its place. As Giandomenico Majone explains, evidence exists only in the context of an argument. There is no evidence without an argument. This may seem like a paradoxical claim as we normally see an argument as dependent upon evidence, not vice versa. The point can be clarified through a distinction between evidence, data and information (Majone, 1989: 46). *Data* are observations about the world (survey or interview responses, for instance, or temperature readings or pollution levels), and *information* is data that has been organised and categorised (an Nvivo report based on codes, or a statistical regression analysis). *Evidence*, on the other hand, is information that is selected to support a certain point in an argument. If data are raw material, information is a new sort of substance created from that raw material. Evidence is 'information selected from the available stock and introduced at a specific point in an argument' with the intention to persuade. Evidence is still important, but it cannot be delinked from the narrative within which it is embedded.

If policymakers select and utilise evidence in the context of narrative, the same is true of those who support policymakers, be they professional policy officers or academic social scientists. The policy analyst is not story-free, but rather engages with policymakers through the intersubjective trading of stories. As Majone (1989: 1) argues, we should see the policy analyst as 'a producer of arguments, capable of distinguishing between good and bad rhetoric, rather than as a "number cruncher"'. Social scientists cannot bracket narrative off, or clean it out of the policy making process. It is not simply a fluffy extra (the stuff of 'missions' and 'visions'), nor necessarily a suspicious act of 'spin' (designed to manipulate) – although it can be both of those things. Narrative is constitutive of the policy process. Fritz Mayer (2014) shows how collective action problems are commonly addressed through recourse to storytelling, including the linking of new stories to 'back stories'. For example, a new policy to devolve (selected) powers from central government to city-regions in England has sought to attach itself to established narratives celebrating 'the great Northern cities' of the Victorian era. The intention is to overcome (or ease) the competitive pressures between those individual municipalities being asked to combine into new city-region structures.

There is truth in the adage that human beings are 'storytelling animals'. Policymakers, and the social scientists who work with them, are no exception. Storytelling cannot be avoided, so it should be taken seriously.

The limits to rationality: heuristics in the policy process

Academic research on the role of narrative in public policy abounds, providing a base upon which social scientists can build in developing interventions to support policymakers. Approaches focusing on the meanings that actors attach to their behaviour (and observations of the world) have a long social science pedigree, associated notably with Max Weber's concept of *verstehen* (understanding). Within the discipline of public administration, many of the 'greats' were attentive to the limits of rationality within public policy. Charles Lindblom (1959) compared the rational-comprehensive model of decision-making to an approach he termed 'successive limited comparisons' (of both means and ends) or, famously, 'the science of muddling through'. Herbert Simon (1947) had argued that policymakers 'satisfice' rather than undertake a fully rational evaluation of the costs and benefits of different options, due both to information insufficiencies and cognitive limitations. Instead, they use 'rules of thumb' or heuristics, which serve to speed up decision-making processes, aiming not for a scientifically optimal solution, but for one sufficient to meet immediate goals. Heuristics provide frames or constructs for problem-solving and are expressed in a narrative style. Resonating with the ambition of this book, the word 'heuristic' comes from the Greek for 'discover'. 'Trial and error', for example, is one of the most fundamental heuristics in human decision-making; expressed in a narrative form, it is explained and passed on to others as 'if you don't at first succeed, try again' or 'learn from your mistakes'. These are more than proverbs; they are actually problem-solving strategies that emerge from the experience of dealing with comparable issues. While heuristics are expressed discursively, they can have very real effects, with a bearing upon the allocation of material resources and differential policy outcomes.

Heuristics offer policymakers opportunities for parsimony and efficiency in decision-making. They also build upon policymakers' own local knowledge and situated meanings (Yanow, 2000; Bevir and Rhodes, 2006), potentially generating a sense of confidence in, and commitment to, decisions. Rules of thumb are generally shared within a particular setting – a specific locality or a type of policy work or a professional role – reflecting what Herbert Lasswell (1949) called the 'contextual orientation' of public policy. However, they can be grouped into broad categories. For example, a 'consistency heuristic' is where a policymaker seeks to ensure that one decision is consistent with another (not perfect, but consistent); an 'educated guess' is where a policymaker draws on what they have observed in the past (rather than undertaking exhaustive research); 'working backwards' is where we imagine a policy problem is solved and then seek to identify those steps that would be need to be taken to reach that point; an 'authority heuristic' is where we follow the position of the person in authority without questioning (as in a military situation); and an 'affect heuristic' is a snap, intuitive judgement.

Research has focused on the use of heuristics in doctors' and patients' judgements (including the differences between them), decision-making within the criminal justice system (from front-line police officers to judges and juries), and in Web design for e-government (eg Heath et al, 1994, Donker-Kuijer et al, 2010). For social scientists working with policymakers, just acknowledging the role of heuristics, rather than trying to trump them with 'science', may be an important contribution. It is also important to evaluate their use critically, analysing whether they continue to be relevant as contexts and policy issues change, and the type of biases that they may build into decision-making. Changing heuristics is likely to be difficult, however, given their status as 'mental short cuts'. Any intervention requires contributions from anthropology (to underpin the detailed observation of decision-making) and psychology (to model cognitive processes, both old and new), as well as the more obvious social science disciplines associated with public policy.

From short cuts to stories: research on narrative in policy making

If the early public administration scholars drew attention to policymakers' use of cognitive short cuts, the subsequent narrative 'turn' saw researchers focusing on full-blown storytelling. 'Policy narratives' are identified, which have a specific setting, a cast of characters (who may reflect archetypes like villains, victims or heroes), a plot (often conforming to well-worn scripts) and a purpose (or dominant normative message) (Hajer, 1995). The interest in narrative has led to a range of novel approaches, which include (but are not exhausted by):

• The 'new public administration', which challenges value-free premises and a focus on explanatory approaches, emphasising instead interpretation and critique. Influencing scholarship for the past 40 years, this broad approach has inspired feminist, postmodern and psychoanalytical contributions to policy research (White, 1999; Ospina and Dodge, 2005: 147).

- Interpretive policy analysis, which focuses on specific policy artefacts (textual and non-textual), those groups for whom artefacts have meaning, the nature of these meanings and the points of contrast and contest between different narratives (Yanow, 2000: 20; Lowndes and Madziva, 2016). The aim is to better understand the interplay between plural sets of meanings, which are themselves associated with different positions of power (Griggs et al, 2014: 17).

- Narrative policy analysis, which (inspired by sociolinguistics) seeks to establish 'meta-narratives' from a comparison of stories, non-stories and counter-stories within a policy field. Meta-narratives are able to encompass major oppositions, providing space for deliberation – as an alternative to seeking consensus (Roe, 1994; Hampton, 2004: 262).

- Narrative policy framework, which specifies narrative elements and strategies as previously neglected variables within explanatory models of the policy process. This approach seeks to measure the impact of narratives on policy outcomes through empirical investigation and statistical testing (Jones and McBeth, 2010; Shanahan et al, 2011: 535–6).

Some of this work comes from a positivist perspective, in which narratives are seen as another causal variable to be considered in seeking to explain and/or predict policy outcomes. It is argued that this variable has been neglected, and its inclusion will allow social scientists to construct more realistic and useful models (Shanahan et al, 2011: 536). However, the narrative turn is more generally associated with research from a post-positivist viewpoint. Here, researchers do not attempt to explain policy outcomes, or establish causation, but rather seek to understand better the way in which narratives and storytelling operate within the policy making process. Rather than quantitative methods and modelling, these researchers develop 'thick descriptions' of narrative in action, using ethnographic methods that aim to situate narratives within their own specific context. Starting with policy actors' own accounts, the researcher is engaged in a process of 'interpreting interpretations', bringing to bear their own social science narratives in this process. In this vein, Mark Bevir and Rod

Rhodes' (2006) ethnographic work in Whitehall seeks to explain shifting patterns of governance with reference to underlying 'traditions' (Whig, Conservative and socialist).

How much have these bodies of research contributed to enhancing policy making in practice? Bevir and Rhodes (2006: 172) argue that policy analysts are able to put together 'resonant stories' from their ethnographic research, which they can share with policymakers to aid reflection on their decisions and actions. Ospina and Dodge (2005: 152) argue that 'Research that takes a narrative turn offers a way to heal the theory–practice divide ... because it may offer information that rings true to practitioners' experience'. However, 'resonating' and 'ringing true' seem rather modest aspirations. Furthermore, such an approach can be highly irritating to policymakers in the sense that researchers may be simply telling them the stories that they themselves told those same researchers! Where is the added value? Can we go beyond this? In this chapter, I will outline a series of techniques that are grounded in research on storytelling and narrative, and can underpin new forms of discovery for policymakers and new opportunities for social scientists. However, first, I summarise six key reasons why narratives are important in policy making.

Why are narratives important in policy making?

First, narratives carry values. They deal with 'why' as well as 'how' questions. Narratives 'distil and reflect a particular understanding of social and political relations' (Feldman et al, 2004: 148). Richard Kearney (2001: 153) argues that 'Storytelling ... is never neutral. Every narrative bears some evaluative charge regarding the events narrated and the actors featured in the narrative'. More specifically, policy making relies 'on the successful activation of the cognitive and moral resources of citizens through signals and appeals that educate and remind people of what is "the right thing to do"' (Offe, 2009: 559). Paul Sabatier (1988: 152) also reminds us that public policy rarely operates just 'through the raw exercise of power', but has to be 'convincing' in terms of the definition of problems and the elaboration of policies. Beyond specific policies, those who promote 'good governance' (whether at the national or global level) confront a discursive as much as a technical challenge as it is narrative that makes possible what Kearney (2001: 150) calls 'the ethical sharing of a common world'.

Second, narratives reflect or even constitute identities, both individually and collectively, and at different levels of policy making (from the global to the neighbourhood). Henk Wagenaar (2011: 573) argues that policy narratives have the capacity to 'create social visions, constitute identities, create publics, and influence individual and group relationships'. For Mishler (1995), narratives are 'culturally shared stories' that 'provide frames for interpreting collective experiences'. Policymakers may seek to link their agenda to established 'back stories' so as to promote their positions as constitutive of shared identities. In management, there is new interest in 'identity leadership': rather than considering the personal qualities of a heroic leader, the focus is on the leader's capacity to share a compelling story with followers, which can mobilise them in pursuit of an organisation's goals (Haslam et al, 2010).

Third, narratives hold the keys to agency. Psychologists refer to narrative as a form of 'agency training' (Bruner, 2002). If we have the story, we are able to act. Going back to Aristotle's poetics, Kearney (2001) argues that 'human existence is in search of a narrative', a 'crafted structure' that makes sense out of the chaos of existence. Stories make possible a 'shareable world' and we are both actors within stories and tellers of others. As we saw earlier, scholars of public administration have emphasised the role of heuristics in facilitating action within complex and contested policy spaces. Neuroscience is now able to identify the chemical bases of 'decision fatigue' and the value of heuristics in reducing cognitive clutter and enabling action. Narratives enable policymakers to frame problems, selecting in and out evidence, prioritising certain characters, settings and plots, while selecting out others. Dominant narratives are, at the same time, contested through interpretation and action. Janet Newman (2005) considers how 'performing citizens' may react to governing strategies by fashioning their own narratives and generating new capacities to act. As John Clarke (2005: 158) explains, actors may be 'called' but may not necessarily respond, choosing instead to 'refuse to listen or tune into alternative hailings'.

Fourth, narratives make policy 'stick', gain traction and endure. As Majone (1989: 31) puts it, 'to decide is never enough'. Policies also have to be explained and justified through narrative, and narratives have to be adaptable enough to secure policies over time, including their implementation and adaptation in the context of changing environments. When narratives become institutionalised, they contribute to policy stability over time (but also to path dependency and its change-hampering effects) (Lowndes and Roberts, 2013: 63). The most robust public policy institutions are secured not just through formal rules, nor sets of established practices, but through convincing and frequently rehearsed stories. Such narratives may have an official life as mission or vision statements, or they may be more informal, infusing decision-making and behaviour on the ground, and being told and retold around the water cooler or in the corridors. Lowndes and Roberts (2013: 70) look at how the National Health Service in the UK is bolstered by the power of story, and how proposals for policy change confront the established narratives (eg 'free at the point of delivery') and the challenge of crafting new ones (eg 'any willing provider'). Moments of major policy change generally involve the collapse of established narratives (and their associated ideas and values), as in the transition from Keynesianism to monetarism in the 1970s (Hall, 1992), or, as Mark Blyth (2013) put it, 'the birth of a dangerous idea' – austerity – in the period following the 2008 global financial crisis.

Fifth, narratives are a power resource. As they carry values, narratives are never neutral. Whose narrative dominates, or what influence it has in the policy mix, is a significant factor. Furthermore, what we could call 'narrative capital' is unevenly distributed among participants in the policy process – politicians, policy advisers, business and community stakeholders, marginalised groups, and individual citizens. These groups have a differential capacity, and opportunity, to devise and narrate compelling stories, and – most significantly – to get them heard. Policy is 'multi-storied' (Hampton, 2004), and negotiating between these stories is a deeply political process.

Finally, narrative provides a point of intervention in policy making. It is a way, literally, of joining the conversation, whether as a social scientist, policy adviser or stakeholder. Narrative interventions may be about supporting policy design and implementation, or they may be about disruption – challenging the values and priorities embedded in dominant narratives, and offering alternatives. We now consider in more detail the forms of discovery that narrative analysis offers to policymakers. A social science approach to narrative can support policymakers in working more explicitly and critically with the discursive resources at their disposal. This chapter explores different forms of intervention designed, respectively, to mobilise, generate and contest policy narratives.

Narrative as meaning, metaphor and knowledge

Typologising the different ways in which narratives operate within public policy enables us to establish a framework for considering interventions. Adapting the work of Dodge et al (2005), we can distinguish between narrative-as-knowledge, narrative-as-meaning and narrative-as-metaphor:

- Narrative-as-knowledge: Narrative is seen as 'a way of knowing'. Actors are assumed to 'think and know through stories' (Dodge et al, 2005: 291). Narratives are seen as containing knowledge. People use stories to draw knowledge from their socialisation and lived experience. Stories enable practical learning. They offer an opportunity to surface tacit knowledge, which can be shared and also generalised to new situations.

- Narrative-as-meaning: Narrative is seen as a 'medium of expression'. People are assumed to be purposeful social agents, who 'create and use stories to communicate meaning' (Dodge et al, 2005: 291), deploying language and other symbolic resources. As such, narratives are a window on beliefs, revealing actors' processes of sense-making.

- Narrative-as-metaphor: Narrative is seen as constitutive, as shaping human beings, rather than simply being used by them. Narrative, in some sense, 'stands for' deeper structures, and provides a way into studying their effects. Narrative is not just a way of knowing, but also a way of being. It has ontological as well as epistemological significance. Through narrative, we get a glimpse of deep social structures that are not visible to the 'naked eye'.

These three approaches can be mapped on to a series of distinctive interventions to support policy making – through mobilising, generating and contesting narratives.

Intervention 1: mobilising narratives

This intervention draws upon our understanding of *narrative-as-knowledge*. It is about unearthing the narratives in use, and their associated tacit knowledge. In work with Alison Gardner, we have shown how narratives help to explain what we call the 'austerity puzzle'. Between 2010 and 2015, English local government lost one third of its budget and yet continued to function fairly effectively. Our research has demonstrated the role of narrative as a policy resource with material effects. Studying the impact of the cuts (in the context of rising public demand), we analysed how local government policymakers are working with key 'traditions', in the sense defined by Bevir and Rhodes (2006), to make sense of and negotiate the demands of austerity. We have identified five key local government traditions – civic, collectivist, professional, commercial and communitarian –

each of which have long historical traditions and are not the property of any one specific political party (for more detail, see Gardner and Lowndes, 2016). Our research shows how, in responding to austerity, traditions were being mobilised, including latent elements, and were in the process of being modified. These traditions were interpreted in the context of specific local knowledge (Yanow, 2000), leading to new hybrid narratives of reform.

In our case study, we looked at the emergence of a policy narrative of 'municipal enterprise', in which the local council has pursued 'commercial' goals (generating additional income) within the context of deeply held 'collectivist' traditions. The local authority had been undertaking overnight vehicle maintenance for other councils and private companies in its garages that were previously closed at night. It had also generated income from investment deals on funds released for an infrastructure project, and was letting unused property and land on a commercial basis. Through the narrative of municipal enterprise, commercial activities were presented as releasing funds and thus mitigating the effect of cuts on local residents, in keeping with the expectation of a strong local council looking after its residents. Policy leaders referred back to the 1980s' story of 'municipal socialism' to give more narrative power to their chosen approach (Newman, 2014). Another hybrid narrative (combining aspects of collectivism with both communitarianism and commercialism) proved less successful in gaining traction. 'Community commissioning' involved establishing market-style contracts with voluntary sector consortia in place of established grant-giving relationships with a wide variety of community organisations. The change has been met with powerful narrative resistance on the part of voluntary bodies and activists, who see the new contracts as undermining both the autonomy and effectiveness of community action, and as a 'cloak' for making cuts.

When we debated narrative strategies with a wider group of local government policymakers (in a series of local and national workshops), participants engaged enthusiastically with the idea of traditions, which they agreed encapsulated forms of tacit knowledge that could be drawn upon in responding to new policy challenges. They pointed to additional local government traditions, including 'community representation' and 'innovation resilience'. One participant contrasted traditions with the 'fads and fashions' that pass through local government, and another described traditions as being like the writing in a stick of rock, running through everything. The concept of traditions was seen as acknowledging the important role of history in local government ('looking back does give us ideas'). One participant noted that even when political control changed in their council, policies were formulated within the context of dominant traditions. It was felt that narratives could be a lot more compelling in supporting strategic thinking than what usually passed as evidence. There was some agreement that constrained resources had actually engendered a turn away from evidence-based policy and had put the politics back into policy making (with a plea for 'stories not spreadsheets' from social scientists).

The feeling in the workshops was that practitioners needed more 'thinking capacity' to self-consciously review the narratives in play within their policy making processes, and to selectively mobilise (and combine and adapt) those narratives that contained implicit knowledge and learning from the past. Creativity can be unleashed by critically examining the range of potential policy stories, each of which illuminates new and potentially productive connections between actors, ideas and institutions. Workshop participants saw social scientists as having an important role in facilitating this process: 'We need a greater understanding of those classes of local government organisations that have been constrained or trapped by traditions and those others that have used traditions to drive change'.

Intervention 2: generating narratives

This intervention is concerned with *narrative-as-meaning*. In comparison with the previous intervention, it is concerned less with narrative archaeology and more with narrative architecture. Constructing narratives, rather than unearthing them, is the focus. We are concerned less with identifying existing tacit knowledge and its future applications, and more with generating new narratives, which allow actors to 'reframe' their situation and unlock new capacities for action – to effect change. Here, narratives function as a 'medium of expression'. This sort of intervention involves social scientists working with policymakers and practitioners to generate new stories, with due attention to settings, characters and plot. From classical dramaturgy, we can think of such narratives as involving elements of logos (an appeal to logic), ethos (ethics), pathos (emotion) and mythos (recurring and familiar plot lines).

An example of intervening in this way is provided by Marshall Ganz's 'public narrative' approach, which reflects the identity, values and agency aspects of narrative that we discussed earlier. Constructing new narratives to achieve change is a hallmark of this type of intervention. Ganz worked with Barack Obama in developing his initial campaign for the presidency, drawing on his experience of working with trades unions and social movements. As Ganz explains:

> Public narrative is the art of translating values into action. It is a discursive process through which individuals, communities, and nations learn to make choices, construct identity, and inspire action. Because it engages the 'head' *and* the 'heart', narrative can instruct *and* inspire – teaching us not only why we *should* act, but moving us *to act*.
>
> Through narrative we can articulate the experience of choice in the face of urgent challenge and we can learn to draw on our values to manage the anxiety of agency, as well as its exhilaration. (Ganz, 2011, emphasis in original)

The approach provides a model for working with policymakers and practitioners, as well as politicians and activists. As social scientists, we have an opportunity to work with policymakers in the explicit authorship of three different sets of stories (paraphrasing Ganz):

- A story of self: here, the task is for policymakers to identify their own personal motivations to engage with the particular course of action, whether derived from previous experience or core values. They have to come up with stories about themselves that will enable others to understand them. 'Choice points' that they have faced in the past may be important.

- A story of us: the purpose of this story is to identify the values, experiences or aspirations that policymakers intend to tap into among the constituencies with whom they work (which may be relatively broad or narrow, depending on the context). Policymakers are asked to identify shared stories that could underpin this process.

- A story of now: the object is to identify the urgent challenges they face, and on which policymakers want to inspire action. They are asked to come up with a vision of successful action, and the choices that it would entail. Policymakers need to identify those with whom they will need to work and specify some initial actions.

The different stories exist in a circular and iterative relationship. We can just as easily start the process by working on the story of now, and then explore stories of self and us within that context. However, all three elements need to be in place in order to produce a 'public narrative'. This is not an approach in which policymakers can hope to remain 'at a distance'; they need to be open about their personal and emotional investments in the policy task. At the same time, social scientists are engaged not in reporting evidence to policymakers, but in creating a 'safe space' for individual and shared reflection, and in facilitating creative processes. As the process has affective as well as cognitive dimensions, social scientists need to employ coaching or even therapeutic skills, reminding us that supporting policymakers is not only a job for those trained in statistics, modelling or cost–benefit analysis. Indeed, Ganz argues that stories capture and express a particular mood or setting (in the manner of a poem, painting or piece of music), and recommends that participants experiment with presenting their stories in different ways. In an initiative to develop shared stories to support public health reforms in England, facilitators worked with participants including clinicians, social workers, and health promotion staff and then employed a cartoonist to draw stories as they emerged, showing visually the links between characters, settings, choices, plot and purpose. Going 'beyond text' is important for social scientists seeking to support policymakers and provoke critical reflection on current practice and alternatives (Beebeejaun et al, 2013).

According to Ganz, we all need to craft our own 'public narrative' because if we do not, others will. This threat (or reality) is all too familiar to public policymakers, who find themselves pilloried or misunderstood by key stakeholders (including elected politicians, business investors, campaigners, citizens and the media), or faced with the challenge of replacing a story of failure with one of success – not just for good public relations, but to provide a framework for new forms of action. If negative stories circulate in the public domain about our city, for instance, this is likely to affect inward investment from both the private sector and central government, and will make it harder for the municipality to recruit and retain good staff. It can affect citizens' expectations about public policy, and their own capacity to influence it. Any city, or government department or public service, that has achieved a major 'turnaround' has engaged with the need to undermine bad stories and craft good ones, perhaps with new and surprising messages that confound general expectations.

The importance of generating authentic and compelling stories of place is evident in the current debate on devolution to city-regions in England. The New Economics Foundation think tank has used the tag 'England's Dreaming' in a project to compare the different arguments for devolution put forward by central and local government and civil society actors (NEF, 2015). Within different city-regions, the extent to which these 'dreams' are explored, and a persuasive shared narrative is generated, is proving critical to the quality of the 'devolution deals' negotiated with central government. Greater Manchester, the pioneer of this round of devolution and the recipient of the most extensive new powers, stands out for the clarity, coherence and passion of its 'story of now' (vis-à-vis other localities characterised by local rivalries, artificial boundaries and fudged bargains between players). The story has been able to mobilise powerful local identities, historical legacies of institutional cooperation, close relationships between political and business elites, and the impressive storytelling abilities of charismatic leaders. This experience stands in contrast to some other localities' efforts to express a shared vision, which are stymied by local rivalries, artificial boundaries and fudged bargains between players.

Intervention 3: contesting narratives

This type of intervention rests on an understanding of *narrative-as-metaphor*. Here, policy narratives are seen as standing for something deeper, as reflecting power relations that generally lie beneath the surface of the policy making process. If our first intervention was about archaeology (surfacing and mobilising narratives), and the second about architecture (generating or constructing narratives), this approach is about demolition. How can we work with policy actors to identify narratives that perpetuate deep-seated inequalities – not just as linguistic expressions, but as frames that organise in and organise out particular concerns and interests? How can we work with them to disassemble these narratives and imagine new stories that are more inclusive, or even empowering? The demolition envisaged here is to be conducted not with a wrecking ball, but through the careful dismantling of dominant narrative infrastructures. (The wrecking ball, however, should be kept in reserve – given the size of the task, its urgency and the likely resistance to be encountered.)

Social scientists intervening to support the contestation of established policy narratives may find themselves working with service users, community groups, campaigners and 'street-level bureaucrats', as well as top-table policymakers. There is a long history of activist scholars who have played a major role in contesting (official or unofficial) narratives around, for instance: 'climate change' (critiquing the neutral language that fails to name global warming as the issue); the policing of violence against women (challenging stories about women 'asking for it' or being complicit with their attackers); and the security case for 'ethnic profiling' (unravelling stories about what a 'suspect community' looks like). Efforts to shift such narratives do not just help policy 'catch up' with wider social change, but can also lead that process of change by framing problems, actors and settings in new ways.

Returning to the Greater Manchester devolution case, we can observe that, despite its official traction, the 'story of us' has been met with concern, even anger, by some communities and marginalised groups within the locality. The setting of the story is contested (do smaller towns like Wigan really *feel* part of Manchester?), the actors have been criticised for representing an exclusive elite (the 'Manchester Men' from business and politics) and the narrative plot has been criticised for prioritising technocratic rather than democratic means, and pursuing goals of economic growth over and above social justice. Narrative analysis reveals that the biases within the Manchester story are present in discourses on devolution in other localities too. Nationwide research on 'arguments in favour of devolution' (policy narratives, in effect) has found that 42% focused on achieving economic growth while only 13% linked devolution to strengthening local democracy and citizen engagement. Moreover, only 7% of narratives addressed inequalities in wealth and power. The research concluded that 'new voices' were needed to contest and revise the dominant devolution narrative (NEF, 2015).

A response to this challenge can be found in the launch by social scientists (with partners) of an 'Action Research Collective' (ARC) for Greater Manchester, which has the aim of 'reconnecting those who have been disenfranchised and excluded from the search for solutions'. The ARC is facilitating 'learn and do' activities (to support innovations in urban governance), live debates, online communities and learning exchange visits (in the UK and internationally). The purpose is to actively stimulate critical reflection among communities and citizens on the dominant narratives of city governance and to 'organise knowledge better to make positive urban transformations happen that are inclusive and equitable'.[1]

In work of this sort, social scientists are operating as narrative provocateurs, providing a framework for contesting the Greater Manchester story and assembling new storylines. In effect, they are unpicking the metaphor, and challenging its assumptions. When social scientists support marginalised groups to formulate 'stories of self', and to contest the putative 'story of us', they make an intervention that challenges deep-seated power relations. While outcomes are never guaranteed, a potentially transformative process has been unleashed. Indeed, narrative analysis can itself be a tool for empowerment

(Hampton, 2004). As Julian Rappaport (1995: 805) explains:

> Stories are not a scarce resource, but often the stories of people who are 'outsiders' are an ignored or devalued resource. Much of the work of social change ... may be about understanding and creating settings where people participate in the discovery, creation, and enhancement of their own community narratives and personal stories.

Limitations of the narrative approach

Having identified possible interventions in the policy process, a consideration of the challenges associated with the narrative approach is needed. Five points are of particular significance:

- The challenge of being taken seriously: this arises from the fact that the narrative approach deviates from the assumptions of mainstream policy analysis; for instance, it does not fit the criteria of non-falsifiability and may have a limited capacity for generalisation.

- Practical challenges: working with narrative involves spending a lot of time in the field, working collaboratively with policymakers and practitioners. Such work does not fit the demands of the quick call from the minister's office for evidence to support a policy position (or options). It is resource- as well as time-intensive, and also requires skills that are not generally prized in the social scientist's training.

- Ethical issues: the outcomes of narrative work do not simply 'belong' to the policy analyst, having been generated collaboratively. Issues of ethics are brought to the fore, in contrast to the policy analyst's typical relationship with the data they collect and analyse. The subsequent academic use of narrative-based policy analysis will have to be negotiated with partners. As we have seen, who 'owns' a story is a highly contentious matter.

- Narrative and power: narrative capital is unevenly distributed. Narratives are not free-floating, or separated from structures of social and economic inequality. One of the roles of academic interlocutors may be to consider critically whose story is dominating, and what weight is given to different stories within the art (rather than science) of policy judgement.

- Institutional design: our three forms of intervention all require a subsequent stage of activity in which new or modified narratives are 'fixed', so that they have traction over future policy initiatives. Institutionalising new narratives is tantamount to changing the 'rules of the game' within which policy issues are framed. However, institutional change is inevitably a slow process, and one likely to be resisted by those who benefit from the status quo (or pursue alternative new narratives).

Conclusion

The three forms of intervention are clearly overlapping. *Mobilising narratives* can lead to the articulation of new stories as traditions are put to work in the service of new objectives. *Generating narratives* is a process that inevitably looks backwards as well as forwards in locating and combining discursive resources from which a 'story of us' can be crafted. *Contesting narratives* is a process that is endemic to all narrative encounters. In conclusion, it is important that social scientists pay attention to their own narratives too, whichever techniques from this book are used. Social scientists tell stories too. We are engaged, as Bevir and Rhodes (2006) put it, in the 'interpretation of interpretations', bringing to bear in this process our own academic theories and traditions. The social scientist is as much a producer of arguments as the policymakers they study. As Majone (1989: 36) puts it, 'propaganda is of the essence'. We need to reflect upon our rhetorical and dialectical skills, as well as our technical and scientific accomplishments. We also need to recognise that our performance of narratives is always 'embodied', with our own gender, ethnicity and class affecting the way in which our narratives are received and interpreted by others.

Social scientists confront, and are implicated in, a multiplicity of stories within any policy space. The question is whether they engage directly with these stories or ignore or dismiss them. However, even where they seek to make stories invisible beneath a patina of 'scientific' policy analysis, they will not succeed in negating their effects. As interlocutors in public policy, social scientists are inevitably engaged in a task of 'active translation' (Durose et al, 2015), involving the negotiation of values and power. The interventions discussed in this chapter seek to make a virtue out of the story 'problem'. A narrative perspective reminds us of the necessarily political character of policy making, and the unsustainability of any clear separation between 'politics' and 'administration'. Such a perspective encourages social scientists to unpick supposedly neutral policy statements in a spirit of scepticism or critique; but it also provides them with new tools for working creatively with policymakers, in 'talking' between (not over) competing values, choices and strategies.

In working with policymakers, we ignore the power of story at our peril. The Greek philosopher Socrates observed that 'the un-narrated life is not worth living'. In this chapter, I have sought to show that the un-narrated policy is not worth having – and probably would not work either.

Further reading

An introduction to narrative policy analysis, with international case studies from environmental, defence and social policy, is provided by Jones et al.'s (2014) *The science of stories* (available as an e-book).

For a case study on how narratives can be mobilised in the service of creative policy making during times of crisis, see Gardner and Lowndes' (2016) 'Negotiating austerity and local traditions'.

On the 'public narrative' approach, pioneered by Marshall Ganz at Harvard, see 'Public narrative: self, us and now', available at: http://marshallganz.usmblogs.com/files/2012/08/Public-Narrative-Worksheet-Fall-2013-.pdf

To see how the approach is being applied in the British National Health Service to improve services and build leadership capacity, see: http://changeday.nhs.uk/ and www.nhsiq.nhs.uk/download.ashx?mid=8801&nid=8800

Ways of challenging dominant narratives about urban governance are being explored by an Action Research Collective in Greater Manchester, see: www.urbantransformations.ox.ac.uk/project/jam-and-justice-co-producing-urban-governance-for-social-innovation/

Note

[1] See: www.urbantransformations.ox.ac.uk/project/jam-and-justice-co-producing-urban-governance-for-social-innovation/

Appear evidence in legislatur – gets to the importance at SS adopting, but has no necessary relationship w/ evidence

SEVEN

Visuals in policy making: 'See what I'm saying'

Leonie J. Pearson and Lain Dare

Let us be clear, the use of visual methods to inform, analyse and deliver policy is not new! Various visual approaches from the social sciences are used to inform politics and political studies. For example, there have been investigations of political party TV advertisements (Robinson, 1976), as well as the influence of visual imagery such as national flags on political behaviour and decisions (Hassin et al, 2007). There is a long history within the social sciences of visual methods, particularly in sociology, anthropology and the arts (see Grady, 2008; Margolis and Pauwels, 2011). However, to date, there is little work that outlines the ways in which the visual components of the social sciences can contribute to policy making and political analysis.

The hyper-visual nature of modern society emphasises the need for policymakers to actively consider the use of visual methods in policy making and policy analysis (see Knowles and Sweetman, 2004; Ball and Gilligan, 2010; Spencer, 2011). The vast majority of human communication is non-verbal (Davies et al, 1990); we are built to process visual information faster than textual information (Holcomb and Grainger, 2006; Merieb and Hoehn, 2007; Semetko and Scammell, 2012). With new technology, there has been a burgeoning of visual information (Uimonen, 2013), described by Gatto (2015) as a data explosion. There was a 4000% increase in visuals in literature from 1990 to 2008 (Google Ngram Viewer, in NeoMam Studios, 2015) and a 9900% increase of visuals on the Internet since 2007 (Google Trends, in NeoMam Studios, 2015).

Visual information shows us ways in which we interact socially and politically (Smith, K.L. et al, 2004). It affects us cognitively and emotionally, enabling us to communicate better about the issues and emotions that affect our thought processes (Van Oostendorp et al, 1999). As such, visual information is a critical and readily accessible 'data' resource for policy-makers, providing rapid insights into evolving social and political issues and consequent policy preferences. However, access to, and appropriate use of, such visual information is dependent on policymakers' and/or research colleagues' visual literacy (Symon and Cassell, 2012). This is perhaps best articulated by Robert E. Horn, from Stanford University's Center for the Study of Language and Information, who said:

> When words and visual elements are closely entwined, we create something new and we augment our communal intelligence … visual language has the potential for increasing 'human bandwidth' – the capacity to take in, comprehend, and more efficiently synthesize large amounts of new information. (Horn, 1998)

This potential of visuals highlights that, despite the growing reliance on the visual in our everyday lives and the long history of visual research methods in social science, there is insufficient understanding and application of visual literacy in policy making.

In this chapter, we focus on the use of visual methods in policy making, with the aim to position visual methods as a useful addition to the policymaker's toolkit. Visual methods are grounded in the basis that 'valid scientific insight in society can be acquired by observing, analysing and theorising its visual manifestations: behaviour of people and material products of culture' (based on Pauwels, 2011: 3). This infers that there is 'meaning' in visual elements, as there is in written text. By positioning visual methods as a useful addition to the policymaker's toolkit, we explore two types of visual methods: those that augment current policy techniques; and those that focus on the meaning of and in visual artefacts.

The chapter is organised into three sections. First, we provide a brief overview of what visual methods are and how they are currently used in policy making, including two case-study examples. We then outline the core analytical and ethical considerations of visual methods, and review the strengths and opportunities that visual methods can add to the policy making toolbox. This chapter will conclude by clarifying for policymakers that an understanding of visual methods will enhance communication and potentially lead to better engagement with citizens, other policymakers and academics.

Context

Social science has strong traditions in investigating visual elements, using both quantitative and qualitative analysis approaches (see Ball and Smith, 1992; Banks, 2001; Grimshaw and Ravetz, 2005; Margolis and Pauwels, 2011; Pink, 2013). There has been a recent rise of visual research methods, described by Pauwels (2011: 382) as a 'fetishisation'. This growth in methods cannot be wholly explained by the correlated growth in technological advances given the often 'low-tech' application of methods and the portrayal of visual artefacts (see Rose, 2014). Another explanation for the rise of visual methods, and, indeed, their relevance, is the importance of visuals in contemporary culture, as previously discussed. Visual imagery is a constant in modern lives, through advertising, online social networking, political lobbying and so on. This accumulation of images embeds visual communication into our psychological and social practices (Ferguson, 2013), highlighting the importance of visual information in our political lives.

Despite this rise in visual information, there is a relatively weak consideration of visuals in policy making, with governmental and political communication dominated by text, and visuals only providing 'glossy graphics' for aesthetic purposes (eg, see the majority of government departmental websites). This is despite the understanding that visuals present many benefits in considering and capturing the complexity of issues, as outlined in Chapter Thirteen on co-design by Evans and Terrey, where 'knowledge packages' are developed with the deliberate use of visuals. In this chapter, we intend to address this gap by providing an insight into the use of visual methods that highlights the benefits and relative ease of application.

Visual methods

This chapter provides a 'taste' of some visual methods most appropriate to policymakers by exploring visual methods in two broad categories: those that enhance common investigative methods, for example, the use of pictures in interviews; and those that investigate visual artefacts or phenomena, for example, asking people to take photographs for data collection. These two 'tasters' provide policymakers with a basic understanding of visual methods as each method requires different analysis requirements and different ethical considerations, both of which are further outlined in the chapter.

Visual methods that enhance common investigative methods

Visual methods are most often used as a compliment to common policy making investigative methods, for example, using pictures to stimulate discussion in an interview, or using images in a survey. The two most common research methods used in policy-based research are document analysis and interviewing, with a predominant focus on 'words' in the analysis. By including visuals within these approaches, we can provide additional dimensions that benefit policy analysis and policy making; both are discussed in the following.

Document analysis with visual artefacts

Document analysis is a form of research in which documents are interpreted by the researcher to give voice and meaning around a topic (see Kress and Van Leeuwen, 1996; Bell, 2001; Krippendorff and Bock, 2009). Generally, three types of documents are used in policy making document analysis:

- Public records, the official records of an organisation's activities, for example, annual reports, policy manuals, strategic plans and so on.
- Personal documents, such as first-person accounts of an incident, belief or experience, for example, calendars, emails, scrapbooks, blogs, duty logs, incident reports, reflections/journals and newspapers.
- Physical evidence, including objects or artefacts found within the study setting, for example, flyers, posters, agendas, handbooks and training materials.

In public policy, there is a strong tradition of document analysis of public records, personal diaries and physical evidence that focuses on the narratives of words (eg Benoit and Laver, 2007; see also Chapters Three, Five and Seven of this book). A clear example of how visuals can add value and provide greater certainty to an argument is found when investigating visual images in document analysis. While documents vary in type, size and shape, most public records, personal documents or physical artefacts include both written and visual imagery. By focusing on both types of data, a policymaker can be more holistic in their understanding of the document and the narratives and issues raised (Bell, 2001). Some examples of which both words and visuals have been accounted for include Fahmy and Kim's (2008) analysis of how the Iraq war was presented to the American and British populations through newspaper pictures, and Dobernig et al's (2010) exploration of the differences between the verbal and visual presentations of the 2009 Gaza crisis in newspapers.

The decision to include visuals within policy document analysis is clearly a case of 'Does it add value to my investigation?' and/or 'Is it appropriate?' For example, fear-inducing visual images of climate change are extensively employed in the public domain as part of the policy making process to connect with the public. Recent work by O'Neill and Nicholson-Cole (2009) identified that these visual images, which are used to attract public attention, are an ineffective tool for motivating genuine personal engagement with the issue, and hence changing behaviour. Importantly for policymakers, the work found that non-threatening imagery and icons that link to individuals' everyday emotions and concerns in the context of this macro-environmental issue tend to be the most effective in engaging the public on climate change. This understanding highlights that having the right type of visual information is an effective part of the policy implementation process.

Another visual documentary analysis approach is the very structured interrogation of the visual image within the document, as described by Bell (2001). Bell states that there are two important aspects of the visual image to consider. The first important aspect concerns the *objective* visual qualities, such as the picture size, picture position in the text, amount of space allocated relative to the text and so on. This 'objective' information is used to discuss the salience or priority of the visual content, while counting how many visuals of the same event occur over different media (ie newspapers, journals, etc) indicates the frequency of the visual media content. The second important aspect concerns the *subjective* visual qualities, which are about the actual content displayed in the visual artefacts. These qualities could include who is portrayed? How many people are presented? What is their relative position in the picture? Are there specific gestures shown? There are also questions about the contextual setting of the image or the place the image was depicted: where is it? What is expected in this place? What is occurring in this place?

Dobernig et al (2010) adopted this style, counting, classifying and coding the images related to the 2009 Gaza conflict in four weekly newspapers. The results identified the number and type of images, and the disproportional representation of subject material, with 42% of images depicting people or organisations related to Palestine, compared to 29% related to Israel. The results of the newspaper document analysis (which included both visual and written text) showed that the conflicting parties are represented differently in the visual and the written text. For example, in both cases, the Palestinian side is associated with individual civilians, whereas the Israeli side is shown with political or governmental officials. In addition, the visual and written content showed an imbalance in how the conflict parties were portrayed as empathy seems to be promoted for the Palestinian side, whereas governmental power is focused on for the Israeli side. Finally, the results showed that reports on Israel dominate the verbal reports, whereas the visual reports favour photos of Palestinians. From the results, it can be inferred that the verbal and the visual level do, indeed, 'speak another language' (Dobernig et al, 2010: 102).

Interviews with visual artefacts

Interviews are a core method within qualitative social science and are used extensively in policy making (see Chapters Five, Six, Eleven, Twelve and Thirteen of this book). An interview is a conversation in which the interviewer questions the respondent in order to gain information. Interviews can be formal or informal, structured or unstructured. They can be conducted one-to-one or in groups, face-to-face or by telephone, Skype or email. They are not 'chats', but have structure, purpose and focus, and are often recorded using a combination of audio, video or written notes for subsequent analysis. Here, we focus on the introduction of 'visual stimuli' into the interview environment, for example, the introduction of a photograph, artefact or other object that leads to both a verbal and visual response in the respondent.

When considering the introduction of a visual artefact into an interview, the most common form is through the inclusion of photographs. This can be done as deliberate methodology, for example, the use of photographs instead of written description in a Q-methodology (see Brown, 1980; Hardy et al, 2014). Figure 7.1 provides an example of a Q-methodology sort where photographs were used rather than text statements to determine study participants' tourism preferences (see Hardy et al, 2014).

Alternatively, photo elicitation uses a more unstructured approach, where a photograph of the issue or place under discussion is introduced in the interview and then discussed. Photo elicitation provides many benefits, including a capacity to 'get inside' an issue and its context, bridge psychological and physical realties, assist in building trust and rapport, produce unpredictable information, and promote more detailed interviews in comparison with verbal interviews (Hurworth, 2004). The data can be coded and analysed in both qualitative and quantitative form depending on the approach desired and the research question under investigation (Lapenta, 2011).

The second way to incorporate visual methods into interviewing is to record the visual outcomes of the interview, focusing on body language and its relationships to the verbal discussion. Atkinson (1984)

Figure 7.1: Q-sort using photographs to determine tourist preferences

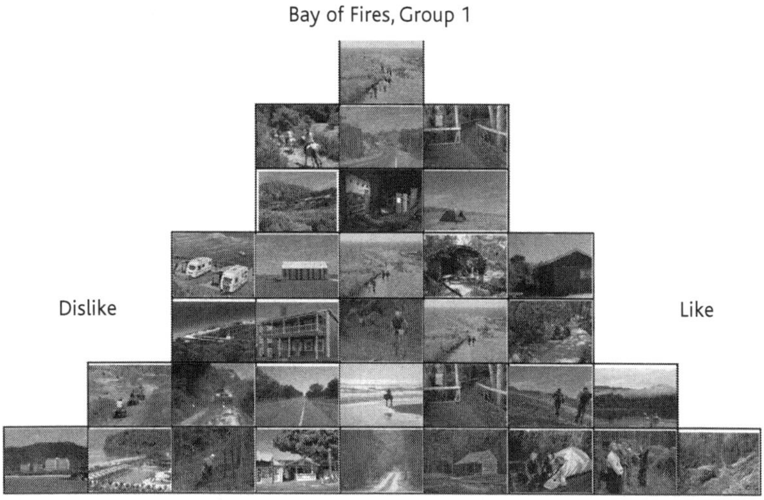

Bay of Fires, Group 1

Dislike   Like

Source: Authors' image.

produced a book on the use of body language, intonation and verbal and non-verbal cues for delivering high-impact political speeches. Based firmly in more ethnographic fields, this work is considered highly complementary and necessary in some forms of analysis, for example, discourse analysis. This inclusion of non-verbal cues as data has been found useful; however, it creates implementation challenges as some respondents do not want to be videoed or act in non-natural ways during the interview due to the visual recording process.

Investigating visual artefacts

Visual artefacts can be investigated as the focus of a policy making exercise, with the visual artefact becoming the object of the research investigation and hence the visual method focus (see Harper, 2002; Moore et al, 2008; Margolis and Pauwels, 2011). A popular visual method useful to policy making is respondent-generated images.

Respondent-generated imagery is where a respondent, subject or person involved in the research is asked to provide a visual image (eg photograph, drawing, video artefact) in the context of the investigation. It has been used extensively with children and youth (Hogan and Pink, 2012) but has had little application in other areas despite its considerable potential given the burgeoning use of the Internet and the personal posting of images (see Chapter Eight on big data). One application of the use of respondent-generated imagery in policy making is found in Australian local governments, where efforts have been made to engage citizens in local identity policy making by asking citizens to enter a photographic competition on 'the best place in my neighbourhood' (Howard, 2012).

In many instances, a policymaker needs to understand not the aggregate societal inference, but a personal response – how will this policy affect a particular individual or family? What aspect of people's lives will change with an adjustment in service provision through a new policy? Respondent-generated images help to understand these personal perspectives on an issue, providing an ability for respondents to: engage multiple sensors in the understanding of an issue; provide individual perspectives that are not fully dictated by a policy or research framing; provide innovative data; and create an environment of control or power that is held by the respondent in the research space (see Van Leeuwen and Jewitt, 2001; Van Dijck, 2008). The weaknesses of respondent-generated imagery include the potential lack of control that a policymaker can have over respondents.

One example of how asking respondents to construct visual artefacts can be used is a small study that investigated how researchers at the Murray-Darling Basin Futures Collaborative Research Network (University of Canberra) understood their influence on policy making in the Murray-Darling Basin (for a study description, see Pearson and Moon, 2014). The approach asked respondents to visually describe (using a whiteboard, pre-coded variables and a marker pen) their research project and how it would influence policy making (see Figure 7.2). These 'influence diagrams' are a visual representation of the respondents' mental map of their research project's effect on policy making. The respondent was asked to provide an 'influence diagram' one week before and after a field trip, to determine if time and/ or the field trip altered their conceptions of how their project influenced policy.

The influence diagrams were then visually assessed for themes and quantitatively coded to determine which variables were used and which way arrows were arranged between variables, and analysis was conducted using statistics and network analysis. Network analysis results were compared with the interview analysis to identify key themes, direct and indirect influence approaches to policy, and engagement with other projects and broader policy issues.

The respondent-generated visuals provided clear data showing that researchers who undertook the field trip had a statistically significant change in their influence diagrams that represented the effect of their research on policy making. The change was found in more links

Figure 7.2: Influence diagrams of a respondent who undertook the field trip, showing before (7.2a) and after (7.2b)

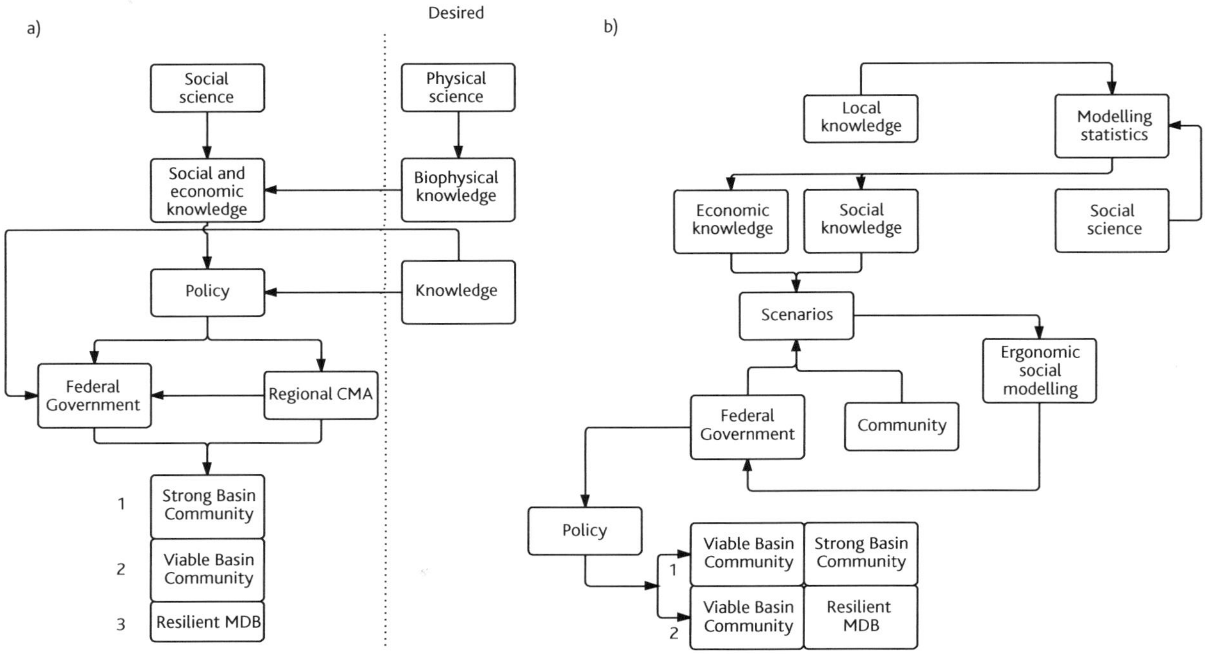

Source: Pearson and Moon (2014: 204). *Note:* CMA = Catchment Management Authority; MDB = Murray-Darling Basin

to other projects, a greater number of ties to pathways that would influence policy and more internally connected projects. Figure 7.2 shows this change, where Figure 7.2a was before the field trip and Figure 7.2b was after, exhibiting more backward arrows (ie going from bottom to top), closer ties between project components and additional pathways to policy influence (ie government bodies or agencies). In addition, the use of respondent-generated visual methods enhanced the respondent experience with one stating '*this was the best fun I've had in an interview*'. The approach also provided novel insights for the respondent as many had not directly considered how their research would influence policy as a systemic flow of issues and ideas.

Analytical and ethical issues in the use of visual techniques

As identified at the beginning of this chapter, the social sciences have a long history with visual data analysis and each separate discipline has developed alternate approaches to the analysis of visual data (for ideas on different approaches and disciplinary biases, see Ball and Smith, 2011). The challenge for any study is to know which analysis approach is most applicable for the study objectives and data collected.

In this section, we outline three approaches to visual data analysis and provide a step-by-step guide for how visual data could be included in policy making. The rationale for focusing on the analysis of visual data is to ensure that its inclusion in policy making is based on a transparent, clear and salient approach.

Social science has a wide range of analysis approaches; however, for policy makers, there are three common approaches that could be of use – content analysis, semiotics and symbolic interactionism – with content analysis being the most popular (for a more extensive discussion of these and other approaches, see Ball and Smith, 2011). As shown in Table 7.1, each approach has different key questions guiding the research, aims, units of analysis, interpretations of the world and researcher skills. For example, research that was interested in analysing visual data for themes would use content analysis; if symbols were of interest, then semiotics would be more appropriate; if the research was interested in how symbols interacted with people, then symbolic interactionism would be the best approach to analysis in the investigation.

Each approach highlights that the policymaker must have visual 'literacy', the ability to see, to understand and ultimately to think, create and communicate visually (see, eg, Kress and Van Leeuwen,

Table 7.1: Comparing approaches to visual studies

	Content analysis	Semiotics	Symbolic interactionism
Key questions	What are the significant categories and themes predominant in any communication?	What do signs mean within sociocultural contexts?	How are meanings created and sustained in social interaction?
Aim of analysis	Identification of patterns of messages. Manifest and latent contents of communication	Discovery of how signs work to convey sociocultural meaning	Analytic description; concept generation and development
Unit of analysis	Drawings, images, photographs and paintings that can be collected and coded into predetermined categories (quantitative) or interrogated for themes (qualitative)	Images analysed for the *signifier* (the sound, image or word) and the *signified*, which is the concept the signifier represents	Participant and direct observation to examine interactional uses of images and objects
How is the social world interpreted through the data?	A web of messages exchanged by senders and receivers	A multiplicity of codes. Certain codes become dominant ideologies	A vast network of interactions between people and objects
Researcher skills	Reading visual imagery for thematic content, and the identification and coding of themes within visuals	Reading visual imagery for symbols and understanding cultural context to identify what they signify	Reading visual imagery to understand the links between an object or visual and people's behaviour, understanding or cultural context
Exemplars	Robinson (1976), Krippendorff and Bock (2009)	Sayre (1994), Wagner (2006)	Charon and Hall (2009), Hassin et al (2007)

Source: Adapted from Ball and Smith (2011: 395).

1996). The visually literate viewer looks at an image carefully, critically and with an eye for the intentions of the research question.

Table 7.1 also identifies the units of analysis. Each of these different approaches requires visual data to be converted from its original state (ie film, photograph, etc) to a state that is conducive to analysis and reporting. The unit of analysis for visual images needs policymakers to understand what it is that they are actually going to investigate within the images. For example, some policy making is concerned with the categories of issues – as such, content analysis is used in visuals, for example, the amount of times that a specific person is portrayed in a set of visual images. Or, perhaps, as investigated in symbolism, there are symbols present in images and we are interested in how these symbols are used and the associated cultural significance, such as the use of bicycles in transport management plans. Alternatively, we may be interested in the relationship between a visual artefact and people's response; by using symbolic interactionism, we can uncover, for example, how a specific policy flyer is received by stakeholders through video recordings and analysis. So, while you can use the same visual data (eg political advertisements), the focus of the investigation (or research question) will drive the organisation and analysis of the data in different ways.

Figure 7.3 outlines the three broad steps used in visual methods for policy making: observation and data collection; data analysis and interpretation; and writing and reporting. The three steps are common to all research methods; however, when using visual methods, there are a few nuances to the tasks in each step.

The first step in the use of visual methods is to identify the 'artefact' collection – the collation of research records. For visual data, this collation of records may be broad as it needs to encompass the spectrum of visuals used in a study (eg film, photographs, autobiographical diaries, respondent imagery, etc).

The second step – data analysis and interpretation – is where visual methods can transform into either a qualitative or quantitative study, or both. Here, the researcher must be clear about the unit of analysis (for different types of unit of analysis, see Table 7.1); these can either be as presence/absence codes, counts of events or qualitative descriptions of themes. The last task in this step is to determine how data will be displayed and what patterns or analysis will be undertaken. For example, we referred earlier to the visual influence diagrams where the data unit was the arrows between variables (see Figure 7.2); these were coded as one-way or two-way arrows and then analysed using network analysis. This is quantitative analysis of the influence diagrams, which was different to the qualitative analysis of the interview that accompanied the respondent-generated diagrams, which employed the content analysis of key themes.

Figure 7.3: Three steps in the use of visual methods in policy making

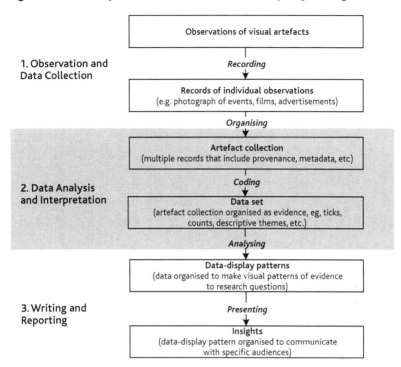

Finally, there is a need to write and report on the research conducted. A benefit of visuals is that *pictures speak louder than words*, so in the conveying of information, the resubmitting of visual data and the construction of new visuals to convey a simple and clear message is often easily achieved. The use of data visualisation to convey policy messages, or research outcomes, can be instrumental for policy analysis as it attempts to make data more accessible, interactive and engaging.[1]

Data visualisation encapsulates the variety of forms to represent statistical and other numeric and non-numeric data through pictures and graphics (eg policy network drawings, graphs and informatics) (Gatto, 2015). Used in conjunction with narratives, data visualisation reduces knowledge gaps between data users (eg policymakers, policy analysts, experts, citizens), supporting evidence-based policy making through the improved representation, communication and interpretation of knowledge (Brandes et al, 1999; Ruppert et al, 2013). Visual data is more manageable than texts and numeric tables, allowing us to rapidly make comparisons, identify patterns and understand the meaning behind the data (Koch et al, 2006).

However, despite the proliferation and demand for data visualisation, there remains a reluctance to accept it as a reliable analysis tool due to the high risks associated with such an accessible and powerful medium (Burn-Murdoch, 2013, in Gatto, 2015). The quality and origin of data representation is important, with the production of visual data being a result of 'complex sociotechnical acts involving a variety of actors and technologies with the persuasive power to shape people's engagement and interaction with the world itself' (Williamson, 2016: 132). Visuals can benefit policy through their accessibility. With access to more data and more technology, data visualisation is evolving from static graphics to more interactive visualisation tools that have become policy instruments in themselves. However, data visualisation must be treated with caution as without sufficient critique, visualised data can 'flatten and compress extraordinary complexity into simplified seductive visual presentations' (Williamson, 2016: 134), potentially damaging public policy processes rather than aiding them.

Ethical considerations

Visual methods that produce images of individuals raise particular ethical issues in relation to informed consent, anonymity and confidentiality, and the law (Wiles et al, 2008, 2011; Pauwels, 2010; Rowe, 2011). Informed consent is based on the premise that research participants are adequately informed of the research objectives and process, and consent to participating. When using visual methods, this would include agreement not only to produce visual images, but also to display those images to different audiences, in different contexts and over different time periods (Wiles et al, 2011). The practicalities of gaining such consent can be problematic, especially in public spaces with a large number of people, where obtaining informed consent is impossible (eg public rallies, sporting events), and, in some cases, permission to photograph public places may be required or it may even be illegal (eg photographs of defence bases) (see Wiles et al, 2011). Similarly, it is often impossible to maintain anonymity and confidentiality within visual methods (Wiles et al, 2011). A variety of techniques are used to maintain anonymity and confidentiality, including the blurring of identifying attributes (see Wiles et al, 2008), only publishing images that do not depict recognisable individuals (see Barrett, 2004; Moore et al, 2008) or recreating imagery with actors (see Hubbard et al, 2003, in Wiles et al, 2011: 698). The dissemination of visual artefacts (eg on the Internet) invokes important legal issues, such as copyright and moral rights. 'Found' images (eg those available on the Internet) covered by copyright may be used in research only with the permission of the copyright owner (see Rowe, 2011). In addition to this, moral rights help to ensure that the image is used within the intent and commitments initially prescribed when gaining consent from the participants (see Rowe, 2011; Wiles et al, 2011). These ethical considerations should not stop the use of visual methods, but rather highlight the need to adequately consider what is needed from the images and hence the need for well-planned visual investigations from the outset.

This section provided a 'taste' of how visual methods can be included in policy making, and focused on the fundamentals of how to undertake the analysis when using visual methods. In doing this, it has outlined three common approaches to analysis, and the necessary steps to consider when using a visual method. In focusing on analysis, we highlight the skills that researchers need to undertake visual methods, including visual literacy. In addition, we have closed with a snapshot of the some additional ethical considerations required when using visual methods. Overall, visual methods can add value and richness to a policy making process focused on the textual or verbal narratives.

Challenges in implementing visual methods in policy making

In this final section, we outline the strengths and challenges in implementing visual methods in policy making. As outlined in Table 7.2, these strengths and challenges are necessarily broad given the range of visual methods and analytical approaches that can be incorporated into policy making.

There are always strengths and challenges with any method and approach. In this hyper-visual contemporary culture, visual materials are an important research medium due to their ubiquitous nature in society and associated accessibility. As such, visual methods provide opportunities for policymakers to explore social and political development in a manner that directly engages with stakeholders and complements existing methodologies. By focusing on visual images and artefacts rather than written words and numbers, visual methods enable the engagement of members of society often marginalised from traditional policy analysis processes.

Further compounding issues of visual literacy is the perceived illegitimacy of visual methods as a research methodology. Despite being well established in other disciplines, policymakers still have a strong preference for evidence perceived to be more 'tangible', predominantly

Table 7.2: Strengths and challenges of visual methods for policy making

Strengths	Challenges
• *Holistic understanding through visual methods.* Visual imagery is part of our societal communication approach and hence its incorporation into policy making expands the policy making toolkit to better reflect the mediums used in society	• *Skills upgrade.* Skills required for 'visual literacy' are not taught to policymakers and need to be added to the toolbox
• *Building on a long tradition.* Visual methods are well established in other social sciences (eg ethnography, media studies); hence, policymakers can pull on these long traditions in application	• *Clarity of visual data organisation.* Visual methods may require extra tasks in the policy making process that could hinder the robustness of the work by novice policymakers
• *Visuals add to current policy approaches.* Visual methods are a new dimension to the call for pluralism in policy making and are complementary to other, more traditional, methods explored in the book, for example, big data	• *Ethics.* Additional ethical requirements in the collection and presentation of some visual data could limit the uptake of the visual methods in policy making
• *Pictures tell a thousand words.* In some instances, there is high potential for a greater impact of policy making if visual images are involved	• *Legality.* (Il)legitimacy of visual methods by practitioners and academics may hinder initial acceptance
• *Engaging better with people.* Using visual methods with respondents creates a new dynamic in data collection that is positive to respondent outcomes, for example, fun or building trust and rapport	
• *Innovation for policy.* Visual methods provide a different approach to getting at an issue as they are able to bridge psychological and physical realities	
• *Boundary crossing.* Visuals can cross cultural boundaries and engage participants that have limited verbal and written skills	

numbers and text through narratives. The strong evidence of the benefits of visual methods has resulted in a growing uptake of visual methods across disciplines and contexts, highlighting the capacity for such methods to be undertaken in conjunction with traditional word- and number-based methods, including those described in the other chapters of this book. Visual methods can enhance these methods through methodological pluralism, providing insights into experiences and emotions not typically available through other approaches, while maintaining the perceived rigour and quality deemed acceptable by policymakers.

Finally, visual methods are able to engage a range of stakeholders that are perceived as at the 'fringe' of the engaged policy group. These stakeholders have barriers to entry into policy making processes because they have different cultural backgrounds, language capacity, functional literacy or are 'scared' of direct engagement with traditional research methods, such as interviews, surveys and so on (Rose, 2014). The use of visual methods to engage these often marginalised stakeholders highlights the need for policy making practices to reflect the broadest set of cultural and social dimensions in which they operate. Sometimes, this is hard, and new, alternative approaches such as 'respondent-generated images' rather than online surveys or face-to-face interviews provide both policymakers and stakeholders with new ways to explore old issues and new ways to engage.

Conclusion

This chapter focused on the use of visual methods in policy making, with the aim of positioning visual methods as a useful addition to the toolkit of policymakers and analysts. It has provided guidance on the types of visual methods available to policymakers, approaches to analyses and the ethical considerations therein. This focus on the 'nuts and bolts' of the use of visual methods in policy making has provided clear insight into what, how and why visuals can add to the policy making process. It is clear that visual methods use a variety of visual materials to generate evidence regarding the exploration of research questions in order to elicit broader understandings of the social world, in particular, the inner emotional and creative interpretations, and to engage with people in alternate (non-text-)based approaches.

The hyper-visual nature of contemporary culture renders visual materials an important research medium, especially in policy making, which has strong links to society and culture. As such, visual methods provide opportunities for policymakers to explore social and political development in a manner that directly engages with stakeholders and complements existing methodologies. By focusing on visual images and artefacts, rather than written words and numbers, visual methods enable the engagement of members of society often marginalised from traditional policy analysis processes. Visual methods provide space for an alternative framing of issues, insights and understandings, using 'new' methods that readily engage and inspire participants, which is important in this era where political engagement is waning.

Opportunities for the use of visual methods in policy making include:

- to complement written text analysis, providing a comprehensive picture of issues or context that is critical in a polycentric approach to policy making;
- to provide policymakers with the ability to explore different sets of data readily found in society (eg images, films, etc) that reflect a broader set of culturally based public policy issues than present in written text;
- to provide the capacity to engage with issues that are not obvious and physical, for example, political concerns;
- to enable engagement with alternative stakeholder groups that are traditionally under-represented in policy making processes; and
- to add dimensions to policy making that reflect the broader visual and auditory stimuli context of society and its various forms of communication.

These opportunities for visual methods in policy making extend from basic application to strategic insights. It is our hope that by including visual methods as a distinct and significant contribution to this book, future policymakers will be able to trial the approach and develop a more refined applied research agenda for future policy analysis.

Further reading

The last decade has seen a boom in the critical analysis of visuals and their role in policy making as 'science'. However, it has yet to make an impact in the practical world; as such, further readings are limited to journal articles and books – although numerous PowerPoint presentations are available online that outline specific methods that may assist future projects. Some great readings to start with are the following:

- For an overview of visual methods, see Margolis and Pauwels (2011) book, *The Sage handbook of visual research methods*.
- For a better understanding of each approach, consider the references provided in Table 7.1, more specifically for content analysis;
- For an example of data visualisation, see Williamson's (2016) description and Pearson's Learning Curve (available at: http://thelearningcurve. pearson.com), and consider the rapid emergence of data journalism (see: http://www.datajournalismhandbook.org/1.0/en/).

Note

[1] See the Organisation for Economic Co-operation and Development's (OECD's) Gapminder, available at: http://prev.gapminder.org/

140

PART THREE:
DEVELOPING DATA MINING

EIGHT

'Big data' and policy learning

Patrick Dunleavy

In early February 2014, during an industrial dispute with management about extending the London Tube's hours of service, many of the system's train drivers went on strike. Millions of passengers had to make other arrangements. Many switched their journey patterns to avoid their normal lines and stations, which were strike-hit, and to use those routes still running a service. Three economists downloaded all the data for the periods before and after the strike period from London's pre-pay electronic travel card system (called the Oystercard), covering millions of journey patterns and linking each journey to a particular cardholder (Larcom et al, 2015). They found that one in 20 passengers changed their journey – an interesting 'flexibility' statistic on its own.

However, after the strike, they also found that a high proportion of these people also stayed with their new journey pattern when the service returned to normal, strongly suggesting that their new route was better for them than their old one had been. They considered two possible explanations of why people could have been using the 'wrong' Tube lines in the first place. One is that they were trying to maximise their welfare all along but had limited their initial search behaviour because of high search costs, so failing to optimise. The other possibility is that Tube travellers only 'satisfice': they had not set out to maximise their welfare in the first place, but were just going with the first acceptable travel solution that they found. The scale of savings made by the strike-hit changers was so high, however, that only the second, 'satisficers' explanation makes empirical sense. The analysts also showed that the travel-time gains made by the small share of commuters switching routes as a result of the Tube strike more than offset the economic costs to the vast majority (95%), who simply got disrupted. The unusual implication here is that economic welfare grew as a result of the strike. One implication might be that disruptions are always likely to have some side-benefits, which should be factored in by policymakers when making future decisions (like whether to close a Tube line wholly in order to accomplish much-needed improvements).

This small case perfectly illustrates the huge advances in social science and public policy understanding that the availability of 'big data' now seems to offer. The economists could not possibly have reliably identified the subset of changing passengers from any conceivable survey of people in person. They needed a huge N of journeys, linked to specific Oyster cards (but anonymous as people), and completely objective and highly detailed in the information on routes chosen. The data involved were also not collected especially for this analysis. Instead, it was routinely generated by Transport for London as part of their administrative operations – checking that people were travelling with valid pre-pay cards with money on them, and at the end of journey, debiting a fare electronically from each card. It is also noteworthy that all the data were digital from the outset, at the point where each Oyster card was read. For the analysis, they were only recoded, not re-entered or handled manually at any stage. Finally, the process of understanding the data was swift. Within a relatively short time, the analysis was complete and able to be presented in timely and accessible ways to policymakers (Larcom et al, 2015).

These are some of the features which mean that the feasible scope of the modern social sciences could rapidly expand because of 'big data'. The societal scale of the effects may be large, as some 'pop social science' treatments have argued (Cukier and Mayer-Schonberger, 2013), and might even 'accelerate democracy' (McGinnis, 2013). However, at this point in time, the effects on public policy still seem to depend a great deal on the complex way in which a set of incentives and constraints on using 'big data' now play out. The argument here is organised into four substantive sections and a conclusion. I first define what the term 'big data' means and consider where it fits within the already-established 'tools of government'. The second section examines the varied and increasingly plentiful sources of big data, and considers how the phenomenon is linked with the digital revolution that is still working its way through many civil society institutions, especially government agencies and the public sector. I next consider how the methods of analysis of the social sciences need to change as a result of big data's arrival. The fourth section considers how 'big data' could alter public policy making, and yet may not do so as much as one might think because of barriers and time lags in its use. The brief conclusions situate these substantial but differently facing implications within a far longer-run tendency of changes in modern information and communication technology (ICT) to be simultaneously centralising and decentralising in their implications.

Defining 'big data'

The philosopher Rob Kitchin (2014a; see also Kitchin, 2014b) notes that what 'big data' means is still vigorously contested and debated (see Boyd and Crawford, 2012; Dumbill, 2012), as with other new and fashionable tech vocabulary:

> Some definitions, whilst simple and clear – such as big data being any dataset that is too large to fit in an Excel spreadsheet – have limited and misleading utility [because] they do not get to the heart [of] what is different ontologically [ie in terms of existence] and epistemologically [ie in terms of knowledge] about big data. And there is a significance difference [here], which is why there is so much hype surrounding these data. For me, big data has [these] traits [see Table 8.1].

This approach helps explain why 'big data' is different from previous very large data sets, like the population censuses conducted every decade for more than a century in many advanced industrial states. Yet, these huge exercises, of course, were the opposite of speedy or 'real-time', often taking years to generate information. Like censuses, 'big data' include whole populations, not any kind of sample – for example, in the London Tube case, all journeys. However, the information is collected and analysable in very timely ways, perhaps even in 'real time'. As the data are very detailed and large-scale, and can often be linked to other information like geographical information systems

Table 8.1: Kitchin's definition of big data

• 'Big data' is 'huge in *volume*, consisting of terabytes or petabytes of data	• 'Big data' **is** high in *velocity*, being created in or near real-time
• 'Big data' is *exhaustive* in scope, striving to capture entire populations or systems, so that *N* = all	• 'Big data' is fine-grained in *resolution*, aiming to be as detailed as possible, and uniquely *indexical* in identification
• 'Big data' is diverse in *variety* in type, being structured and unstructured in nature, and often temporally and spatially referenced	• 'Big data' is *relational* in nature, containing common fields that enable the conjoining of different data sets
• 'Big data' is *flexible*, holding the traits of extensionality (so we can add new fields easily)	• 'Big data' is *scalable* (so it can expand in size rapidly).

(GIS), many more causal processes can be analysed in far more detail than is feasible with any survey method.

An alternative view of 'big data' argues that their essential features stem from being by-products of digital transactions. It is the digital properties of the data that make them easily re-combinable and scalable, which facilitates their retransmission, storage and manipulability – all these are more general properties of many digital artefacts (Anduiza et al, 2012; Jensen et al, 2012; Constantiou and Kallinikos, 2014; see also Kalinikos, 2006; Kallinikos et al, 2010). According to Jensen et al (2012), digital artefacts can be rendered in different archival structures without destroying the original artefact, which can be recovered later on. Unlike surveys or other forms of bureaucratic record-keeping, the 'big data' analysed are the native digital objects themselves (eg the journey 'traces' essential for operating the London pre-pay card system) rather than representations or codings of them. The data can be subject to lossless copies and recombined without destroying the original.

The collection of digital objects is often relatively unobtrusive. For instance, commuters in the London Tube example knew only in a background way that their journey details were being recorded – and they had no chance of altering their 'data', as they could have done with a survey question. Numerous operationalisations and relations between data can be imposed without re-contacting subjects or otherwise producing response bias from iterated queries. Modern data storage capacities are also more scalable with big data, so that their collection and analysis can be automated, continuous and enjoined with other systems.

In public management terms, it is worth locating 'big data' (as defined earlier) in a somewhat modified and extended form of the 'toolkit' of government sketched by Hood and Margetts (2007) in Table 8.2.

The key change that I make here is to distinguish as two categories things that Hood and Margetts treated as one. These are:

- basic bureaucratic capabilities, of precise recording, classification of cases and information, reliable retrieval of information, and impartial and effective implementation – the *organisation* infrastructure needed for any effective administrative apparatus in a basically Weberian mode; and
- the developed *expertise* needed if government is to do essential but inherently complex technical tasks – like keeping government ICT safe from Internet hackers, or determining safe limits for nuclear energy operations, or determining whether or not a new drug can

Table 8.2: The extended 'tools of government' (or NATOE) framework

Code	Label and resources included	Detectors (finding things out)	Effectors (getting things done)
N	**Nodality** – government's central location in civil society information networks	Citizen trust, generating civil society notifications to public agencies	Broadcast information and warnings, targeted messages
A	**Authority** – law, regulations, norms coercively enforced	Legal/regulatory requirements to report statistics or information	Prohibitions, tax raising and requisitions
T	**Treasure** – finance, property, conscripted resources	Tax-funded research and investigations	Subsidies, grants, tax exemptions, incentives, transfers, welfare state benefits
O	**Organisation** – basic bureaucratic administrative competences	Maintaining an information collection network	Capacity to implement policies on the ground
E	**Expertise** – esoteric or highly developed technical knowledge and skills, organised in productive ways	Specialist scientific, research and analysis capabilities	Design, development and calibration of new scientific or engineering solutions or remedies

be approved as safe. What is needed here is a combination of rarified professional talent, often extensive capital equipment and highly sophisticated research/scientific types of organisation.

The role of 'big data' within government is concentrated most in the expertise row (E), where later sections show that talent acquisition and effective deployment are considerable problems. In highly professionalised systems, like health care, sophisticated data analysis can boost already-established expertise in key ways (Bates et al, 2014; Moja et al, 2014; Sinsky et al, 2014). It has also already opened up potential for government agencies to develop genuinely 'free' (not just taxpayer-funded) services, where scalable information provision allows marginal consumers to be added at zero (or near-zero) marginal cost – a capacity that has transformed Internet economics (Anderson, 2009). 'Big data' are also highly relevant in the nodality row (N here), where government must continuously compete in information terms with the major social and economic interests that it is seeking to regulate or influence. The state cannot afford to be blindsided by better-informed societal interests, for if this happens, the government's central role in society's information networks may be compromised or called into question. Monitoring participation and grievance-raising as it happens can also let the government intervene proactively before problems get out of hand (Hale et al, 2014).

'Big data' can also contribute to the other three tools in diverse ways through:

- improved basic organisation (O) – for instance, a border control agency upgrading its basic immigration scanning ability with biometric passports;
- better deployment of subsidies and grants (T) – for instance, a welfare agency using data analytics to target transfers and employability help preventatively at people most at risk of becoming long-term welfare-dependent; and
- improving regulatory capabilities (A) – for instance, a police force adding the capacity to decrypt digital records kept by drug merchants on mobile phones or memory sticks, or gaining an ability to monitor social media being used by rioters to coordinate their behaviour, something London's police failed to do in major August 2011 riots (*Guardian*, 2012).

The main sources of 'big data'

The massive amounts of new information becoming available to policymakers come from two major sources:

- 'Administrative data' – a broad category including governmental records and tracking information but also data from commercial and business sources.
- The 'digital residues' – the 'electronic footprints' of behaviour patterns, meanings and memes – created by our contemporary civilisation.

Administrative data

A 2013 government taskforce in the UK reported on the prospects for encouraging greater use by researchers of administrative data:

> Government collects and holds a vast amount of data as part of the normal transaction of government business. Similarly, government collects data for the purpose of producing statistics about the current state of the economy and society. The ability to link and analyse data held by

government has the potential to add new insights to our understanding of how society and the economy performs and to reduce the need for separate data collections where we ask, for statistical purposes, for the same information that has already been provided for administrative purposes. (BIS, 2013: 4)

Following a UK government commitment to improving data-sharing, a rather complex apparatus for encouraging academic researchers to make greater use of administrative data was put in place, later on reorganised as the Administrative Data Research Network (ADRN, 2016). At first, most take-up of these new opportunities was by health researchers (perhaps 90%), followed later by education (perhaps 5%). More economics-, finance- or transport-focused applications came much later on, in part because the ADRN framework is relatively restrictive and oriented a lot towards protecting individual identities.

Administrative data in government are all collected for transactional purposes, rather than being designed from the outset as a data set for analysis by researchers (eg conducting repeat social science surveys), or forming part of the carefully constructed and evaluated national statistics reporting. Major longitudinal surveys are very expensive and large-scale social surveys, asking respondents for the same fixed grid of information over successive years. Questions have to be specified in advance. National statistics generally operate by requiring business or civil society organisations to file regular reports with government, filling in forms with numbers that are then checked and aggregated – for example, to form a picture of the latest pace of economic activity in a country.

Table 8.3 shows some pros and cons of administrative data sets against these main alternatives. Administrative data typically record objective behaviours, but not people's opinions or meanings. They can often be collected unobtrusively and non-reactively (so you do not need to worry about people 'faking' survey responses or 'dressing up' statistics to try and make them look better). However, the items recorded may not be exactly what research is interested in, but only indicators often or usually associated with what the focus of interest is.

Some observers have identified 'missing data' as a problem of administrative data (Smith, G. et al, 2004). However, in fact, technologically recorded data will often have less of a problem here than longitudinal surveys as computerised recording devices can be very comprehensive in what they track (so long as they are working). However, tech-gathered data may often lack some central identifier,

Table 8.3: Some advantages and disadvantages of using administrative data in a 'big data' mode

Characteristic	Advantages of administrative 'big data'	Disadvantages compared with other data sources (eg national statistics or longitudinal surveys)
Scale	Large- to massive-scale collection. Often comprehensive for a whole population	Analysts cannot over-sample those sub-populations of particular interest
Disaggregation by geographical area	Gives a reliably granular picture at the small-area level	None
Frequency of updating	Updating occurs regularly (sometimes continuously) with all new transactions or contacts – usually annually, quarterly or even more often	Updating is on an externally fixed cycle and cannot be adjusted to capture specific events
Vulnerabilities	Achieving consistency in data reporting is a key compliance aspect for the managers and staff of agencies. Accuracy is required and inaccuracy may have seriously adverse consequences	Managers or staff may nonetheless 'massage' numbers where they can, so as to make their units' performance look better. Implicit knowledge combined with some space for discretion in classifications may make this hard to spot
Quality checks	Managers check returns and data, focusing on case-by-case consistency. Internal audit will selectively highlight inconsistencies affecting performance	Data quality is rarely cross-checked or tested using social science or statistical techniques or sophisticated data analytics – although external auditors may make more rigorous checks once in a while
Metadata	May be limited or inconsistently applied across organisations	Later analysts may not have access to the implicit knowledge used in choosing metadata tags
Coverage of the population	Captures people who normally resist being included in conventional surveys	Excludes people living 'off the grid' or not transacting with government agencies
	Government incentives or coercion limit non-responses or incomplete data	Coverage may vary over time if administrative rules change the costs and benefits for transactors
Data generated	Normally covers actual behaviours	Rarely captures intentions or perceptions
		The variables collected make sense for administrative reasons, but are not necessarily defined in useful ways for wider analysis

(continued)

Table 8.3: Some advantages and disadvantages of using administrative data in a 'big data' mode (continued)

Characteristic	Advantages of administrative 'big data'	Disadvantages compared with other data sources (eg national statistics or longitudinal surveys)
Mode of collection	Less obtrusive than a separate survey. Penalties for misrepresentation. And cross-checks of documents may enhance accurate factual data	Some reactive components (eg recall of historic factual data)
Identification	Machine learning may let analysts compensate for missing registry links or identities	Beyond the original collection agency, most data may be available only in anonymised forms, not linked to key registers

Source: Own analysis but draws on Smith, G. et al (2004).

making it useful for some purposes but not others. For instance, police forces can be notified immediately of traffic jams by mobile phone companies when their data show long lines of geographically static phones forming along major highway locations, triggering real-time warnings to other drivers and highway agency ameliorative action. However, anonymised mobile phone numbers do not tell policymakers where the car drivers (perhaps suffering repeated delays) have come from or are going to. Some more extensive data collection is often needed to get full value from administrative data sets.

One useful factor behind researchers' new interest in administrative data from government is that countries like the UK and Australia have made relatively firm commitments to '*open data*'policies – making available information already collected at taxpayers' expense so that it can be accessed and reused by other actors in society, especially businesses, universities and civil society organisations (Cabinet Office, 2013; Margetts, 2013). The UK's site[1] provides an overview of progress in this area and a wider openness agenda. Some work may be especially relevant for social scientists, for example, on the National Information Infrastructure project.[2]

The G7 group of countries have also formally pledged support for such policies, in the belief that the costs of data provision are already outweighed by direct benefits (Houghton, 2011) and that in the longer term, it can help fuel innovation, especially by small and medium-sized enterprises (SMEs). SMEs are often shut out of government sector ICT contracts by huge integrated ICT systems, giant contract sizes, demanding capability requirements and civil servants' precautionary desires to contract only with very large system integrator companies

(Dunleavy et al, 2006). Yet, smaller firms may have innovative and creative capabilities that are only weakly present in large public sector bodies or big system integrator companies.

A good example of the potential here again comes from Transport for London, who struggled over many years to find ways of reliably communicating bus arrival information to passengers waiting at bus stops, long after Transport for London itself was able to track its buses' movements in geographical space (for an overall view of this problem, see Gammera et al, 2014). The official solutions focused on a centralised ICT system that re-sent bus arrival information to electronic signs at bus stops, not altogether successfully. The quite expensive shelters also had to be funded by advertisers installing the electronic link as part of displaying rolling or static adverts, a viable solution only for well-used bus stops besides major roads. However, once Transport for London's real-time bus information was made available for outside programmers to access, it was not long before several competing small businesses developed mobile phone apps that told customers very accurately when buses would arrive at their own local bus stop – an especially useful facility for customers when it is raining or there is bad weather and where their bus stop has no shelter. Similarly, the computerisation of Land Registry data generated a huge potential for value-added services letting consumers know accurate house prices, organised successfully by a central government website in the UK (Land Registry, 2016) and (less well) by the private sector in the highly fragmented USA (Newcombe, 2014).

This example also illustrates a particularly strong and useful form of open data provision that occurs when government, business, academics or non-governmental organisations (NGOs) commit to creating an Application Programming Interface (API). Here some of their 'big data' can be regularly (perhaps even continuously) downloaded in bulk, for free and possibly in real time by other users (as with the bus geo-positioning information mentioned earlier). At other times, the API grants other users access after a short delay, which is key to safeguarding the data collectors' commercial advantages, but may still be much better than official statistics' typically long time lags. Providing APIs is especially valuable because researchers, businesses or NGOs have the assurance that the data stream will flow regularly and without interruption, and so they can reliably base their own operations on its accessibility. Of course, external re-users need a good deal of software and statistical expertise to download data from an API. However, they do not need the time-consuming special permissions needed with much administrative data (eg accessing anonymised versions of people's tax or health records). In addition, APIs are very time-saving for expert users because they 'support code reuse, provide high-level abstractions that facilitate programming tasks, and help unify the programming experience' (Robillard, 2009: 27). Users can also undertake reanalysis without having to let the primary data compiler know what they are doing (whether government or big private companies like Twitter or Facebook), and without having to alert the subjects of the analysis. Overall, the shift to widespread use of open data and APIs 'allow[s] web communities to create an open architecture for sharing content and data between communities and applications. In this way, content that is created in one place can be dynamically posted and updated in multiple locations on the web' (Wikipedia, 2016a).

A third way of accessing 'big data' is feasible even when information is not being routinely made available in electronic form. The technique of *Web-scraping* allows researchers (typically, expert journalists, academic researchers and PhD students) to visit public websites displaying data or statistics in regular slots and a predictable fashion – as, for instance, many local authorities and health sector bodies do in reporting on their performance (Bradshaw, 2014). A simple program is written that visits each of the relevant websites in turn and pulls off or 'scrapes' the same data in each, allowing it to be re-aggregated and analysed. Other aspects of public sector bodies' sites can also be recorded – for example, how government ministries link to different internal and external organisations, as mapped by Escher et al (2006) in a comparison of how foreign ministries in liberal democracies make use of digital communication capabilities.

Sometimes, administrative data can only be accessed in anonymised ways, for privacy reasons or because of commercial restrictiveness (see later). So, it often *lacks connections to key 'registers'* or key files that users within government do have access to. This 'incompleteness' is quite characteristic of administrative 'big data' and means that researchers have to be ingenious in finding new ways around the lack of name tags or unifying registers' ID numbers. When plentiful data can be obtained that nonetheless lacks key registers, either social science theory connections or machine learning may offer a partial solution (see later).

Digital residues

It is a truism of our modern digital civilisation that everything leaves a trace, an electronic footprint or record created as part and parcel of a massive flow of digital information (Siegler, 2010). Governments have not been slow to compel mobile phone companies and Internet service providers to log and track every phone call and website visit or email in different ways, some focusing only on the metadata of linkages, others on their content as well. Despite some companies' resistance (*Huffington Post*, 2015), and efforts in Europe by the European Union (EU) to guarantee a measure of citizen privacy (European Union, 2016), by and large the Snowden affair shows that all these records can then be hoovered up by intelligence and surveillance agencies such as the US's National Security Agency or Britain's Government Communication Headquarters (GCHQ) (*Guardian*, 2016; Snowden Surveillance Archive, 2016). The agencies mainly use the data in hunting for evidence of terrorist activities and personnel or financial flows, or for information on criminal frauds, money laundering or illicit bank transfers. However, with zero public accountability, concerns over the indiscriminate accessing of metadata or message contents remain severe.

Away from such 'dark side' uses and concerns, however, digital residues are now often recoverable by ordinary social science researchers or by appropriately qualified teams working in public policy agencies. A first key source is *accessible text records*, which have multiplied in the digital era. For example, the micro-blogging site Twitter has assumed huge centrality in the news and information systems of many liberal democracies. And the somewhat harder to access patterns of communication on Facebook are a huge repository of information previously mined for better-targeted advertising, but now available for far more multipurpose analysis.

Greatly improved programs for text analysis mean that far more information can now be recaptured from text communications. For instance, stock market firms and financial reporting systems have long been analysing Twitter traffic relevant for financial markets, using techniques of 'sentiment analysis' to try and detect turning points in trading before they become obvious in changing behaviour patterns (Pang and Lee, 2008). The logic here is that if people become economically pessimistic, they are more likely to sell shares and less likely to invest. So, it is valuable for market actors to know that this is becoming an emergent feature of current trends *before* that pessimism converts into mass sell actions on the markets. Central banks have also begun to undertake somewhat similar text analyses, but this time on the lookout for emerging threats to financial stability or evasions of the regulatory net (Bholat et al, 2015). Similarly, intelligence agencies increasingly find that a growth in terrorist 'chatter' on aligned websites has some value in allowing predictions of major operations threatening security (Joachim, 2003). Finally, in the UK's serious urban riots of August 2011, the police force in the city of Manchester were able to monitor would-be rioters' chatter on Facebook and Blackberries (which were encrypted), and broadcast dampening messages of their own about their readiness on the same networks. Thus, they did a lot better at preventative policing than forces that lacked this capacity – like London's Metropolitan Police (*Guardian*, 2012).

Mining masses of text for relevant memes or distinctive ideas and vocabulary is now an essential aspect of many governments' efforts to maintain nodality. To stay in the centre of society's information networks, government officials (and social science researchers assisting policymakers) must increasingly be experts in 'big data'.

Nor are digital residues confined to text. Increasingly, sophisticated systems now allow the massive recording of audio files from phones or other sources, and of images or videos from CCTV systems or other systems – such as the UK's Automatic Number Plate Recognition (ANPR) system that tracks cars across main highways (Police UK, 2016). With storage very cheap (even almost 'free' now), search programs can also scan for objects of interest either in real time – as with US cities' programs that use facial recognition software to try and track the movements of known criminals via CCTV cameras (Gates, 2011: 63–96) – or in relatively swift retrospective (eg in criminal investigations).

Many of these developments mean that government agencies or social science researchers can often collect text or other digital data series that rather resemble administrative data in some aspects. For instance, they may often be anonymised or lacking an authoritative register. However, on the other hand, they contain a great deal of potentially useful text, image or sound information, if only they can be decoded. We are still at the beginning of working out how these capabilities will affect the traditional Weberian model of government bureaucracy. Currently, these agencies show an overwhelming emphasis on reducing all data about behaviours to highly parsimonious classification text (or now dots and dashes on computer discs). This stance reflects an inherited dominant assumption that storage is expensive and analysis will be relatively rarely undertaken. Yet, bureaucratic form-filling loses tremendous amounts of information in the process of forcing people to condense answers into minute scraps of text. Why not instead use a videoed or audio-recorded interview with an agency script prompting for answers, from which key responses can be extracted via analysis programs – leaving the whole digital record intact for possible later reanalysis? Already, the Australian Tax Office (ATO) employs digital voice recognition to grant or deny individuals access to their tax records, and employs voice analysis software in its contact centres to detect when people phoning their staff are under high stress (eg perhaps because they are lying about aspects of their tax affairs). In future, advanced bureaucracies may well record and store digitised video and audio transactions in lossless ways.

Social science methods and the analysis of 'big data'

The advent of 'big data' has created a great deal of uncertainty about the evolution of the social sciences from two major sources: (1) the growth of new methods and approaches, radically different in character from past approaches; and (2) controversy about the continued importance of theory.

New methods and approaches

Many of the characteristics of 'big data' reviewed earlier mean that how they are analysed has to change radically. Very large-N data sets can be processed far more effectively and extensively than conventional small-N (under 5,000 cases) survey data sets. In traditional social science, even longitudinal surveys typically have too few cases to allow the intense dissection and multiple variables and categories that analysts often want to evaluate. Also, in regression or multivariate analyses, it is common to 'run out' of the variance needed to test complex models. In 'big data', by contrast, it is possible to focus analysis precisely, and to understand complex patterns of behaviour and factors affecting multiple, relatively small, subgroups of the population (like the 5% of Tube passengers who found better routes to work as a result of the exogenous shock of a strike).

Traditional social science with small-N data sets also traditionally placed a lot of emphasis upon significance testing as a way of knocking variables out of contention in the model-building and model-testing sequences (Wasserstein and Lazar, 2016). Through convention, analysts looked for variables significant at a 5% probability (p) level in multivariate model building, and regarded variables significant at a 1% p-value as gold-quality components (Radziwill, 2015; Wasserstein and Lazar, 2016). This approach has always been controversial, for five main reasons, neatly summed up and linked to five modern critics by Cook (2008):

1. Andrew Gelman: In reality, null hypotheses are nearly always false. Is drug A identically effective as drug B?

Certainly not. You know before doing an experiment that there must be some difference that would show up given enough data.

2. Jim Berger: A small *p*-value means that the data were unlikely under the null hypothesis. Maybe the data were just as unlikely under the alternative hypothesis. Comparisons of hypotheses should be conditional on the data.

3. Stephen Ziliak and Deirdra McCloskey: Statistical significance is not the same as scientific significance. The most important question for science is the size of an effect, not whether the effect exists.

4. William Gosset: Statistical error is only one component of real error, maybe a small component. When you actually conduct multiple experiments rather than speculate about hypothetical experiments, the variability of your data goes up.

5. John Ioannidis: Small *p*-values do not mean a small probability of being wrong. In one review, 74% of studies with *p*-values of 0.05 were found to be wrong (see also Ioannidis, 2005).

In 'big data' sets, the problems of significance testing simply disappear, however, because dozens of possible associations between variables (maybe even all or most associations) will pass the 1% or 5% standards, simply because the data set *N*s are so large. So, significance testing is no use at all in winnowing or evaluating models – as perhaps it never should have been. How, then, do you distinguish a preferred model when so many variables can no longer be discarded?

In an article on 'new tricks for econometrics', the Google chief economist Hal Varian (2014) outlined a different, competitive approach to model testing. A large data set might be divided randomly into, say, 10 parts and different model streams evaluated in different parts by their ability to predict the behaviours or patterning being researched. So, here, model development is competitive, and model performances are compared across different subsets of the same massive data set. Empirical competition winnows out dud models and promotes high-performing ones, not significance tests or theoretical considerations.

At root here, perhaps, is an approach that values 'control' over 'causation'. The traditional approach (often over-focusing on regressions) tries to develop a causally developed explanation of phenomena that are the focus of research, where the set of 'independent' variables are conceived as (somehow) *producing* the effects analysed, such that a rerun of the same factors in the same situations will reproduce the results being analysed. Yet, real predictions are rarely attempted (Taagepera, 2008), and, anyway, social situations never rerun from the same point (Gleick, 1987). As the Greek sophist Thrasymachus insisted (in a parody of an earlier dictum of Herodotus): 'You can never step in the same river once'. The alternative approach focuses on *control*, being able to manipulate 'explanatory' variables as effectively as feasible, so as to produce desired results and interpretations. Given the complexity of social life, at least some analysts are now sceptical that causality can be uniquely established.

The control perspective suggests that the acid test of 'big data' analyses is not the backwards-looking interpretation of what has already happened – traditional social science's almost exclusive focus. Instead, the digital and 'big data' context of much policy making and administrative implementation opens up scope for a particularly ambitious form of the experimental approach discussed in small-N forms by Peter John in Chapter Four of this book – randomised control trials (RCTs). *Online* RCTs with 'big data' have all the virtues that Peter discusses but a lot fewer barriers and difficulties because the availability of huge data sets allows the evaluation of the very small-scale effects that are all we can realistically expect as a result of experimental stimuli. Online RCTs can also often be undertaken at low cost and in real time by government agencies or businesses.

For example, in the UK, getting 1.9 million people a year to pay court fines promptly is an important aspect of the conduct of court services. Where fines are not paid promptly, far greater expense is caused for the government in chasing unpaid debts using contractors, and far greater costs also result for the offenders involved. Now people's willingness to pay may actually be influenced by quite small factors – such as the design of reminder letters sent to them, the briefness and clarity with which the consequences of non-paying are explained, and the ease or convenience of paying immediately (eg via credit card over the phone or online). An online RCT might come up with one or more treatments (such as one or more new and 'improved' or redesigned forms of reminder letter). These are sent to large, randomly assigned treatment groups, and their performance in improving the prompt payment of fines is then compared with a randomly assigned control group. At the end of such an experiment, we may know that treatment B works better than A or C, and generates a worthwhile saving for government finances compared with the status quo reminder letter sent to the control group. However, we may still be none the wiser (beyond some intelligent guesswork) about exactly why letter format B works so well and other ideas less well.

An ambitious agenda claiming to resolve this problem is associated with 'behavioural public policy' studies and behavioural economics, much of which has actually been developed by psychologists. Their claim is that social science can now exhaustively explain the origins of dozens of different 'anomalies' or 'fallacies' that affect individual citizen or customer behaviours, influencing them to deviate from what abstract rational choice models predict that they should do. In the UK, the Behavioural Insights Team, in partnership with the Cabinet Office, claimed to use online or other 'big data' RCTs as part and parcel of generating comprehensive behavioural insights into why citizens sometime behave suboptimally and how to 'nudge' people unobtrusively into making better choices through structuring how options are put to them (Halpern, 2015). This extended the well-known Sunstein and Thaler (2009) arguments about how to 'nudge' people unobtrusively into making better choices through structuring how options are put to them (originally called 'paternalistic libertarianism'). Some social scientists have enthusiastically endorsed the potential for such techniques allied to experimentation to produce useful additions to our knowledge of 'what works' (see, eg, John et al, 2013).

Yet, the jury is still very much out on whether behavioural public policy is anything more than a developed set of descriptive narratives that can be cited in post hoc justification by analysts discovering that particular control effects work – exactly the way that 'behavioural insights' are used in marketing by private sector firms. Around 60 economic 'fallacies' have now been identified in behavioural economics and psychology, and there is an even larger list of 'cognitive biases' when social and memory biases are considered (Wikipedia, 2016b). So, it is almost certain that several apparently relevant behavioural or other cognitive biases can be cited to 'explain' almost all effects discovered in big data and online RCTs, thus suggesting an ability to 'control' or shape behaviour in some way.

The track record of behavioural insights being applied in government and public policy contexts is also a relatively short one and it is not clear from most studies if 'Hawthorne effects' have been controlled – that is, 'treatment' effects arising from customers just meeting for the first time an innovative, different or experimental approach to policy development. So, the first time we send people due to pay court fines an improved reminder letter, we may get a noticeable gain in the desired behaviour – more people pay promptly and without having to be expensively chased. However, next year, that 'improved' letter is the new normal. So, will what worked last year shows results again on repeat? The most likely scenario of 'behavioural insights' using 'big data' is that researchers or policy analysts within government get stuck on an escalator of introducing new innovations every period to counteract the 'wearing off' of past innovations that become overfamiliar. In other words, the government will have to continuously 'market' public services to service users or regulatory targets, in almost exactly the same way as private firms must continuously use marketing techniques to attract customers' attention. In this scenario, we may get better at controlling or prompting citizens' behaviour, but not necessarily in understanding why. If so, then 'behaviour science' peters out in the same kind and level of insights as private sector marketing, where the premium is on creatively stimulating clients with new or unfamiliar materials, not on building up a cumulative or well-founded body of knowledge.

Different kinds of problems may arise with the application of 'machine-learning' techniques in big data contexts (Armstrong, 2015). This is a form of automated engineering software that copes with the 'incompleteness' of much big data by computers working through automatic algorithms that allow them to 'learn' from the associations of what variables they do have about other variables that they do not have. Over several or many iterations, the software improves how it categorises the information being handled, and works out better how to construct associated variables that can speak to the underlying identity of different groups of people, behaviours or assets covered in the data: 'Large datasets may allow for more flexible relationships than simple linear models. Machine learning techniques such as decision trees, support vector machines, neural nets, deep learning, and so on may allow for more effective ways to model complex relationships' (Varian, 2014: 3).

For example, from a health 'big data' set, we may not have access to people's individual identities. However, by associating symptoms and disease problems together, the robot analysis may 'learn' a great deal about the characteristics of different groups and thus bridge across the non-availability of the identities. (This capability is one reason why releasing even anonymised health data sets is still highly controversial).

Machine learning is 'concerned primarily with prediction', but it is also closely linked with data mining, which primarily focuses on summarising data and extracting interesting findings (Varian, 2014: 5). However, machine learning also has relevance for other areas, such as making estimations and improving hypothesis testing.

The continued importance of theory

In an interesting critique, the US political scientist Nicholas Christakis (2013) pointed out that the structure of disciplines in the contemporary social sciences has endured remarkably unchanged for decades. By contrast, discipline-based and university departmental structures in the science, technology, engineering and mathematics (STEM) subjects have changed radically (sometimes several times, as in biosciences) to reflect new methods and foci of study. Christakis argues that the development of new fields will (or at least should) produce similar changes. Key contemporary developments might be a shift to studying the influence of genetics on social behaviours, the advent of neuro-economics or the development of 'big data' analysis towards software engineering and mathematical analysis (instead of past social science methods and packages adapted to far smaller N, survey data sets).

Elsewhere, in the field of empirical sociology, some observers have speculated on the coming crisis produced by sociologists being locked out of many 'big data' sources by, on the one hand, commercial confidentiality in business examples and, on the other, by government privacy restrictions and administrative non-adaptability (Bélanger and Crossler, 2011). The main casualty of the crisis is again likely to be survey-based work, which, in many respects, can no longer 'compete' with the insights that 'big data'-owners can command:

> To give a simple example of the merits of routine transactional data over survey data, Amazon.com does not need to market its books by predicting, on the basis of inference from sample surveys, the social position of someone who buys any given book and then offering them other books to buy which they know on the basis of inference similar people also tend to buy. They have a much more powerful tool. They know exactly what other books are bought by people making any particular purchase, and hence they can immediately offer such books directly to other consumers when they make the same purchase. (Savage and Burrows, 2007: 891)

Yet, as the data universe changes rapidly, the authors also think that there are important theory and professional 'ideology' barriers to sociologists accessing many 'big data' sources. They see a 'danger [of sociology] taking refuge in the reassurance of our own internal world, our own assumed abilities to be more "sophisticated", and thereby I chose to ignore the huge swathes of "social data" that now proliferate' (Savage and Burrows, 2007: 887).

The wider debate here leads to the ambitious claims of the ICT writer Chris Anderson (2008) that 'big data' ushers in 'the death of theory' because in the digital era, everything in contention between rival schools of thought in social science can, in principle, be explored and tested, using our vastly expanded armoury of information and methods of analysing it:

> This is a world where massive amounts of data and applied mathematics replace every other tool that might be brought to bear. Out with every theory of human behaviour, from linguistics to sociology. Forget taxonomy, ontology, and psychology. Who knows why people do what they do? The point is they do it, and we can track and measure it with unprecedented fidelity. With enough data, the numbers speak for themselves. (Anderson, 2008)

Widely rejected by social scientists as almost half-baked in conception (Williamson, 2014), this simple prediction may nonetheless have a degree of force, certainly in the way that public policymakers approach research issues. A good example is the kind of 'predictive policing' programs developed by some US social scientists for cities like Los Angeles (Perry et al, 2013). They use machine-learning and data-mining techniques to hunt for data associations that will allow them to identify possible crime suspects or traffic accident problems, and then analyse the behaviours of people involved. From there, the analyst can suggest to police patrols very specific locations and times that they should be in particular small 'boxes' of the city where known offenders were previously spotted and might be expected to return; or particular zones and times where the presence of police patrols may help deter drunk or drug driving. The theory behind these models is often pretty slender (eg offenders are creatures of habit and hence tend to revisit the same locales at the same times of day). However, if they seem to work in offering better arrest records, crime prevention/deterrence effects or impacts on cutting accidents, then policy administrators and politicians will still want to deploy them.

The mainstream social science rebuttal of such examples has been to argue that 'big data' analyses, run directly by software engineers or 'big data'-owners, only explore or test 'common sense' kinds of propositions – in many cases, validating the blindingly obvious, and failing to control for the inherent variability of social behaviours.

A now-classic example is the Google algorithm that for a period of some months and years successfully predicted where flu outbreaks would take place in America, using a big data set of people's daily flu-related queries to the search engine (Ginsberg et al, 2009). For a time, this even seemed to work faster and better than the US government's elaborate system for recording and notifying the incidence of diseases, run through the public health regulatory system (by the Center for Disease Control [CDC]). However, the apparent association did not last – the advent of a different strain of flu made the Google-based model perform very poorly, forecasting almost twice the level of flu in 2012 than the CDC system found (Lazer et al, 2014). The official recording system proved resilient, while the 'big data' alternative had key problems. So, the conventional wisdom now is to 'pooh-pooh' the 'death of theory' and to claim that the real future lies with 'big data' analyses informed both by strong theory and improved data analysis (Williamson, 2014). Whether such a view is well founded remains to be seen.

Using 'big data' in policy making

The examples already mentioned give a good sense of how 'big data' has already begun to be used in a wide range of public policy settings, both by social scientists and by professional analysts working for state agencies or consultants. However, these 'classic' cases of impacts are also potentially unrepresentative of the public policy landscape as a whole. To give a broader picture, it is worth briefly considering an admittedly anecdotal summary of central government departments and major agencies in the UK. The most advanced organisation in terms of using 'big data' seems to be GCHQ (the UK's electronic surveillance agency), which is also known to be using machine learning to assist in 'big data' searches. For other intelligence agencies, their scientific or analytic capabilities are less evident. Medical researchers in academia and the National Health Service (NHS), funded by the UK's Medical Research Council, have also accounted for around 90% of the applications to use administrative data, and for the large bulk of publications including a mention of administrative data. The Government Data Service has also used machine learning to predict traffic flows on its major site and to identify anomalous times or event periods (GDS, 2014).

Some large civil government agencies with lots of transactional data are using 'big data' analysis a fair amount to analyse policy problems, and have begun making their data accessible to researchers and also using machine learning a little bit. The UK's tax agency (Her Majesty's Revenue and Customs) and Transport for London are prominent here. However, other departments with massive transactional data have only just begun to think through the issues and their data is still closed to most research – notably, with the Department for Work and Pensions (the UK's social security and labour market ministry), and the Ministry of Justice, which sits at the apex of the legal structures and runs prisons. Some 'big data' are being analysed around crime issues by the Home Office (responsible for police forces). However, many Whitehall departments running substantial policy fields (like education, business and regulation, policing, transport, and the environment) have neither ready access to 'big data' resources of their own (except longitudinal surveys in some cases), nor the highly skilled staff or developed and stable research contacts in universities to have yet mastered 'big data' analytic capabilities. Even highly numerate and analytically oriented departments operating in environments with plentiful 'big data', such as the Bank of England, setting UK interest rates and running financial resilience regulation, have only just begun to explore 'big data' possibilities. They remain very dependent upon the national statistics system for the coverage and timing of their policy information (Bholat, 2014).

For much of government, a key driver behind developing the capacity to do 'big data' analysis lies in the incessant competition between state agencies and private sector businesses (and even civil society NGOs) over shaping public policy and regulatory interventions. If the government is to retain its nodality, a central location in society's information networks, and if ministers and officials are to speak with authority on issues, then state agencies cannot afford to fall behind in their capacities to acquire and analyse timely information. For instance, the competition between regulators and regulatees is incessantly changing as regulated firms and industries constantly innovate in developing new products and services. In a recent study of *The impact of the social sciences*, Bastow et al (2014: 133) quote executives from a major ICT company discussing how research can shape policy development:

> I don't know if we are getting ahead of universities. But we are getting ahead of the government, that's for sure. I was at a Treasury thing yesterday with another colleague, and we were talking about datasets and so on, and this guy from the Treasury was saying 'That's all very well, but we survey 1000 people every week, and I feel pretty confident with

that. How robust is your data?' And we were just like, 'Well
this graph here is based on 207,000 people from yesterday'.
So we are getting ahead there.

The 'arms race' character of government keeping up is also obvious
in fields like police forces trying to keep pace with criminals and
anti-social forces, and by the 'dark side' world of government versus
terrorists, or security systems versus hackers. However, it also applies
far more widely to innovations – for instance, where regulatory
agencies are supposed to be monitoring or controlling the constantly
innovating activities of private sector firms in key sectors of the
economy like financial institutions or stock market trading using
computer algorithms (Government Office for Science, 2012).

Yet, the barriers to the large-scale deployment of 'big data' methods
in government and in policy-related social sciences are also substantial.
Despite the growth of APIs and government pledges to open up data to
outside users, substantial privacy barriers remain in areas like medical
and health research (where patient confidentiality is sacrosanct). In
taxation also, citizen privacy is a key concern in the Anglo-American
democracies; but in Norway, personal tax submissions are public
documents (for these cases and a useful survey of global practice, see
Devos and Zackrisson, 2015). Legal and constitutional protections
for citizens and businesses have generally failed to keep pace with the
capabilities for data surveillance by government intelligence agencies,
which can broadly do what they want in many countries.

Yet, this whole area of citizen privacy still remains littered with
restrictive rules and regulators. Although normally insufficient in the
UK or the US to provide citizens with worthwhile safeguards against
state intrusion into their private lives, these barriers and provisions
are nonetheless often enough to create major difficulties in releasing
even anonymised data in sensitive areas. In addition, many different
government agencies, and large and small businesses, have faced massive
problems either over mass data records going missing or being lost, or
in hackers proving able to access and download sensitive information
on a large scale (*Huffington Post (Australia)*, 2015). These have all added
to the difficulties of moving to 'open data' arrangements and of getting
researchers (or even other government agencies) access to many kinds
of 'big data'.

The other substantial problem for civil government, and for
university social science quite acutely, is that they tend to be at the
back of the talent queue in recruiting personnel with the right kinds
of training and skills to be good at 'big data'. In most advanced

industrial countries, the social sciences have generally not been generating their own specialists in the area. They have mostly had to rely on a trickle of computer scientists, software engineers and analysts coming across from STEM sciences like medicine and ICT. Arguably, the social sciences are now converging strongly with these two and other STEM disciplines (Bastow et al, 2014: ch 1; Dunleavy et al, 2014), so these flows may increase. Yet, business demand for 'big data' experts is soaring, and the most interesting and innovative projects are being undertaken by giant firms like Google, Amazon or Apple. So, ordinary civil government departments (not intelligence and defence agencies) have major difficulties in finding talented staff (or even recruiting well-qualified consultancy firms) to undertake regular 'big data' analysis. The university sector is often in a position to help here, along with some NGOs and small- and medium-sized agencies. However, government departments in big nations (like the UK and the US) are often reluctant to let them into policy making and implementation systems long-term, and do not want to become dependent upon them (as they are with many consultancies supplying staff for complex ICT roles).

For the social sciences, there are also risks inherent in becoming too closely engaged in applied work for policymakers, especially in fields where the emphasis is upon achieving simple predictive control rather than necessarily advancing causal understanding informed by social or economic theory. Some authors hark back to the role that the early social sciences played from the late 19th century through the 1940s in generating a toolkit of statistics and methods of analysis that greatly enhanced the powers of big government. For example, Robertson and Travaglia (2015) recently argued: 'We run the risk in the social sciences of perpetuating the ideological victories of the first data revolution as we progress through the second'.

Conclusions

Like many other technological and ICT-related developments before it, the advent of 'big data' has ambiguous implications (Bloom et al, 2009). On the one hand, the new information-access opportunities can be decentralising by placing into the hands of relatively junior (even grass-roots or street-level) public sector staff the capacity to make far better informed decisions (Von Hippel, 2006), and enhancing the competencies to deliver public services that are better attuned to citizens' needs. On the other hand, 'big data' clearly potentially enhance the communications or network control capacities of central decision-makers, as well as their ability to shape social behaviours and achieve timely (perhaps even real-time) effects. This latter capability may be differentially developed only by large corporations, on the one hand, or in 'dark side' areas of government like security and intelligence, within a climate of weak legal and constitutional protections for civil liberties and personal privacy. Here especially, there is a large potential for citizens' resistance (and guerrilla hacking) to slow 'big data' advances across civil government.

Yet, if the development of 'big data' competences could be broadened via accessible university research, and if the multiple tensions around data security and privacy issues could be better handled in the future, then this somewhat dystopian future is not automatic. There remains a considerable potential for fruitful and balanced advances in social knowledge, linked with innovations in theory-based social science. 'Big data' are also an important area of potential advance in government, especially with strengthened protections (on which, see Crawford and Schultz, 2014). In Anglo-American democracies especially, reform here could set the stage for the growth of more agile, expert and research-based central state policy making, and for the more sensitive, personalised, effective and timely (even preventative) delivery of public services.

Acknowledgement
I am deeply indebted to Dr Michael Jensen of the Institute for Governance and Policy Analysis, University of Canberra, for several detailed conversations about 'big data', from which I learnt a huge amount.

Further reading
To get a good sense of how to engage with 'big data', see Kitchin (2014b), Cukier and Mayer-Schonberger (2013) and Bradshaw (2014).

For some interesting examples of how to use 'big data', see Bates et al (2014) and Larcom et al (2015).

Notes
[1] Available at: https://data.gov.uk/

[2] See: https://data.gov.uk/blog/progress-national-information-infrastructure-project

NINE

Cluster analysis in policy studies

Jinjing Li

Introduction

Social scientists and policymakers alike rely heavily on statistical analyses to seek patterns in data collected from our changing world. Collecting information about the complexities of the world surrounding us and understanding the links between intricate sources of information can be a daunting task. Hence, over the last few years, numerous actors in the policy sphere have turned to statistics tools to inform their decision-making and provide their decision processes with credibility. Besides regressions, factorial analyses and other multivariate statistical techniques that are widely adopted in the field of political science and policy studies (Pennings et al, 2006), less known statistical tools can provide different and complementary insights. This chapter focuses on cluster analysis, one of the less adopted, yet powerful, statistical techniques that can be applied in policy making processes and the social sciences generally. The utility of this method will be discussed by various examples in the context of policy research.

Compared with typical regression techniques, cluster analysis deals with sorting data and seeing patterns that are data-based and can be less assumption-driven. It is an explorative technique in nature; thus, you can go on a more open search to your questions compared with regression analyses, where the data generation process must be assumed beforehand. Cluster analysis is a bottom-up, grounded analytic form of theory building in that it seeks connections between data through the power of careful statistical analysis rather than through preformed theories. Compared to standard regression analysis, it is an inductive rather than deductive hypothesis-testing approach. The value and primary purpose of the inductive approach is to allow research findings and potentially policy insights to emerge from the frequent, dominant or significant themes inherent in raw data, without the restraints imposed by structured theories or methodologies. With other approaches, there is a danger that key themes are often obscured, reframed or left invisible because of the practices or assumptions of the analyst and the demands of experimental and hypothesis-testing research. So, cluster analysis provides an inductive starting point but from a quantitative and replicable base. It brings into play qualities only normally associated with more bottom-up qualitative analysis. In an era where accessing and using big data may become more important to policy making (as discussed in Chapter Eight), it may be that the searching capacity provided by cluster analysis will become more important. Cluster analysis is a useful tool for policymakers eager to approach a topic with an open mind and a data set.

So, what is cluster analysis? Cluster analysis is a collective term covering 'a collection of applied statistics techniques for discovering "natural groups" in data' (Anderberg, 1973: 10-24). It aims at sorting different objects (or observations) into groups based on their degree of association with each other. The technique is particularly useful in forming typologies – a common task in research (Ahlquist and Breunig, 2012). It has had many applications in academic studies, ranging from DNA analyses (FitzGerald et al, 2004) and fraud detection (Sabau, 2012), to identifying welfare regimes (Saint-Arnaud and Bernard, 2003), political system change (Schrodt and Gerner, 2000) and voting behaviours (Jakulin et al, 2009). Compared with the qualitative approach in grouping identification, statistical-based cluster analysis can produce replicable work and offers a potentially less subjective grouping. So, the challenge taken up in this chapter is to argue that a method with a strong academic pedigree could also be of great use to policy making. This chapter provides an introduction to cluster analysis, covering its basic concept, and discusses the key assumptions and choices available in a cluster analysis. This framing of cluster analysis is followed by the real-world uses of the technique, with a particular focus on the field of policy-related studies. The concluding discussion looks at the scope and limitations of the method.

Concepts in cluster analysis

As an empirical approach to developing taxonomies, cluster analysis aims to identify categories in which policy-relevant occurrences can be placed (Miller, 1998). Clusters are defined by investigators and data analysts as a function of meaningful classifications in which for a given element in a set of findings, there is 'small within-cluster variation relative to the between-cluster variation' (Dillon and Goldstein, 1984: 158). Usually, clusters are formed by data points that can be grouped since these are very close to another in the first place. As cluster analysis generally aims to create manageable categories for analysis and evidence for decision-making, within-cluster and between-cluster variation analysis is determined by measures of similarity or dissimilarity (Miller, 1998). Due to its properties and differences of degree, cluster analysis is an extremely versatile method that can be applied to a range of policy contexts, especially those in which extensive or standard data are not easy to come by.

The result of a cluster analysis is sometimes visualised, as in Figure 9.1. Broadly, what this hypothetical example shows is two clusters. The data points in Cluster 1 are closer to one another than the data points in Cluster 2, which are, in turn, closer to one another than the data points in Cluster 1. In effect, cluster analysis helps you to group data and to begin to make sense of it. So, imagine that the data refer to a group of citizens, where one group (Cluster 1) are getting lower costs and higher benefits from a policy and another group is getting lower benefits and higher costs from a policy. Cluster analysis lets you see those groupings and then go on to analyse their characteristics.

Cluster analysis is different from standard regression models in that due to the method's inductive nature, it is not necessary to define

Figure 9.1: An example of data points with two clusters

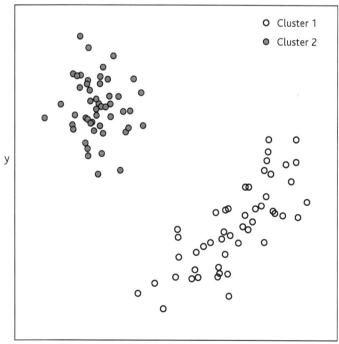

a dependent variable prior to analysis. This feature is why it can be referred to as an unsupervised classification as we do not know the grouping of the data prior to the cluster analysis. It generally has lower requirements as to the number of observations compared with traditional statistical approaches. Hence, it can be extremely useful for analyses in which observation numbers are restricted due to small population sizes (such as countries) or a limited number of available cases (eg political system change). However, it needs to be noted that a small number of observations would result in less robust clustering. Cluster analysis can be used with all common data available to policymakers and social scientists as the technique is flexible enough that it can be used for both traditional quantitative data (such as numeric values in a survey on household incomes or crime rates) and qualitative data (such as texts, interview data or verbatim comments in studies on political attitudes or voting preferences collected at polling stations). The clustering of the text is usually more technical and requires more complex computational methods but the fundamental principles remain.

Several types of clusterings and clusters can be found in the realm of cluster analysis. Clusterings can be either *hierarchical* (sets of nested clusters with sub-clusters) or *partitional* (non-overlapping cluster subsets). These two different types will be discussed in more detail further along in this chapter. At the same time, clusters can also be exclusive (ie one observation is assigned to one cluster only), *overlapping* (ie one observation can belong to two different groups at the same time) or *fuzzy* (ie every observation is part of every determined cluster along a spectrum of between 0 and 1). In a *complete* clustering procedure, every observation is assigned to a cluster, while *partial* clustering may not include all observations, such as outliers, and force them artificially into a specific category (Tan et al, 2006). The most common form of clustering in the field of policy studies is complete clustering, which is also the focus of this chapter.

Cluster analysis procedures

Generally speaking, cluster analysis involves the following steps. First, prepare the data. This is the step when the researchers select the data and define the variables that should be included in the analysis. Second, define a measurement of the similarity or distance between two observations. Third, a cluster algorithm needs to be decided upon and the clusters should be formed. Last but not least, the clusters formed by executing the previous steps need to be validated. Let us look at each step in turn.

Selecting the data

The selection and preparation of the data would vary based on the research question. For instance, we may use a collection of Likert-scale questions to describe the political tendency of an individual if we want to study whether there is any cluster of political views. The selection and the coding of the variables are generally guided by the theoretical and practical concern, which is outside the scope of cluster analysis. For the purpose of this chapter, we mostly focus on the key choices of a cluster analysis once the data has been defined.

Measures of distance

Defining the 'similarity' or 'distance' measure is a crucial part in establishing meaningful taxonomies in cluster analysis. In general, the measure maps the distance or similarity between two observations into a single numeric value. 'Similarity' and 'distance' measures are often complimentary to each other. In many cases, the multiplicative inverse of the distance, or one minus the standardised distance, is used as similarity. The choice of the distance measure should match the nature of the data and the data types (binary, continuous, ordinal, etc) and its meaning. The choice of distance measure can sometimes be subjective, but the measure should reflect the degree of closeness of the observations in a sensible manner. Below are a few examples of the most popular distance measures.

Manhattan, Euclidean and Minkowski distance

The choice of the distance measure can be as simple as plain differencing, for example, the distance between a data point with a value 5 and a data point with a value 2 can be assigned as 3. When there is more than one value attached to a single data point, one has to weight the importance of each dimension and convert the values into a single number that can represent the distance of the two data points. A simple way to do this is to sum the absolute differences in all dimensions. The measure calculated using this absolute differencing approach is also referred to as Manhattan distance. If you sum the square value of the differences, however, it becomes the commonly used Euclidean distance. Minkowski distance is the generalised version of these common distance measures (Han et al, 2011). Mathematically, if there are two observations, x and y, and both have n attributes $(x_1 \ldots x_n)$, $(y_1 \ldots y_n)$, the Minkowski distance between the two points can be defined as:

$$d = \left(\sum_{i=1}^{n} |x_i - y_i|^q \right)^{1/q}$$

where q is the parameter for the distance function. The measure d is the Manhattan distance when $q = 1$ and Euclidean distance when $q = 2$. Euclidean distance is mostly used for continuous variables, while Manhattan distance can also be applied to binary variables.

Correlation distance

Another method to measure the distance between two multivariate data points is to use a Pearson correlation coefficient. The coefficient indicates how two sets are related and the degree of the correlation. A Pearson correlation coefficient has a maximum value of 1.0, where two data points are moving in the same direction perfectly, and a minimum value of −1.0, where two sets are moving completely towards the opposite direction. As the distance measure in a cluster analysis has to be positive in most cases, some minor adjustment is required. There are a few variations of the adjustment procedure (Glynn, 2005). For instance, one may use the absolute value of the correlation coefficient as the basis of the distance. In this case, the distance measure can be expressed as:

$$d = 1 - \left| \frac{cov(x, y)}{\sigma_x \sigma_y} \right|$$

where $cov(x,y)$ is the covariance between x and y, and σ_x denotes the standard deviation of x. Alternatively, one may adjust the distance of the negative correlations to ensure a positive distance value, as in the following case:

$$d = 1 - \frac{cov(x, y)}{\sigma_x \sigma_y}$$

Cosine distance

Cosine distance is another popular distance measure when dealing with high-dimensional binary data (Huang, 2008). The measure is particularly popular among text clusters as texts are often coded as a series of binary values, where the existence of a word is coded as 1, and 0 otherwise. The high dimensionality and unequal length between data points make it hard to use traditional measures such as Euclidean distance. Cosine distance becomes a suitable candidate as it can measure two documents with unequal length. Cosine distance measures the angular differences between the directions that the observation represents instead of the raw geometric distance. Mathematically, Cosine distance between two observation points x and y can be described as:

$$d = 1 - \frac{\sum x_i y_i}{\sqrt{\sum x_i^2 \sum y_i^2}}$$

If there is no negative value coded in the variable, the value of the cosine distance always ranges from 0 to 1, where 0 means that two observations are identical, and 1 indicates that two observations are very different.

Clustering methods

With the distance function defined, one needs to decide on the algorithms that generate the clustering. There are different cluster algorithms but the most common ones are the hierarchical clustering algorithm and the partition-based algorithm. Other algorithms, such as the density-based algorithm, grid-based clustering and model-based clustering, are also used, but to a lesser extent in the field of social science. This section captures these different methods in a simple way.

Hierarchical clustering

Hierarchical clustering algorithms, as the name suggests, create a hierarchical order of the clusters defined by the analyst, whereby one cluster can be broken down into smaller clusters. As one of the most popular techniques within cluster analysis, hierarchical clustering requires distances to be calculated between all potential pairs of observations. This requirement can place a computationally heavy burden when clustering a very large number of observations. In addition to the distance function between observations, hierarchical clustering algorithms require some inputs of the intra-cluster measure to reflect the distance between two clusters. The common methods include:

- *Single link* method, where the distance between two clusters is defined as the shortest distance between observations in two different clusters.

- *Average link* method, where the distance between two centroids is the average distance of all possible pairs of observations, with one observation in the pair taken from the first cluster and the other one from the second cluster.
- *Complete link* method, where the furthest distance between observations in two different clusters is used as the distance between two clusters.
- *Ward* method, which is different than the earlier ones as it is based on the variance approach to minimise the total within-cluster variance. At each step the two clusters with the minimum cluster distance are merged. It implies Euclidean distance between observations.

Hierarchical clustering techniques can either start with one cluster that is refined until most observations are turned into their own cluster (ie divisive method), or start with one cluster per observation and agglomerate until only one cluster remains (ie agglomerative method). The name of hierarchical techniques is derived from the fact that results are linked to previous stages of analysis, creating results that can be represented in a tree-shape. One advantage of hierarchical clustering algorithms is that one does not need to decide the number of clusters before running the clustering. The algorithm returns all possible numbers of clusters in one go. The hierarchical scheme is commonly represented via dendrograms, as shown in Figure 9.2, which shows the branching of the clusters.

Partition-based algorithms

Partition-base clustering is another type of clustering method, where the data is split into different groups (partitions) without forming any hierarchical order. The algorithm evaluates various partitions by some criterion, for example, minimising the sum of squared errors. Contrary to the hierarchical clustering algorithm, the number of clusters is usually chosen before the clustering computation.

K-means is one of the most popular algorithms in this category. The standard K-means algorithm works by randomly initialise select k observations as the centre of a cluster (centroid), and assign rest of the observations to the nearest cluster based on the distance to the centroids. The centroid is recomputed once the assignment finishes and, in turn, all observations are reassigned to the nearest cluster. The whole process reiterates until the grouping of the data no longer changes. The method has the advantage of being relatively efficient, but it can be sensitive to outliers and ends with a local optimum

Figure 9.2: An example of a dendrogram created in a hierarchical cluster analysis

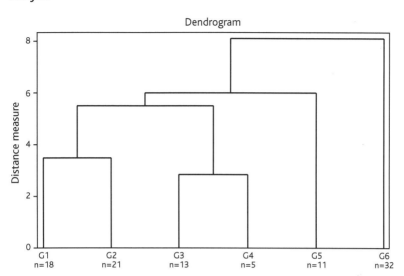

solution. It may be necessary to cluster the data multiple times with different initialisations in order to search for the global optimum.

Other clustering algorithms

There are also other types of clustering algorithms used, these include the density-based approach, grid-based approach, model-based approach, pattern-based approach and so on. Most of the clustering algorithms take as input some parameters, such as the number of clusters, the density of clusters or some form of initialisation parameters. Model-based clustering algorithms can be very powerful and computationally heavy, but they are also popular in applied econometrics, topic modelling and so on. Depending on the exact research question, one may find a density-based approach or model-based approach more appropriate for the research.

Assessing cluster quality

While assessing the quality of the cluster analysis is not part of the 'clustering' procedure *per se*, it is one of the most important steps of cluster analysis as validation serves the purpose of verifying whether the number of clusters derived from the data corresponds to a meaningful grouping. While the determination of the final number of clusters is the crucial final result on which policy advice will be based, this can also be a difficult task. Most cluster algorithms require the user to specify the number of clusters, which is an inherently subjective task. This step is sometimes required before any cluster can be formed, as in the case of non-hierarchical clustering such as K-means. Deciding on the number of clusters suitable for the data and evaluating the quality of the clustering is therefore an important part of the cluster analysis.

One method of assessing the quality of the clusters involves applying a theoretical solution, which consists of determining a given number if there are some theoretical reasons why a certain number of clusters should emerge. Alternatively, the number of clusters can be derived empirically by exploring the 'optimal' number of clusters. It is common to evaluate the quality of the clustering result by some sort of validity indices (Rendón et al, 2011). A number of statistical tools can be used to test the significance of the groupings and to evaluate whether the current classifications are 'optimal'. Of course, in the space of social science and public policy, it is important that the generated clusters can be interpreted and are meaningfully different from each other.

There are three approaches that can be used to evaluate and determine cluster validity (Halkidi et al, 2001). The first evaluation criterion consists of benchmarking the results of a cluster analysis to results derived from other studies in similar fields of investigation. While a previous review of the literature usually guides analysts in determining the problem to be solved and the relevant variables, post-analysis benchmarking can be useful for validating results. External benchmarking usually checks the resemblance of the clusters to the known groupings. A number of indices are used for this purpose, including the Czekanowski–Dice index (Dice, 1945; Sørensen, 1948), Rand index (Rand, 1971), F-measure (Han et al, 2011) and so on.

The second validity criterion consists of validation by comparing the resulting clusters to other cluster outcomes derived from the same algorithm but not necessarily from within the same policy field, research area or sample size (ie parameters). This type of method usually checks for the stability of the cluster formation.

The third evaluation criterion benchmarks the results obtained from the cluster analysis against information derived during the analysis but does not refer to external sources for validity. This approach is common among explorative studies as no external benchmarking is available. Generally speaking, such a validation technique follows the idea that the optimal grouping means high heterogeneities between clusters and high homogeneities within clusters. A number of statistical indices were developed for this purpose. Desgraupes (2013) and Charrad et al (2014) list some commonly used indices:

- *Dunn index*: an index that is based on distance between clusters and cluster diameter measurement (Dunn, 1974).
- *Davies–Bouldin index*: an index that analyses the dispersion of a cluster and dissimilarity between clusters (Davies and Bouldin, 1979).
- *Silhouette-statistic*: evaluating average dissimilarities between observations to determine the most appropriate data structure and to propose potential cluster structures, but it is only valid for first-choice estimations (Rousseeuw, 1987).
- *D-index*: a graphical derivatives-based approach (Charrad et al, 2014).
- *SD index*: which estimates cluster scattering and separation between clusters (Halkidi et al, 2000).
- *Maulik–Bandyopadhyay index*: developed by Maulik and Bandyopadhyay (2002), allowing for refinement of parameters in the method developed by Dunn (1974).
- *Score function (SF)*: a validation method for assessing single cluster solution validity (Saitta et al, 2007).

While there are many tools that have been developed in the literature to assess the quality of the clustering, it should be noted that different methods of validation can lead to different results. The research team has the task of bridging the empirical result with theoretical or policy expectations. In short, cluster analysis, like other forms of statistical analysis, cannot avoid the need to make some assumptions based on wider reasoning and experience, but it does still deliver a more bottom-up approach that, to a large extent, enables the data to speak to researchers and policymakers.

Uses of cluster analysis in the policy context

The use of cluster analysis in different policy areas will be illustrated in the following section, based on different units of analysis: individuals, organisations and geographic units (ie regions and countries). The aim here is to show the range of issues that cluster analysis might be useful at addressing.

It would be common in a policy debate to want to know more about the attitudes or behaviour of the citizens affected by a policy. An example of how cluster analysis can provide this kind of insight is offered in the following, based on the work of the author with colleagues at the University of Canberra (Stoker et al, 2014). In 2014, we undertook a survey to explore how Australian citizens judge their polity. The survey itself was designed to provide a representative sample across a range of age cohorts that were labelled Builders, Boomers, Gen X and Gen Y. The data were gathered in a survey of 826 individuals across various demographic profiles. A number of items in the questionnaire were designed to extract the political views of the participants. These are presented to participants as a series of true or false questions. The study respondents fell into five to six groups depending on the question that was the focus of attention. The clustering was achieved by applying a hierarchical clustering method. Stoker et al (2014) validated their classification by both computing the D-index, which suggested that further increasing the number of clusters will no longer improve the homogeneities within clusters, and by examining the interpretability of the clusters and the statistical differences on a wide range of views and other variables. The statistical tests suggested highly significant differences between clusters. The study further explored the link between birth cohorts and the political view clusters and suggested a gradual shifting of political preferences across generations.

Broadly, while with such a substantial sample size, other types of statistical analysis could have (and have been) carried out, this type of study allows policymakers and analysts, for example, to develop targeted 'cluster-appropriate' communication strategies. Cluster analysis was attractive because we faced a challenge about how to make sense of public opinion on issues of democratic practice and performance that, for most, lack everyday salience. Other forms of statistical analysis might have assumed too much about how members constructed their understandings in relatively unfamiliar territory for them. Our solution was to use the tool of cluster analysis, which we argued enabled us to garner insights into complex arrays of opinions and expectations about democracy among citizens. There are many other policy settings where institutional or policy unfamiliarity would be characteristic of public opinion – reasonably so since the public has everyday concerns to occupy their thinking – so an attraction of cluster analysis in these settings is that it helps build a bottom-up picture of how citizens put the pieces together. It that sense, it aids policymakers by giving them a more unvarnished and less predetermined picture of public opinion.

Another study based on individual data was conducted by Filsinger et al (1979). In this early example of cluster analysis, the research was designed to create a classification of religious individuals. The data were gathered using the Religiosity Scale (De Jong et al, 1976), which was administered in a questionnaire format to 547 undergraduate students at Pennsylvania State University. A total of 37 items were chosen from the Religiosity Scale, a measurement device based upon a previous factor analysis of these data (De Jong et al, 1976). A sample of 220 was selected for the study. The authors chose the seven-cluster solution for interpretation, and named seven types of religious individuals: outsiders, conservatives, rejectors, moderately religious, marginally religious, orthodox and culturally religious. Filsinger et al (1979) validated the clusters via a discriminant analysis and by comparing the statistical differences of the mean values between different clusters on key variables. The authors suggested that the empirical typology of religious individuals is well supported. From a policy point of view, the determination of clusters of attitudes can be important when considering policy reforms.

On the organisational level, a study conducted by Semetko and Valkenburg (2000) investigated the representation of European politics by performing a hierarchical cluster analysis of news items issued by media organisations. Identifying types of news organisations and media items (ie ideas and discourses) is necessary for policymakers to understand how their policies are received and interpreted. Broadly, being able to classify the responses of various organisations using cluster analysis could be a useful tool for policymakers in, for example, responding to large-scale public inquiries or parliamentary or representative assembly investigations.

As for country studies that apply evidence-based and policy-relevant cluster analysis to the policy sphere, one example is the welfare regime clustering by Saint-Arnaud and Bernard (2003). The study used a number of the policy indicators that measure the specificity of social situations to cluster a few advanced economies. The authors used hierarchical cluster techniques and generated seven groupings based on interpretability and close resemblance to known cluster groupings in the literature. This research demonstrates the use of empirical data to systemically group social policy patterns without imposing strong subjective judgements. Another study focusing on countries as the unit of analysis was conducted by Wolfson et al (2004). In their article, the authors identified clusters as a function of aggregate measures of political, economic and conflict-related attitudes. An innovative aspect of their analysis involved the use of cross-sectional data for a number of countries participating in the 'Data Set on National Attributes' over five collection periods to create clusters within and across years. A similar approach was adopted by Brzinsky-Fay (2007), who focused on the transitions between education and working status of high school graduates in 10 European countries. The authors used an optimal matching algorithm for this purpose and obtained eight distinct sequence types that corresponded to the theoretical typology developed by Sackmann and Wingens (2003). The results offered insights into the variations of the school-to-work transitions in Europe, linking the findings of clustering with education policies and training systems.

Where policymakers are engaged in the process of policy transfer or policy learning from other countries (Dolowitz and Marsh, 2000), it is possible to see how the capacity that cluster analyses gives to cluster the experiences of different countries might support a process of more sophisticated learning. There is a tendency for policymakers to make strong assumptions about which countries are most likely to be the best for their country to learn from but a cluster analysis, with its approach of looking at data rather than assumptions, might lead to a rather more open-minded search.

Strengths and limitations of cluster analysis

Cluster analysis as a method of data analysis has strengths and limitations, just as with all statistical techniques. Before opting to use cluster analysis for policy development and implementation, analysts and decision-makers need to ensure that cluster analysis is the appropriate method for their information needs.

The advantages of applying cluster analysis to policy-relevant topics have been extensively explored in this chapter. The method, as discussed, can contribute to creating typologies and taxonomies in areas of scant previous knowledge, cope with a small number of observations, and be adapted to suit a large number of policy-relevant situations and research contexts. Hence, one of the major advantages of using cluster analysis can be tracked to its versatility, and its capacity to be combined with other methods of investigation. While cluster analysis certainly can be applied as a standalone analytic tool, the approach is also a useful base for subsequent and more in-depth data exploration.

Cluster analysis has been successfully combined with qualitative comparative analysis (QCA), a well-known and established method for comparing policy differences and similarities at a national level (see Chapter Five in this book). In Haynes's (2014) study, the author proposed using clusters as a basis for determining more robust theoretical groupings and variable relationships by means of QCA in the context of Eurozone countries' macroeconomic policies. The method is also readily accessible for applied researchers as modern statistical packages often have easy-to-access data-clustering tools.

Statistical Package for the Social Sciences (SPSS), Stata, Statistical Analysis Software (SAS) and R all have modules that allow users to run popular forms of cluster analyses.

Despite the significant work carried out to ground cluster methods in statistical and mathematical research, it seems that this approach is still less developed than factor analysis in the field of social science. Cluster analysis is predominately used to form typologies of complex multivariate data in research and can be used to detect novel aspects of the data, while factor analysis looks at extracting the 'core' factors, with imposed statistical assumptions. While the goals of the two methods differ, they do relate mathematically. Principal components are actually the continuous solution of the cluster membership indicators in the K-means clustering method with a restricted distance measure (Ding and He, 2004), although the result interpretations can be a bit difficult.

Even though clusters can improve understanding of data information by reducing the information to manageable categories, the results need to be interpreted carefully due to implicit assumptions. Additionally, some cluster algorithms are developed in a heuristic manner that was not extensively validated in the literature. This aspect is particularly important in the realm of policy- and decision-making as the use of overly simplistic information can lead to unintended results for researchers and policy.

Additionally, while cluster analysis can be straightforward to use in many modern-day statistical packages, researchers should be aware of the implicit assumptions that the analysis brings, such as distance, the property of each cluster and so on. Different algorithms, in many cases, will form different solutions. While this is not a unique problem to cluster analysis, selecting the algorithms and measures that are appropriate to the research question is of utmost importance. From a technical point of view, cluster analysis aims to find patterns in the data, while the analytical methods used artificially place observations in groups. As these cluster groups are usually not apparent in alternate modes of data exploration such as scatter plots, the results may not seem transparent. Therefore, results must be carefully inspected post-analysis to verify whether cluster groups are plausible and were not imposed by the method. The interpretation of results will always have to be carried out by the person(s) carrying out the analysis.

Conclusion

Cluster analysis is a powerful, yet not overly complex, inductive statistical method that can form meaningful categories and patterns in data observations without imposing the need for time- and cost-intensive data collection. As many forms of information can form the basis for cluster analysis, the method is versatile and can be used to test hypotheses in an efficient manner. The method is widely used in many academic fields and policy areas and can help to reveal patterns of multivariate data that may not be immediately apparent due to unexpected properties and complexities of the information available. This method can be particularly useful in the field of policy studies, where complex, exploratory questions are the norm. Policy contexts where cluster analysis may be relevant include: where public opinion is important to a policy decision but where that opinion may be only partially formed or set; where a public inquiry attracts a multitude of organisational responses that need to be sorted; or where a policy transfer demands a better understanding of how the approaches of different countries to the policy question can be categorised.

Cluster analysis offers a useful tool alongside formal statistical methods for initial, further and in-depth data exploration to start policy debates and to provide valuable leads for further analysis. The method, as illustrated in this chapter, can also be very useful in validating existing theoretical typologies, as in the case of political attitudes or voting preferences, where voter categories can be established. As with most statistical methods, cluster analysis imposes its own methodological assumptions, as explained in this chapter, where the results can be misinterpreted should these assumptions be violated or the method's aim be misunderstood. As all good policymakers and analysts will know, the choices made prior to data exploration will affect the final cluster groups emerging from the data. Therefore, it is important for policy analysts, decision-makers and applied researchers to understand the method's assumptions, both explicit and implicit, to validate the result against other methodological approaches and to critically assess its utility for a given context.

Further reading
Interested and inclined readers can further their understanding and explore different variants of cluster analysis by consulting relevant literature. For instance, a comprehensive textbook-style overview of cluster analysis can be found in Everitt et al (2011). Current and up-to date developments of the technique, including its applications in the fields of social and political science, are best tracked through journal publications.

As for the practical implementations, cluster analysis can be performed in many statistical software packages, including R (different packages/package depending on the cluster method, eg, the hclust function for hierarchal clustering), SAS (CLUSTER Procedure), SPSS (through the analysis menu) and Stata (cluster and clustermat commands). There are even add-ons allowing basic cluster analysis in Microsoft Excel, although these add-ons are generally less powerful and less flexible compared with the cluster analysis modules provided by the dedicated statistical software. Specific instructions can be found online or in the manuals accompanied with the software.

— who is this for? these do's stats but not cluster analysis - is that a large group?

— that said, nice clear overview

TEN

Microsimulation modelling and the use of evidence

Robert Tanton and Ben Phillips

Background

Microsimulation is a form of modelling that operates at an individual unit level, and then aggregates up to get results for higher levels, either geographic or demographic (eg results for couple families). By aggregating the individual-level data taken from surveys or administrative records, microsimulation modelling can identify the results of a tax policy change on incomes by family type, and which income groups are most affected by a policy change. For policy analysis, this provides a very powerful tool that cannot be replicated with any other type of model.

The method was first developed by Guy Orcutt (1957). This forward-looking article predicted models that incorporated individual behaviour, using inputs and outputs based on operating characteristics (equations, graphs or tables that determine outputs or the probabilities of possible outputs from the unit). The model was further developed by Orcutt (Orcutt et al, 1961) and others (Hoschka, 1986; Morrison, 1990; Harding and Polette, 1995).

Microsimulation models now have a firm place in the social sciences, being used for policy modelling (Bourguignon and Spadaro, 2006; Percival et al, 2007), population projections (Van Imhoff and Post, 1998; Booth, 2006), demographic modelling (Booth, 2006), small-area modelling (Ballas et al, 2005; Tanton et al, 2011) and data imputation, for example, when income estimates are not available (Figari et al, 2011).

Many countries now use microsimulation models for analysing tax/transfer policies and this is one of the main applications of microsimulation models. Euromod in Europe (Imervoll et al, 1999) and STINMOD in Australia (Percival et al, 2007) are examples of tax/transfer microsimulation models.

The primary advantage of microsimulation models over other models used in the economic and social sciences like Computable

General Equilibrium (CGE) or cluster analysis (see Chapter Nine) is that because they operate at the individual level, they can be used to investigate distributional results, so distributions of income can be calculated, rather than just a summary measure like a mean. This was used to powerful effect by Tanton (2011), who was able to use a spatial microsimulation model to compare the frequency distribution of incomes in two suburbs in Sydney, Australia, to identify the reason for differences in poverty rates. This analysis pointed to a high proportion of older people on pensions in one suburb compared to another, leading to a higher poverty rate.

So, while microsimulation models can provide aggregate results, the previous example shows that they also allow the user to drill down into the distribution of the results, providing more information to help explain a particular aggregate result. One caution here is that as the user drills into more detail, the number of records that the results are being based on can rapidly reduce, meaning that the results can become meaningless.

Microsimulation models can also be as simple or as complex as required, and can easily be expanded. In the social sciences, this is essential due to the complexity of people and societies. Simpler models in the social sciences, like aggregate regression models, have to make assumptions, or cannot take into account behaviour, in the way that microsimulation models can. Other models in the social sciences, like agent-based models, are useful for studying human behaviour, but they tend to be experimental, rather than empirical (although some recent work on empirical agent-based models is now available; see, eg, Boero and Squazzoni, 2005).

As an example of this complexity of models, the model of the tax/transfer system in Australia (STINMOD), has had expenditure, childcare and carbon pricing added over the years. Behavioural change can also be implemented, as outlined by Orcutt (1957). Caution needs to be expressed here, however, as increasing complexity may mean increasing error.

While microsimulation models have great advantages over other models in the social sciences, they can be even more powerful when they are combined with an aggregate model, for example, being able to get distributional outcomes from a CGE model (see Vidyattama et al, 2014), and using regression models to impute new variables into a microsimulation model (see Schofield et al, 2014).

Basics of the method

To describe the method, we have used a case study of an Australian tax/transfer microsimulation model called STINMOD, a static microsimulation model of income taxes and cash transfers created and maintained by the National Centre for Social and Economic Modelling (NATSEM) at the Institute for Governance and Policy Analysis at the University of Canberra. STINMOD can be used to analyse the distributional impact of current tax and transfer policy or to estimate both the fiscal and distributional impacts of policy reform.

There is a range of microsimulation models apart from the static tax/transfer model described in this chapter, and a description can be found in O'Donoghue (2014). Different types of microsimulation models include behavioural models, dynamic models, spatial models, labour supply models, transportation models, health models, environmental models, and firm and farm models.

Tax/transfer microsimulation models, by predicting the winners and losers of policy and by how much, along with a range of other outcomes, are often highly contentious and controversial. The modelling outcomes can and do play an important role in shaping public policy and perceptions, as well as the outcomes of policy. There is an important role for a model such as STINMOD in providing government, academics, the media and the public with an evidence base for important policy making and policy shaping.

A static tax/transfer model like STINMOD applies a number of rules to a unit record file from a survey. For STINMOD, this unit record file comes from the Australian Bureau of Statistics (ABS). The rules are applied to the individual-level data on the unit record file, financial values are inflated and demographic populations are benchmarked to published demographic totals from the ABS. This forms the base file, from which changes can be made.

When a tax or transfer change is made, the incomes are recalculated based on the new transfer rules, and the tax paid is recalculated based on the new tax rates and cut-offs. New incomes and taxes are therefore calculated for everyone on the survey, and these are aggregated to get a national total. The change in income and tax compared to the base file can then be calculated, and as long as family type, or tenure type, is on the base file, estimates can be derived for these groups of the population. This process is shown in Figure 10.1. More details of each of these steps can be found in the section on how to use the method.

The static microsimulation model only estimates the 'day after' effect of a policy, or what the state of the world is straight after the policy

Figure 10.1: Example of a static tax/transfer microsimulation model

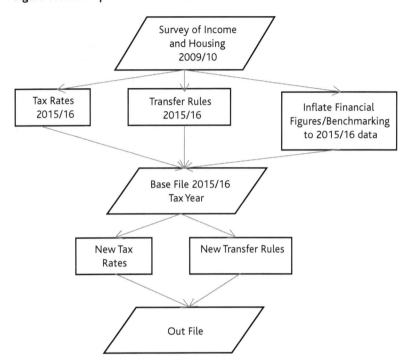

is implemented. With an income change, we may expect people to change behaviour (eg increase hours if income is lower due to higher taxes). This is not modelled in a static tax/transfer model.

While STINMOD is a static model, tax/transfer microsimulation models can also be behavioural, dynamic or spatial. A behavioural tax/transfer microsimulation model extends the richness of modelling to incorporate responses to policy, such as increased hours worked by the secondary earner in an income unit. These models have an obvious advantage over a simple static model such as STINMOD as they incorporate what is the object of much policy change (behavioural change). The drawback is that the behavioural component is often subject to a large degree of uncertainty and may 'muddy the waters'. It is worthwhile having a sense of the magnitude of such impacts, or 'elasticities'. For example, a change in childcare benefits may have a significant impact on female participation, whereas a change in aged pension payments may have little behavioural impact (at least in the short run).

It is possible within STINMOD to incorporate a behavioural component, and such changes could be derived either through a typical behavioural-style model (such as an econometrically estimated labour supply function) or through scenario-type modelling. The results from these models would then affect the people, families and households in the microsimulation model, and the overall effect could be aggregated. Behavioural tax/transfer models include the MITTS model in Australia (Duncan and Harris, 2002) and other models overseas (see Bourguignon and Spadaro, 2006).

Dynamic models, such as Dynamod or APPSIM (Keegan and Kelly, 2009), introduce another layer of complexity to modelling – time. These models usually start with a sample file or a census file and dynamically age records into the future. Individual records are created, die or may be transformed through time. Such models are especially important where there are strong cohort changes through time. As an example, it is highly likely that the current cohort of 65 year olds who enter their retirement years will have different superannuation balances to the 65 year olds who enter retirement in 50 years' time. A static model such as STINMOD (in its standard form) would assume that the superannuation balances of 65 year olds are effectively unchanged in 50 years' time (with the exception of the usual uprating of values with inflation and real returns on assets). A dynamic approach models the superannuation balances of 15 year olds today for each year into the future and would incorporate through their lifetime the many policy changes which inevitably mean that they will have very different superannuation balances in 50 years (when they are 65).

Dynamic models are generally very complicated and best used for long-term modelling that incorporates significant demographic change. Dynamic models are ideal for the sort of modelling used in The Treasury's Intergenerational Report (Commonwealth Treasury, 2015), which considers fiscal pressures from the predicted ageing of the Australian population for the next 50 years.

Spatial microsimulation models, such as NATSEM's SpatialMSM model, consider the geographic implications of policy change. SpatialMSM is based on a STINMOD base file that has been matched up with regional ABS census targets at a small-area level. The model retains the full richness of STINMOD but can be used for small areas such as postcodes in Australia by using weights developed for the specific postcode.

The map in Figure 10.2 provides an example of output from a regional microsimulation model where the spatial impact of changes to a transfer policy was simulated (see Tanton et al, 2009). This policy change was an increase in the aged pension for single-person families

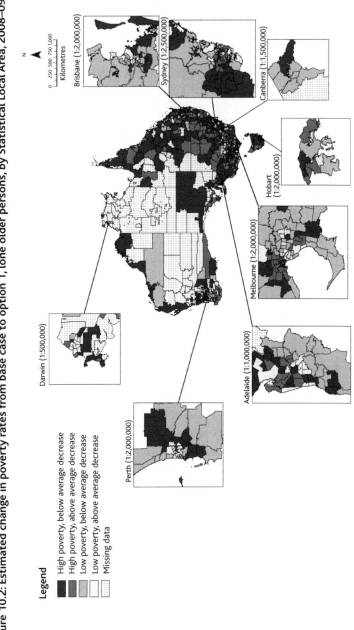

Figure 10.2: Estimated change in poverty rates from base case to option 1, lone older persons, by Statistical Local Area, 2008–09

Legend

■ High poverty, below average decrease
▨ High poverty, above average decrease
▩ Low poverty, below average decrease
□ Low poverty, above average decrease
▦ Missing data

Darwin (1:500,000)

Brisbane (1:2,000,000)

Sydney (1:2,500,000)

Canberra (1:1,500,000)

Hobart (1:2,000,000)

Melbourne (1:2,000,000)

Perth (1:2,000,000)

Adelaide (1:1,000,000)

N

0 250 500 750 1,000
Kilometres

Note: Brisbane has been aggregated to wards and Canberra to Statistical Sub-Divisions to allow comparison with other Australian Statistical Local Areas.

from 60% to 63% of the couple pension. The change in poverty rates is shown in Figure 10.2. This map shows that the greatest impact of the policy change was in high-poverty areas (the darker coloured areas), which were also in regional areas of Australia.

Spatial microsimulation models are particularly useful for developing estimates of measures such as poverty and housing stress at a regional level before and after policy change or, indeed, without even considering policy change. Administrative data or census data are often not detailed enough to provide such estimates or to relate such estimates to other important policy variables.

Microsimulation is widely used within the Australian government and, to a lesser extent, in academia and the private sector. Within government, the main users of microsimulation (relating to social and economic policy) are the Federal Treasury, the Department of Social Services (DSS) and the Department of Employment.

How to use the method

For use in policy modelling, a reasonably detailed understanding is usually required of a statistical computer program. The STINMOD model uses the SAS statistical package, which is specifically designed for the statistical analysis of large data sets. A range of other programs that are capable of handling large data sets and manipulating such data sets are also available, such as R, Stata or Statistical Package for the Social Sciences (SPSS).

The base file for any microsimulation model is a unit record file of persons, families and households. Most of the time, the base survey being used will be out of date due to delays from the statistical agency producing the data. The user will want to model the current tax/transfer system, so will need to inflate any incomes and costs, using either wages growth or the consumer price index. If the model is predicting into the future, then projections of wages and prices growth will also need to be applied.

The survey will also have been benchmarked by the statistical agency to the population in the year that the survey was conducted. This means that the survey weights (applied to inflate the survey population to a national total) in the base survey file will need to be adjusted so that the survey sums to the national population figures for the tax year being estimated. These weights also need to be adjusted so that demographic (age, sex) estimates are reasonable, and the number of welfare recipients matches external administrative data. This means that a complex iterative reweighting procedure needs to be conducted, and STINMOD uses the GREGWT SAS macro developed by the ABS (Bell, 2000) to conduct this reweighting.

With a base file that now has a set of weights aligned to demographic, economic, taxation and welfare benefit benchmarks, policy simulations can now be made. STINMOD models all of the major tax and transfer payments received by households in Australia. The major payments modelled include:

- Pensions – aged, disability, carers, single parents, veterans;
- Allowances – unemployment, youth, parenting payment couple;
- Family payments – family tax benefit part A and B;
- Personal income taxation and medicare; and
- Childcare.

There are also a number of supplements and other elements of the tax and transfer system that are not covered in this chapter.

For all of the programs mentioned earlier, the detail in the survey data is used to simulate entitlement and eligibility. For eligibility, we establish whether a person is eligible for each payment. For example, for the aged pension, details on an individual's age, income, assessable assets, partner income, citizen status and the year at which a person arrived in Australia are on the base file. The STINMOD program then calculates whether the individual satisfies the rules (legislation), and if they do, they are then flagged as being eligible for the aged pension. After passing eligibility, the entitlement is calculated based on unit income and assets.

For a disability payment and carers and veterans, there is not enough survey information to determine eligibility. For these payments, eligibility largely relies upon the receipt of payment on the survey. Entitlement is then calculated based on the same way as the aged pension – upon assessable income and assets.

Allowances take a similar approach, with eligibility code and entitlement code based on the legislation of the day. Family payments are also calculated in a similar manner. As we have all the information required for eligibility in the survey data, we do not rely on the actual payment response in the survey but are able to independently calculate these payments.

Childcare is more difficult. The ABS survey data provide most of the information required; however, a challenge is that only partial information is provided on hourly costs for children. A significant amount of recoding is required to impute hourly rates and hours used for each childcare child.

Taxation is calculated using a person's personal taxable income. Private incomes are aggregated across a range of sources and taxable welfare payments are added. Tax deductions are estimated and removed, including rental investments, which are deducted from gross income.

Microsimulation models such as STINMOD can be used to compare existing and alternative policies. Running all the modules listed earlier with parameter changes reflecting a new policy (eg an income eligibility change for a pension) provides the 'out file' (see Figure 10.1). The out file is a simulation of the policy. The difference between the existing (base file) and alternative (out file) policy data sets represents the policy impact. In STINMOD, this is typically the difference in variable disposable income. Where a family (income unit) has a larger disposable income in the alternative out file, the family is labelled a 'winner'. Where the alternative policy provides a lower disposable income, the family is labelled a 'loser'. For some families, there may be no change in income as the policy change simulated does not affect their family. A simple aggregate across all families provides the share of winners and losers and those where there was no change.

By considering the total change in disposable income, we can estimate the total impact on all households. This impact is also equivalent to the fiscal impact for government. This total impact can be averaged across all households to find the average household impact. A powerful use of a microsimulation model is the ability to provide distributional outcomes of policy change. Instead of just considering the average impact across all families, a microsimulation model can consider the impact for different population groups, like single-parent families. This is because the model is based on individual (and actual) families. As an example, were a flat tax applied, STINMOD could compare the existing policy with the new policy (flat tax) and consider the impact by income levels, for example, the impact on low-income couples with children or high-income single persons.

As a worked example, in Australia, tax rates are applied to individuals and are calculated as marginal tax rates. To calculate the amount of tax payable as at February 2016, an algorithm such as the following would be applied to every person on the base file:

If gross income > 18,201 and gross income < 37,000 then tax = 0.19*(gross income − 18,200); else

If gross income > 37,001 and gross income < 80,000 then tax = 3,572 + 0.325*({gross income} − 37,000); else

If gross income > 80,001 and gross income < 180,000 then tax = 17,547 + 0.37*(gross income − 80,000); else

If gross income > 180,001 then tax = 54,547 + 0.45*(gross income − 180,000); else

Tax = 0

To simulate a tax policy change, any of the income cut-offs, or tax rates, could be adjusted, the formula applied again to the whole data set and a new unit record file (out file) created. Using the base file and the out file, the difference between the current policy and the proposed policy can be calculated. These differences for each household can then be aggregated and the overall impact calculated, or the impact on low-income families or single-parent families can be calculated, depending on what data are available in the original unit record file.

Note that this is a very simple example of how a microsimulation model can be used. As described earlier, the tax/transfer system is usually much more complicated than applying marginal tax rates. In Australia, complications include a low-income tax offset, which affects tax for low-income earners (those earning less than $37,000 a year in the 2014–15 tax year), but it does not affect the medicare levy (which is calculated as 2% of taxable income before the low-income tax offset is calculated). However, there is a medicare levy reduction for low-income workers, which means that there is no medicare levy paid if income is below $20,896, and only part if income is between $20,896 and $26,121. To complicate these matters even further, these income cut-offs are different for seniors and pensioners.

Examples of its use in the social sciences

Microsimulation models are used extensively in the social sciences. Areas where they are used include:

- economics (analysing economic policies like tax and welfare policies);
- demography (modelling demographic change and potential results of changing parameters like birth, death and marriage rates); and
- health (modelling mortality, health and disease).

One of the first large dynamic microsimulation models was based around modelling demographics and economics. Dynasim, built by

The Urban Institute in the US, was started in 1969 and was being used for policy simulations in 1976. The model was intended as a general social science research tool that, given the microsimulation base, could develop and grow as needs developed (Zedlewski, 1990).

The model team was led by Guy Orcutt, and included modules to estimate demographic change (deaths, births and migration), family formation and dissolution, education, labour force characteristics (hours worked, wage rates and unemployment), social security and pensions, property income, taxes, and savings and wealth (Orcutt et al, 1976). As examples of the analysis that the model was capable of, the model was used to study the implications of gender equality on the labour market, and the impact of divorce on the distribution of income (Orcutt et al, 1976).

Microsimulation models have also been used extensively for estimating labour supply (for a review of this literature, see Aaberge and Colombino, 2014). These models are usually based on labour supply theory, and will include formulae for determining labour supply, hours worked, budget constraints and utility maximisation. These models may also incorporate behavioural responses to changes in the labour market, for example, the change in behaviour resulting from an increase in wages.

Demographic models are usually dynamic microsimulation models, so include births, deaths, migration, marriage and so on. The complexity of many of these life events (marriage, moving, labour force participation) means that microsimulation models, with their bottom-up approach starting with individuals and families, are ideal. Demographic microsimulation models have been around since the 1970s, with the development of SOCSIM (Wachter et al, 1978). Other examples of demographic models are spatial microsimulation models (Tanton, 2014), which derive demographic data for small areas. Spatial microsimulation models are used in models of urban environments based on individuals and households, and the interactions between them (Birkin et al, 2009), which can then be used to provide insights into housing markets, as well as in models projecting demographic characteristics to estimate the demand for different services into the future (Harding et al, 2011).

Microsimulation has been used extensively in the health field, covering health expenditure (Schofield, 1998; Lymer et al, 2006) and health conditions (Edwards and Clarke, 2009; Lymer and Brown, 2012). Showing the complexity that microsimulation models can achieve, POHEM is a dynamic microsimulation model that simulates diseases and risk factors, health-care costs, and health-related quality of life (Wills et al, 2001). Spatial microsimulation has also been used in the health field for estimating disability levels and the need for aged care (Lymer et al, 2009). Microsimulation models have also been used to look at the relationship between social capital and health (Mohana et al, 2005).

When to use the method

As stated in the introduction, microsimulation models are one of the few types of models that can provide distributional results (so, winners and losers of a policy). They can also be as complex or as simple as required. Having said this, even the simplest of microsimulation models, with no behavioural or spatial element, is still fairly complex.

The method is ideal for when 'what if' scenarios are required – for example, what would happen if the birth rate changed? Or, what would happen if a particular tax policy changed? Given the complexity of designing and creating these models, there needs to be a number of 'what if' scenarios to justify these models. The models are also data-intensive, requiring regular updates to the base data. For these reasons, the best way to use microsimulation models is to continuously run and use the model, implementing different scenarios that may build on the model. As an example in Australia, recent interest in childcare policy has meant that childcare is now built into the STINMOD tax/transfer model.

The risk with microsimulation models is that they are built for one project, and a lot of time and money is invested into the model, which then does not get used after the project finishes. The other risk is that the models are so complex that only a handful of people can run the model, and when they leave an area, the model is useless unless someone can come in and understand it. This means that detailed documentation for microsimulation models is essential.

What is its value added for policymakers, social science and citizens?

Microsimulation modelling is of considerable use to policymakers, businesses, lobbyists, the media, academics and the general public. This kind of modelling is heavily used by government departments such as the Treasury and the Department of Social Services for the purpose of better understanding the impact on society of new and existing policies. Standard economic and econometric models rarely have the level of detail found within a microsimulation model and are unable to provide results at the fine-grained level often required by policymakers.

A key value of microsimulation modelling is the ability to model a range of policy changes at once. Policymakers, particularly within government, can often use administrative data sets to understand relatively simple changes to a specific policy, such as a simple change to the aged pension. Where a microsimulation model stands out is when multiple policy changes are being made and there is interaction between different policies, as we saw with the tax changes, the low-income tax offset and the medicare levy.

A prime example would be the introduction or changes to a new tax, such as a carbon price or the Goods and Services Tax (GST). Such taxes would likely have a larger relative impact on low-income households and those without earned income. As a result, governments would usually provide a compensation package that would involve increased government payments and lower personal taxation. The combination of increasing some payments and also altering personal income tax rates is the type of policy change that, realistically, only microsimulation models using detailed microdata can handle.

An example of the use of a microsimulation model is the recent work undertaken by NATSEM on the 2015–16 Federal Budget in Australia. This Budget incorporated a large number of policy changes to both the welfare and taxation systems. STINMOD was used to model all of these proposed changes and to calculate the impact on families.

While the Budget papers do provide an aggregate Budget impact for each Budget 'measure', they only provide an aggregate and do not provide any detail on the impact felt by different household types. The Budget papers may, for example, estimate that the total savings from the Budget were $20 billion over the forward estimates, but they do not estimate which groups are impacted the most from such savings.

The NATSEM modelling using STINMOD does provide detailed estimates of the winners and losers from the Budget. In Table 10.1, the impact (for 2018–19) on families with children for each income quintile of the changes suggested in the Australian Commonwealth Budget of 2014–15 is shown. The columns show the percentage of families who lose and the percentage who win from the suggested Budget changes. As can be seen, most families are worse off from the suggested Budget changes – most of which are reductions in payments that go to families with children. The table also details the actual average financial impact. The table shows that the average impact on the lowest income category is $2,450 per year, or a 5.4% reduction in disposable income.

Table 10.1: Outcome from the 2014–15 budget on couple families with children

Family type	Income quintile	% loser	% winner	Millions impact	Impact	Disposable income	% change
Couple/ children Q1	1	92.1%	7.9%	−368	−2,450	878	−5.4%
Couple/ children Q2	2	80.9%	19.1%	−446	−2,280	1,216	−3.6%
Couple/ children Q3	3	86.7%	13.3%	−892	−1,601	1,550	−2.0%
Couple/ children Q4	4	77.3%	22.7%	−177	−207	2,111	−0.2%
Couple/ children Q5	5	94.5%	5.5%	−203	−225	3,760	−0.1%
ALL	ALL	86.2%	13.8%	−2,086	−784	2,416	−0.6%

The NATSEM analysis using STINMOD was discussed heavily in the major daily newspapers, television and in Parliament in the days and weeks after the Federal Budget. The STINMOD analysis is an important contribution to the debate on the appropriateness and impact of the Budget each year.

Limitations of the method

There are a few limitations to the microsimulation method that need to be raised. They are:

- the steep learning curve for microsimulation modelling;
- the resources required to create and maintain a microsimulation model; and
- the use of survey data as the base for the modelling, particularly when measuring income and tax.

Regarding the steep learning curve, this is mainly due to the complexity of microsimulation models. Many people unfamiliar with microsimulation models consider them a big calculator, and while this analogy may be helpful in understanding what a microsimulation model does, like many analogies, it oversimplifies the actual model. As we saw earlier, the order in which taxes and transfers are modelled is important, and will give different results (just as the order of operations affects the result from a calculator), and there are interactions between different taxes and benefits. This means that the modeller needs to have an in-depth knowledge of the tax/transfer system and how it operates.

In particular, tax offsets like the low-income tax offset, which reduce the tax payable, rather than taxable income, complicate the calculation of the final tax due from a household.

The resources required to design, program and maintain a microsimulation model are significant. The complexity of them depends on the type of model, but a recent dynamic microsimulation model designed and built by NATSEM took about 35 full-time equivalent staff and cost $4.4 million over five years.

In terms of maintaining a microsimulation model, this is also expensive as staff time and data are required. The models need to be kept up to date with the latest data, and unless some planning has gone into model handover when a staff member leaves, models can become unusable as the data they use becomes out of date. A model also needs to have continuous use and funding for it to be maintained.

Finally, if the model uses survey data for the base data (as many microsimulation models do), then the limitations of the survey will flow through to the model. For example, in many surveys, incomes or Centrelink payments will be underestimated by respondents, or different sources of income may be misreported (eg the respondent may forget that they receive a small amount of income from a part-time cleaning job). These can partly be corrected at an aggregate level by benchmarking to other administrative data, like income data from the Tax Office.

Conclusions

This chapter has argued that microsimulation models are a useful tool for social researchers wanting to model different 'what if' scenarios and to look at the impact of different policies on social outcomes. The power of microsimulation models is that they allow the study of the distributional impacts of a policy reform, and provide these estimates before the policy is implemented. These types of models have been used in many areas of the social sciences, including economics, demography and health.

However, there are risks with microsimulation models. Even the simplest models are complex pieces of code, and they are data-intensive, requiring unit record survey data. A complex model such as STINMOD requires a deep understanding of the underlying survey data and a broad range of economic statistics and auxiliary data such as administration data. Maintaining such models requires knowledgeable staff with specific statistical and computer programming skills. Maintenance alone does require significant investment in time and effort.

Development of such models also requires significant investment in human hours, with new developments often complicated by data restrictions or complexities. STINMOD was recently enhanced with the addition of a childcare module. The most complex element of this work was not the actual modelling of the childcare system (which is complicated), but ensuring that the underlying survey data were of a form amenable to modelling and also relevant to the current financial year and future years. Childcare is a policy area where demand has increased sharply and the composition of use has also changed. Incorporating such changes (beyond the old survey data) requires benchmarking to administrative data and projections of these benchmarks and prices into the future. It is not unusual for a skilled team of researchers to take months to develop such new capabilities.

Modelling complex systems using microsimulation is rarely straightforward; however, once the model is appropriately developed, the potential for policy modelling and understanding the complexities of policy are significant. Models such as STINMOD make a contribution to policy and analysis on many of the biggest policy challenges facing a nation. Likely areas for policy modelling in Australia using such models in the near future include: climate change; changes to the goods and services tax; changing the tax mix and other taxation reforms; and pension modelling.

Further reading
The best place to start learning about microsimulation is the International Microsimulation Association (IMA) website, available at: www.microsimulation.org

This website has links to conferences and workshops, a link to the *International Journal of Microsimulation* (with all issues available free online) and links to other useful websites, including the National Centre for Social and Economic Modelling in Australia, the Luxembourg Institute of Socio-Economic Research and Teagasc in Ireland.

The International Microsimulation Conference is held every two years, with the last one in 2015 (so the next one in 2017). In the off-years, conferences are also held in Europe. The IMA website has information on these conferences.

As outlined in the section on the limitations of the method, microsimulation has a steep learning curve. The models can have complex interactions, and need to be planned and designed before being programmed. Programming the model is relatively straightforward given modern object-oriented languages, but the programs will still be long and complex. There are some languages designed to simplify this coding by using standard procedures and a simplified coding language, like Modgen from Statistics Canada (available at: http://www.statcan. gc.ca/eng/microsimulation/modgen/modgen), but many models now use either Java or Python – for example, JAMSIM is a microsimulation tool that uses Java (see Mannion et al, 2012).

Probably the best book on microsimulation at the moment is one recently published by O'Donoghue (2014). This book is an edited collection that covers all forms of microsimulation modelling.

Books coming from the International Microsimulation Conferences contain papers presented at those conferences. There are two books: one from the 2007 conference (Zaidi et al, 2009); and one from the 2011 conference (Dekkers et al, 2014).

For dynamic microsimulation, an introductory article is Li and O'Donoghue (2013). For spatial microsimulation, a special issue of the *International Journal of Microsimulation* was published in 2014, with papers on spatial microsimulation from the 2013 microsimulation conference. An introductory paper is Tanton (2014). An introductory text on spatial microsimulation is Tanton and Edwards (2013).

PART FOUR:
BRINGING CITIZENS BACK IN

ELEVEN

Citizen social science and policy making

Liz Richardson

More productive relationships between policy, social science and citizens are needed to address complex policy issues, but they have often eluded the best efforts and intentions of those actors. Citizen social science is one approach being used to open up social science methods to members of the lay public. Citizen social science takes many forms, but, in essence, it is about greater hands-on involvement of lay people in scientific research: doing it, designing it, understanding it and debating it. Applied in the right way, citizen social science has untapped potential as a positive development in its own right, and as a tool for more direct policy use. Participatory approaches to both research and policy are designed to enhance research at the margins – whether this is with traditionally under-represented groups or sensitive, controversial and complex topics. An attraction of citizen social science is that it offers something that feels fresh and innovative and could grab the public interest. It is underused in social science directly related to public policy research, and new opportunities for creative policy problem solving arise from this gap.

Additional energy and resources are generated by wide involvement in discovery aimed at addressing complex collective problems. As well as this, it has potential for additional forms of expertise to be added to our grasp of complex policy choices. Societies are witnessing more decentralised, diffuse and engaged worlds in policy and governance, as well as policy spaces where citizens play ever-more significant roles in civic leadership. In this context, the integration of research into policy making demands that models for social science match these democratic innovations by sharing scientific knowledge beyond elites and specialist groups. Citizen social science is also emerging as a viable technique for discovery among hard-to-reach groups, helping groups with less formal power to be more clearly heard in research, and in policy making.

This chapter first sets out some context and basic descriptions for citizen social science, and how the method could relate to policy making. After a brief outline of how citizen social science links to other citizen engagement approaches, the chapter looks at practical issues for those considering doing a policy-related citizen social science project: options for levels and types of participation; whether and how the outputs and outcomes are affected by the nature of the participation; and what kinds of data it is feasible to collect. It then offers three illustrative vignettes of citizen social science projects on specific policy areas, before concluding on how the use of the technique might be expanded in the future.

What is citizen social science?

What is now called citizen science has a long history, including the activity and adventures of the 19th-century Victorian amateur 'gentleman' scientists, largely focusing on the natural sciences and medicine. Citizen science has grown in popularity internationally as a way to crowd-source intelligence and harness collective energies for scientific purposes. Emblematic examples include annual surveys of birds in the US and the UK, which are conducted by members of the public who record bird species seen in their gardens and yards during a nominated survey week. In Manchester, England, the Turing Sunflowers project carries on work in the memory of scientist Alan Turing, using sunflowers to look at Fibonacci sequences in nature. It illustrates how citizen science can generate mass public engagement with science, with around 12,000 participants in seven countries growing sunflowers, counting seeds and uploading data.[1] Zooniverse has somewhere around 30 projects at any one time asking participants to help identify or classify different pieces of data, from images of wildebeest to telescope pictures of the Milky Way, and claims over one million registered users.[2] One of the key features of citizen science is also suggested by these examples, that it can collect or analyse large amounts of easily standardised data that would otherwise be extraordinarily complex, labour-intensive or expensive to do in other ways (Gommerman and Monroe, 2012: 2). Citizen science has typically had the benefits of operating on a large scale with mass citizen involvement in research, using an empirical and scientific approach to research.

Why does this chapter refer to citizen *social* science? Citizen science has been dominated by natural science – counting shellfish, bees, water quality, acid rain, birds, weather patterns, stars and planets. Many of these, particularly earth sciences and environmental studies, are directly relevant to public policy and offer critical intelligence. For example, in the field of environmental governance, organisers of the Audubon Bird Count argue on their website that their work has contributed to 'the implementation of policies that safeguard birds, other wildlife and the resources that sustain us all', including 'innovative policies that balance habitat protection with green energy development on millions of acres'.[3]

Alongside these policy contributions from citizen science in the natural sciences, there are policy questions for which the social sciences are also needed, and uniquely placed. Citizen astronomers can help us find out how galaxies form, but should we invest public money trying to find out? What level of public support is there for investment in space exploration? Does this change when investment options are compared to alternative uses? How do these opinions and preferences differ between groups? What might alter those preferences? There are many well-established social-scientific methods for measuring stated as well as revealed preferences, such as the big data methods discussed by Patrick Dunleavy in Chapter Eight of this book. As also set out by John Dryzek, there are innovative techniques for exploring if and how public views might alter through the process of deliberation. Citizen social science can complement and add to the wide range of available approaches.

How could citizen social science enhance approaches to policy making?

Policy faces challenges of ever-increasing complexity, which have been described as 'wicked' – cutting across many different issues (Jervis and Richards, 1997) – and 'squishy' – involving politics and human behaviour (Strauch, 1975). For many, including the author, policy-oriented citizen social science is part of a broader advocacy of the use of the widest possible range of assets to gather, interpret and use evidence for policy. It is based on the idea that a combination of political leadership, coupled with quality evidence, and blended with direct experience, is well suited to tackling complex public policy challenges (Durose and Richardson, 2016). Public debate over science in mainstream policy is more commonly associated with unresolved controversies over the veracity and application of scientific knowledge to topics including climate change, genetically modified food, alternative energy generation, the safety of vaccines, educational methods, equitable economic growth, and effective and efficient health-care provision, to name just some of the most obvious examples. Alongside disputes over the 'facts' of how to best achieve policy goals, there are value choices also being made about preferences for policy goals, and who benefits and who loses. When citizens and policymakers look for ways to frame and judge these issues, social science competes with political ideology, vested interests, folk wisdom and historical precedent. These challenges suggest a gulf between policy, members of the public and evidence, and underline the need for new methods of discovery that attempt to bridge these gaps. Social science could potentially also help break through these impasses by offering ways to understand politics, interests and competing framings, and ways to structure, evidence and debate value choices.

Public policy is moving in parallel towards even more citizen engagement, as well as to the principle of policy making informed by science and evidence. Values underpinning democratic debate and those of scientific enquiry are, or ought to be, natural bedfellows. Both demand a commitment to reason giving, transparency, openness to critical scrutiny, reasonable scepticism and the welcoming of conflicting views (Jasanoff, 2009). Therefore, public debates about policy choices, and policy making underpinned by social science, need not be seen in opposition. Ideally, democratic debate on policy choices would be open and transparent, involve citizens in policy dialogue and deliberation where relevant and feasible, and allow all participants to have conversations that are evidence-informed.

Citizen social science may be of particular value where there are specific blockages in public policy processes. These include: a low level of public trust in science; controversial, highly contested and/or highly specialised technical debates; particularly intractable policy problems; histories of distant or negative relationships between policymakers, scientists and the public; gaps in intelligence and evidence; policy areas involving groups that could be perceived to be marginalised from the mainstream; and data that are more challenging to access in conventional ways (Richardson, 2017).

The technique is potentially well-suited to otherwise 'hard-to-reach', 'hard-to-research' and 'hard-to-hear' topics and groups usually under-represented in conventional methods. For example, the Kinsey Institute study of sexual behaviours asks citizens to anonymously upload personal data of a very sensitive nature, with potential policy applications in preventative and public health fields.[4] Households with lower incomes, women and people from a minority ethnic heritage are some of the groups who have lower levels of trust in science generally (Sturgis and Allum, 2004; Gauchat, 2012). These are also groups who traditionally lack formal power in decision-making processes, and are less likely to engage in other forms of political voice. Citizens have long used science in lobbying campaigns to challenge policymakers and powerful vested interests on charges of environmental damage,

damage to human health, social injustice and other disputed policies or decisions (Coburn, 2005; Stoudt and Torre, 2014). Some citizen social science projects are also being jointly and collaboratively organised by policymakers and public bodies together with citizens and civic organisations. Another part of the popularity of citizen social science for policy organisations and for academics is that it offers a way for the resources of academic institutions to be used for social purposes. Citizen science can be used to bring together social scientists based in universities with lay researchers, and to contribute to the opening up of social-scientific methods beyond the academy.

How does citizen social science build on existing approaches to citizen engagement?

Citizen social science evolves what already exists. From a policy or practitioner perspective, citizen social science is also a close cousin of public consultation and engagement. People involved in public policy making are often experienced and adept at consulting and negotiating with citizen and user groups and members of the public, using techniques from the social sciences such as focus groups, questionnaire surveys or inviting open responses to policy proposals. Citizen social science builds on this expertise, adding enhanced levels of citizen input, a collaborative and evidence-based approach, and a strong focus on scientific methodologies. There are also traditions of citizen science in the social sciences, such as the mass observation projects in the UK from the 1930s onwards in which members of the public recorded detailed observations of everyday life and opinions.[5] An extensive, rich and varied tradition of community-based participatory research is arguably also another forerunner or reference point, although the relationship between participation, participatory research and scientific methods has, at times, been rather troubled (Richardson, 2013). For practical purposes, citizen social science is a variant of community or participatory research, distinguished by its emphasis on the strict application of empirical scientific methodologies from mainstream social science.

Practical issues in doing a citizen social science project

To more fully exploit the potential of citizen social science, more citizens need to be involved, but, crucially, more policymakers and academics need to take a lead in generating research and policy opportunities. Here, we look at some of the practical issues for those considering doing a citizen social science project: how to choose the level and type of citizen involvement; whether the degree or nature of citizen input matters, and, if so, for what aspect of the work; and what sorts of data it might be feasible for citizen social scientists to collect.

How to choose the level and type of citizen involvement

There is no single definition or model; citizen science is where non-professionals are actively engaged in some way in scientific research (Richardson, 2014). Engagement can be at different points in the research process, from the research questions and research design, through to data collection, analysis, writing up, dissemination and policy application. Some of this is dictated by the nature of the research and data, for example, projects that use citizen scientists to manually classify existing data sets, composed of images of stars, wildebeest or cells, which (as yet) cannot be processed by computer software programs. Citizen scientists' engagement has also been seen by some writers along a continuum of citizen control of the research. At the 'lowest' point, volunteers collect data or 'crowd-source' for projects designed and controlled by professional scientists. At a 'higher' level of citizen control, in collaborative or 'extreme citizen science', lay people make an input into the core research aims and problem definition (Goodson and Phillimore, 2012; Haklay, 2013).

However, for others, continuums of control – however neutrally conceived, carefully explained and horizontally presented – have always struggled to get away from connotations that higher levels are preferable. For those who wish to make no assumptions about which types of participation are more desirable, there is still a range of pragmatic choices based on a continuum of levels of technical challenge and research skills needed for all those involved. Broadly speaking, data collection, while time-consuming and resource-intensive, is at the lower end of technical challenge and specialist research skills demanded. Towards the medium points of the continuum are co-designing research tools, looking at policy implications of research and data analysis. At the higher levels are governance and oversight of research, identifying research problems, designing research methodologies and co-authorship (for a more detailed practical guide, see Richardson, 2017).

Does the degree or nature of citizen input matter?

Those considering a citizen social science project might want to understand whether the degree or nature of citizen input matters, and, if so, for what aspect of the work and its outputs and outcomes. We consider possible implications for: the quality of the research; the impacts on the citizen scientists; and the policy leverage of the findings.

Quality of the research

Fundamentally, the quality of the research should be equal whoever undertakes it, so as to meet accepted scientific criteria for the methodology and be well-implemented. Citizen social science is about opening up social science methods to a broader set of participants than academics, paid researchers and university students. So, in one sense, the level and type of citizen involvement should not produce either a better or a worse piece of research. However, as with any real-life research project, the skills, expertise and perspectives of those doing it make a difference. Additional and complementary forms of experience and expertise should strengthen the research, for example, in hypothesis generation, or the design of the research instruments (such as topic guides). Good social scientists already try to pilot their research methods or instruments, or to test their interpretation of the data on the subjects or participants, and this approach simply extends this principle of piloting. Science that integrates lay knowledge may also be made more methodologically rigorous than it would otherwise have been. This is illustrated by studies that suggest flawed research designs, partly due to the lack of inclusion of local knowledge, such as a study of the measurement of radiation and its effects on sheep in one area after the Chernobyl disaster that failed to include sheep farmers' knowledge fully in sample selection (Wynne, 2004: 66–7).

Impacts

When it comes to the impacts on public engagement with policy and science, the evidence is mixed. Projects have claimed that participants have experienced increased well-being and behaviour change as a result of participation (Davies et al, 2013), though these evaluations are not usually done using randomised controlled trials (RCTs) (experimental methods are discussed by Peter John in Chapter Four of this book). Beyond these general personal benefits, if one aim is to incorporate an evidence base into public discussions of policy, then citizen social science would hopefully increase public trust in and knowledge of science. Looking at the relationships between attitudes towards science and factual scientific knowledge, another study found that positive attitudes are strongly correlated with actual scientific knowledge, independent of other factors such as political knowledge. For those at the highest level of political knowledge, moving from the bottom to the top of the scientific knowledge scale alone results in an increase in favourability of attitude towards science of almost 30 percentiles (Sturgis and Allum, 2004: 65). However, one study using data from the British Social Attitudes survey (BSA) (Barnett et al, 2007) did not find evidence that positive attitudes towards public involvement in science fostered greater trust in science in the area of genetic technology, such as cloning. Those who believed in high-level public involvement were less likely to think that these technologies should be allowed than those who did not (Barnett et al, 2007). So, it may be that active engagement in doing science means that participants are more informed and positive about science, but also more wary of some sorts of technical interventions as a result; or, perhaps, simply that people who are wary of science also believe in citizen accountability.

Policy leverage

Is the degree of the policy leverage of research affected by the level or nature of citizen involvement? Looking at the field of deliberative approaches, citizens are more likely to accept policy proposals that have been decided by other citizens, even if they themselves were not directly involved. This suggests that there may be some positive effects on the public acceptability of proposals informed by citizen science rather than conventional science. Another possible argument is that citizen social science may help bridge the gap between evidence and policy for political decision-makers as the findings and policy implications have already been discussed by voters and constituents. Lessons from conventional science suggest that the policy leverage of research is dependent on the co-construction of the research, the awareness of political contexts, an ability to apply research to policy and practice, and the effective transmission or translation of the results.

What sorts of data might it be feasible for citizen social scientists to collect?

Not all projects will involve new data collection; some may focus on analysing existing material, of which there are many underused sources for policy purposes, for example, correspondence between residents and a local government organisation, existing administrative records, local media articles, historical archives, discussions on hyper-local websites or relevant Twitter hashtags, minutes of community forums, records of local civic projects or groups, and so on. Big data and moves towards open data have created new ways for citizens to mine large data sets for policy purposes, such as through citizen 'hactivists' holding 'hackathons' with open data. In one example,[6] the results included new software applications to manipulate open data for public benefit, such as 'Sat Lav', an app to find the nearest public convenience,[7] and an idea for visualisation tools that plot traffic accidents against the location of speed cameras.

However, the opportunity to discover some entirely new data is one of the things that excites many people considering undertaking such work. Previous primary data collection projects can be roughly divided into those which ask citizens to: provide their own views; collect observable data about themselves or their environments; and collect data from other people. The growth of citizen social science is accelerated by new digital technologies because they offer access and control for large volumes of data collection and the ease of recording and handling data for volunteer researchers, although old-fashioned 'analogue' citizen social science is equally possible and valid.

Crowd-sourced data

Examples of the different types of data collection include a self-complete Web survey in the UK in 2011, which asked people about their understandings of social class (Savage et al, 2013). It is claimed that it is the largest survey of social class ever conducted in the UK, with 161,400 Web respondents, a level of response helped by a partnership with the British Broadcasting Corporation (BBC). This might be categorised as 'crowd-sourced' data, although, in some ways, the participants were doing similar tasks to respondents in a conventional research project. Public policy research has long been dominated by public opinion data, some of which overlap with public consultation. Online computer simulation games are being used to conduct interactive public consultation and dialogue processes, while simultaneously collecting public opinion data through the recording of gameplay. Participatory Chinatown[8] is a simulation game with virtual residents in Boston's Chinatown. Players act as one of the characters reacting to urban planning proposals, for example, for new residential or commercial developments, based on their character's demographic and other characteristics. Some Web applications allow mass participation in games that simulate classic theories of public policy, for example, different ways to get individuals to act for the collective good. Several are based on Nobel prize-winner Elinor Ostrom's (1990) work on dilemmas of how best to conserve and manage scare resources.

Observable data

Observable data collection has been fuelled by innovations made possible using participants as mobile data collection points. In one community 'bio' mapping project, participants walk around their local area wearing a special device that records emotional arousal signs, which are then used to create a map showing places where people had high or low levels of arousal. Maps are annotated by participants to explain the arousal patterns and create 'communal Emotion Maps'. Over 2,000 people in 25 cities have taken part so far, including San Francisco, East Paris and parts of London (Nold, 2009). Other projects use applications available through people's own smartphones to record noise or images, which are also geo-codeable, such as MapLocal, and can be used, for example, for community-led neighbourhood planning (Durose and Richardson, 2016: 141–8). In cities in Brazil, Nicaragua and Mexico, residents in the poorest areas are using a digital game on their smartphones called Dengue Torpedo to identify and report incidents of dengue, creating a map of the locations and allowing the targeting of disease zones.[9] Participatory mapping is also one of the techniques used by a group doing what it calls 'extreme' citizen science.[10] Smartphone and tablet applications have been designed for people with limited literacy to collect and analyse environmental monitoring data, such as deforestation or poaching, with a longer-term aim of creating 'intelligent maps' with novel approaches to the visualisation, analysis and editing of spatio-temporal data, comprehensible for non-literate users.

Perception data from other people

The illustrative vignettes in this chapter include examples of citizens collecting opinion data from other people. Where citizen social science involves volunteers collecting data about other people's attitudes, opinions, preferences, perceptions and behaviours, this presents specific challenges. Research that involves what the jargon calls 'human subjects' is traditionally seen by universities as an especially fraught area requiring additional regulation, for example, in the form of elaborated ethical approval procedures. Taking water or soil samples, or photographing disease in plants and trees, may raise problems of access, equipment, technical knowledge and identification, and potential damage caused by fieldwork. However, citizen scientists are unlikely to be embarrassed or intimidated to approach a tree or river. Neither is an inanimate research subject able to feel offended or liable by the researcher's actions. Nor has the soil or tree any literacy or income barriers to their participation in the research, and their written informed consent is not demanded by university ethics committees. These issues should not prevent citizen social scientists collecting primary data from other people, but do reinforce the need for careful briefings, training and support where needed, as well as carefully thought-through protocols.

Illustrative vignettes of citizen social science

This section describes the process, context, details of the research and use of the data for three illustrative examples. The first vignette gives an example of where the technique has been used to recruit volunteers from groups that tend to have low levels of trust in science, which was initiated by a public housing provider. The second offers a project led by the third sector, where volunteer researchers explored a sensitive topic with marginalised groups of respondents, and also had more engagement of the citizen social scientists through the research process, including in analysis and report writing. The third presents a wholly citizen-led and -organised piece of work, and suggests how a more co-productive model of citizen social science might operate, and how research can be incorporated into policy development and social change. The third vignette also provides a challenge back to 'traditional' models of research, which separate research from policy and citizen mobilisation for change. All three show how universities and others might work with partners to share knowledge on research methods for wider public benefit.

Citizen social science with people on lower incomes and with lower trust in science

This example is of a partnership between a group of universities and a public housing organisation called Family Mosaic. The partnership had the broad aim of encouraging more forms of civic participation, including volunteering for citizen social science. With a substantial asset base of housing stock and rental income, and a relationship with the people who live in the homes that they own and manage, public housing organisations can make some policy decisions directly, for example, choosing to invest surplus income into social inclusion projects. Part of the policy agenda that they were advocating was a strong role for public housing organisations in supporting tenants and others to gain skills and become civically active.

Context

Family Mosaic provides and manages subsidised social rented housing and low-cost homes for sale, with around 24,000 homes in ownership and management. Around 70% of tenants receive a state subsidy for their housing costs, and also get welfare payments for living costs. Of the people living in their homes for whom they have this data, around half have a black or minority ethnic heritage. A public housing provider was selected to focus on households from manual backgrounds, from lower-income groups and with people with minority ethnic heritage, all of which are groups that typically have lower levels of trust in science (Sturgis and Allum, 2004: 63). Family Mosaic also has its own research team, and sizable research programmes, mostly conducted in-house, with some external expertise from universities and others. The organisation had previously used RCTs to evaluate some of its interventions, and places great store in high-quality research and evidence. It also plays a strategic policy role for the sector in that region, with their chief executive officer (CEO) previously chairing an influential lobbying network of social housing providers in London. For the universities, this work was one part of a larger programme of research using a series of field experiments, using RCTs to test different interventions to stimulate and increase volunteering. One of the experiments to recruit volunteers offered citizen social science as one of the volunteering options. Aims for the citizen research included gathering additional perception data on motivations for and barriers to volunteering.

Research

Co-design of the citizen science research was done by the partners, including the research aims and research questions, and specific instruments that the citizen social scientists would use. To enable more co-design of future work, respondents were asked what additional research topics should be included. Of the 75 people who expressed an interest in citizen social science, 25 signed up to be volunteer citizen social scientists after receiving more detailed information. Of those, 15 collected 49 responses in total from seven areas across greater

London. The research topics covered questions about people's civic participation and how this could be encouraged. Each researcher received a researcher 'Starter Pack' in the post, which included: a copy of the interview guide and showcards; written instructions on how to target the desired sample, ask the questions and record the data; stationery for manual recording; university-branded identification; and low-denomination supermarket vouchers for use as a thank you for respondents, or to contribute towards fieldwork expenses. Each researcher then recruited their own sample, collected the primary data and uploaded it electronically through a user-friendly and simple software package. Data quality was reviewed by the two lead researchers, for example, checking how far each respondent's answers appeared to use unique language and the relevance and length of the responses. One researcher's responses were judged as being of low quality, and a note was added to the data set. Five of the researchers then attended a day-long analysis workshop where the academic and a researcher from the housing organisation provided training on quantitative and qualitative analysis. The group then coded a sample of the data to create the analysis framework for the qualitative data. The subsequent coding and write up was done by the paid researchers.

Use of data

Specific findings from this small-N qualitative study have been used to sense-check and illuminate quantitative data collected by the organisation on barriers to volunteering. There are a series of proposals for practical projects to incentivise volunteering, which the evidence is being used to inform. In addition, the project has been seen as a useful proof of concept by the organisation as it develops additional ways to engage its users.

Citizen social science on a sensitive topic with 'marginalised' respondents

This example is of a partnership project between a policy lobbying group, the Greater Manchester Poverty Action Group (GMPAG), and a university based in a city-region in Northern England. Like other universities, the University of Manchester, where the author is also based, is developing links with policymakers in the city-region, engaging with the public on research and trying to mobilise its resources to contribute to the social and public good. At the same time, the devolution of budgets and decisions from central government to the city-region had generated concerns that there needed to be a more equal focus on economic growth and productivity, as well as a greater equity of outcomes. One of the ways in which the partners believed that inequality might be tackled was the greater use, accessibility and transparency of data. These two sets of strategic drivers formed a supportive backdrop to the citizen social science project.

Context

GMPAG is a network made up of local authorities, housing providers, universities, voluntary and community organisations, and Manchester-based charities and philanthropists. It is coordinated on a voluntary basis by a local think tank and research consultancy. It was set up in 2013 to continue the work of the Greater Manchester Poverty Commission, and to help implement the Commission's recommendations, which had widespread support from these agencies across the city-region. One of the recommendations was to make data on various indices of poverty more accessible, specifically, through the creation of an interactive website for public use. Some of the logic behind this is that the greater public availability of evidence enhances the quality of public debate on policy.

Academics worked with GMPAG on the website by processing existing quantitative data on a range of poverty indicators into useable forms for a lay public. They also added commentary on the data to aid interpretation. Citizen social science was proposed by the partners to supplement the available statistical data with qualitative research on the perceptions and experiences of poverty. Some precedents for this already existed in the poverty testimonials collected by the Commission.

Research

One of the GMPAG partners is the Anglican Church, and they offered to recruit volunteer researchers from their trainee clergy and other networks such as community-based associations. A total of 19 researchers were recruited, of whom 15 completed the fieldwork. The research design, including research aims and questions, sample, research instruments, and plans for analysis and writing up, was co-designed by the university academic working together with the partner organisations, some of whom also have extensive knowledge of, and experience in using, research methods. The citizen social scientists were sent research 'Starter Packs' in the mail, as with the first example, and subsequently used the same process as detailed in the first example, including an analysis day involving around 12 people to develop a coding framework for the qualitative data.

The volunteers were each asked to interview people with experience of poverty about those experiences. Researchers recruited their own quasi-purposive and snowball samples following the protocols provided. In total, there were 81 responses across eight local government areas in the city-region. Several of the volunteer researchers helped to code the full data set, drafted sections of the findings and made comments on the final report.

Where the findings made a contribution to the field, it was to restate the importance of mixed methods, and including qualitative material on often harrowing accounts of experiences of poverty alongside the statistical data. Some of the qualitative material was also original and spoke directly to the relationship between evidence and policy, asking about perceptions about if and in what ways evidence played a role in creating positive social change.

Use of data

A senior politician active in decision-making in the city-region has expressed his support for the project as a whole. Partners presented the work at a research conference for faith organisations, with some interest from other practitioner organisations in using the techniques with vulnerable groups, for example, people with terminal illnesses receiving palliative care. There is an agreement to apply for funding to continue the partnership between the university and GMPAG, for example, through a placement-based PhD studentship. GMPAG was awarded funding for one year for a full-time post to continue the project and implement projects based on the findings.

Citizen-led and -organised citizen social change

This example is led by a community organisation called the White Rock Trust as part of their work on community-led neighbourhood planning. This group of citizens led the creation of a masterplan for economic rejuvenation in the neighbourhood, drawing in external expertise as needed. White Rock Trust conducted a public consultation process and commissioned technical experts, leading to a series of plans for redevelopment and investment in the neighbourhood. White Rock Trust is also acting as one of the organisations delivering the plans, for example, through community land-ownership and the community-led redevelopment of buildings for affordable commercial and residential use.

As with all three vignettes, the group have agreed to the use of their work as a vignette in this chapter. White Rock Trust's members recognise many of the features of their work as those seen in citizen social science. However, they do not refer to their own work as 'research' as they argue that research, by itself, will not create sufficient social change. Instead, they use citizen-generated evidence alongside other policy tools, integrating and blending the use of evidence into citizen-led change.

Context

White Rock Trust is based in a seaside town on the south coast of England. It is a community organisation that has one paid member of staff, over 400 members (of whom just under half live or work in the immediate neighbourhood) and a core of around 30–40 active volunteers. A board of volunteer trustees oversee the organisation. One purpose of the Trust is to maximise and capture the benefits for the neighbourhood of local amenities and visitors to their town. A statement of their values explains their approach to combining science with other forms of expertise and leadership:

> we want to combine local knowledge, technical expertise, creative input and political will to achieve a better place with strong ongoing community engagement of both residential and business communities. This goes beyond 'consultation' to local leadership and delivery of place management services.[11]

The neighbourhood that the group works in is in need of renovation and economic growth. There are new facilities and investment going into the neighbourhood, for example, a £14 million grant won by the Trust to rescue the destroyed historic Hastings Pier, and the challenge was to capture the benefits of the investment for local businesses and residents.

Research (community-led planning process)

Open public neighbourhood planning workshops held at the start of the process acted as what researchers would see as focus groups. These initial workshops were used to understand public perceptions of critical issues in the neighbourhood, which would be explored in more depth using different approaches – in research terms, generating hypotheses for further research. One of the topics generated by the workshops was the need for improved pedestrian access to and through the neighbourhood and its assets, such as local shops, restaurants and parks. Participants also articulated possible theories of change of policy outcomes that would be anticipated to result from better footfall (ie numbers of people visiting the neighbourhood) and flow management (ie how people move through the neighbourhood to take advantage of services and amenities). Projected policy outcomes included improved profitability for local businesses, a reduction in vacant properties, increased employment for local people and improved amenity for local residents.

A member of the group conducted a series of what they call 'listenings'. If these were conventional research, they would be a street survey using a face-to-face interview to collect data in response to open-ended questions on a questionnaire. The 'questionnaire' was an established instrument that had already been trialled, used nationally and externally validated.[12] However, the listenings are explicitly and deliberately not about 'researching' people's views and then taking the results 'away' for others to create change. Listenings reject traditional research or consultation exercises, which exacerbate the gap between people and policy, and leave citizens in a passive position. Instead, the listenings help people to clarify what they care about and what action they are willing to take, while also generating what researchers would see as useful opinion data. Asking questions using the listenings is designed to mobilise potential citizen contributions to co-producing ways to improve the neighbourhood. One person conducted all of the listenings; this was not a researcher, but a community organiser.[13] What might have otherwise been 'interviews' were instead seen by the group as opportunities for a conversation and trust and relationship building with people in the community.

In social science terms, the method used to target people for listenings could be interpreted as a blend of a purposive and convenience sample covering different streets in the neighbourhood at different times to target potentially different sets of respondents. They used a basic quota sampling system for numbers of respondents per location, and then for gender and age samples for the responses overall. The listenings were conducted over 24 months, and 400 responses were collected in total.

Observational data were in the form of a series of guided walks around the neighbourhood in groups, each respondent with a map, and a request to identify a suitable route from the railway station to the pier and the positive and negative features on the way. The responses were recorded on the maps using an agreed key and written annotations. The guided walk sites were selected based on areas that had been identified by groups' local knowledge as particularly problematic for pedestrians to navigate.

An analysis day was then held as an open public event, inviting anyone interested to help analyse the data from the workshops, listenings and guided walks; 15 people attended. The author was invited to co-facilitate the session in order to bring in external academic expertise on training citizens in qualitative analysis techniques. Practical exercises introduced the idea of thematic analysis, and then participants worked in small groups to do an initial blind code of different samples of the data. Participants then pooled the coding frameworks and reconciled any differences in order to agree a coding frame that was then used to code the qualitative data. Four volunteers from the day then took the data home and coded it using the agreed coding framework. They also counted the number of respondents making comments under each code, and recorded the analysis in a spreadsheet. Following the analysis, the group sought brief additional advice from the academic on how to interpret the analysed data and produce findings. Another series of public workshops were facilitated by the group to produce the findings in a participatory way.

Citizen social science was one element in a wider set of policy analysis and research activities on footfall and flow management. Other activities brought in technical expertise, for example, the group developed a framework to identify all public spending within the neighbourhood, commissioned a 3D model of the area to show elevations in this hilly area relevant to pedestrian movement and also worked with urban planning consultants.

The findings of the research are specific to the neighbourhood and were not designed to speak to a wider debate. The value and contribution of this research lies in its use as an example of the process of citizen-led social science combining evidence and social change.

Use of data

Unlike more static conceptions of research, the group are using the findings as an underpinning framework for continued 'listenings'; they say the findings represent 'what we currently think that people think'. Through additional community conversations, new material has been generated to test the level of agreement with existing data – in research terms, an ongoing process of falsification – and also ways that new data amend, challenge or expand their framework.

Policy action taken so far include the group commissioning an architect to develop proposals to encourage pedestrian flow through an area identified as poorly performing. This has led to the 'Walk this Way' project, a series of relatively low-cost creative proposals for transforming the space and guiding pedestrians through more effectively.

Expanding the use of the tool: where next?

Illustrated by the vignettes is the ability for the local variation and application of citizen social science. From the discussion in this chapter, some of the intuitive appeal of citizen science, and citizen social science, can hopefully be understood. It offers untapped potential to open up policy debates to public debate and a firmer grounding in scientific evidence and research. It increases the pool of social science tools for policy discovery. A coda to this is that cynical uses of the technique as crude cost-saving measures risk discovery and rejection by citizens, and it should therefore be seen as an additive rather than substitutive option where circumstances warrant.

Despite the popularity of the technique internationally, much of the use of citizen social science for policy is still limited to a relatively small number of flagship pilot projects by early adopters. Expanding its use into a more mainstream technique is likely to require support, such as the following:

- A commitment to opening up policy processes to citizens, to dialogue and deliberation, and to more transparent and evidence-informed policy making.
- An iterative approach that tries to be reflexive. Numerous tough challenges arise from attempts to implement citizen social science, which need to try and design robust research, work with groups with little or no experience or training, and possibly marginalised groups, while speaking to policy. Therefore, expectations need to include the need to pilot and iterate work, incorporating lessons in each new iteration.
- Careful thought about the range of circumstances in which the technique is applied. Some of the appeal is the use of the technique in extreme cases, and it is suited for research that would be hard to achieve in more conventional ways. However, its currency may be damaged if it becomes something that is solely associated with more

intractable policy areas, hard-to-research issues or very marginalised groups. It could also serve as a popular approach for opening up policy areas that have become over-primed, for example, or where existing lines of debate are over-trammelled, overfamiliar and stale.

However, the vignette of citizen-led citizen social change is also instructive if this tool is to gain more policy traction. That example presents some deep challenges to conventional models of research, which see the research process as standing outside those of policy or social change. Citizens doing this work rejected this division and instead posed a model that blended action with evidence. Their more participative social science matched their moves towards a more participative society and citizen-led action. Residents were not simply asked for their opinion of what policymakers should decide, but were asked what contributions they could make themselves, which added to capacity for policy problem solving. This points the way towards new ways to blend action, research and social experimentation with social-scientific methods.

Moves towards a more participative society demand a more participative social science, but this may be easier said than done. These are not merely changes in technocratic processes; there are shifts in power associated with more co-productive policy approaches, of which citizen social science is one, which also need to be borne in mind (Durose and Richardson, 2016). Old values operating under conventional policy processes separate out different forms of expertise, privilege technocratic expertise and keep citizens at arm's length. New values of power operating under more co-productive policy processes actively draw in as many forms of expertise as possible to iterative, open, 'incomplete' processes, underpinned by wide participation generating extra problem-solving capacity. It may be that a fuller expansion of citizen social science will only occur alongside a shift to new values of power, supported by more co-productive policy processes.

Further reading
A detailed practical guide to designing participatory forms of policy research can be found in Richardson (2017). An accessible background text on participatory research is also Goodson and Phillimore's (2012) *Community research for participation: From theory to method.*

The following websites cover some of the best-known citizen science projects: http://www.turingsunflowers.com/results/; https://www.zooniverse.org/; http://www.audubon.org/about-us

These are examples of what could be considered citizen social science (see: http://kinseyreporter.org/; http://www.massobs.org.uk/) and 'extreme' citizen science (see: http://www.ucl.ac.uk/excites).

Examples and principles for novel co-productive approaches to policy and research can be found in Durose and Richardson's (2016) *Designing public policy for co-production: Theory, practice and change.*

For more information on citizen-led approaches, the following websites are relevant, including the 'listening' survey in the citizen-led vignette (see: http://rslm.org/what-is-rslm/) and community organising as one approach to citizen-led social change (see: http://www.corganisers.org.uk/; http://www.citizensuk.org/).

Notes

[1] See: http://www.turingsunflowers.com/results/

[2] See: https://www.zooniverse.org/

[3] See: http://www.audubon.org/about-us

[4] See: http://kinseyreporter.org/

[5] See: http://www.massobs.org.uk/

[6] See: http://opendatamanchester.org.uk/tag/hackathon/

[7] See: https://www.youtube.com/watch?v=JZcUEXJ0MhY

[8] See: http://www.participatorychinatown.org/

[9] See: https://www.denguetorpedo.com/

[10] See: http://www.ucl.ac.uk/excites

[11] See: http://www.whiterocktrust.org.uk/

[12] See: http://rslm.org/what-is-rslm/

[13] See: http://www.corganisers.org.uk/

TWELVE

Deliberative policy analysis

John S. Dryzek

Deliberative policy analysis prizes communication of a particular sort amid the disagreement that pervades public policy processes. What role, then, should deliberation play in the policy process? There are several possible answers to this question. These answers include seeing deliberation as:

1. a limited input into analysis of the relative merits of policy options;
2. a means of resolving conflicts across relevant actors and interests;
3. a form of public consultation;
4. a unique source of valuable inputs into policy processes; and
5. a comprehensive aspiration for whole systems of governance.

I will argue that the first four of these alternatives may have their merits, but also some substantial limitations. These limitations point to the necessity of the fifth alternative, which means that, in the end, deliberative policy analysis has to involve the thoroughgoing analysis, critique and reform of systems of governance. Deliberative inputs into intrinsically non-deliberative processes are of correspondingly limited utility.

Before discussing these five possibilities more systematically, I will say a bit about what deliberation involves, and how it is rooted in the broader idea of deliberative democracy.

Basics

Deliberative policy analysis can be located as part of the 'argumentative turn' in policy analysis (Fischer and Forester, 1993; Fischer and Gottweis, 2012). This turn treats public policy making as primarily a matter of communicative practice (as opposed to instrumental calculation or the aggregation and reconciliation of interests). Deliberative policy analysis has a particular set of standards that it can apply to the evaluation of communicative practices. While it is not the only such source of standards, this kind of analysis can draw on a well-developed body of work in deliberative democracy.

Deliberative democracy sees governance in terms of effective, inclusive and transformative communication encompassing citizens and policymakers. The core idea is that the legitimacy of collective decisions rests on the right, capacity and opportunity of those subject to or affected by a decision (or their representatives) to participate in consequential deliberation about the decision.

What, then, is deliberation? The origins of deliberative democracy owe something to philosophical schools of thought that emphasise reason-giving in pursuit of consensus. However, the field has long outgrown those roots in order to welcome forms of communication such as rhetoric, the telling of stories and humour. Yet, the welcoming of these forms has to be conditional. Deliberation cannot involve threat, manipulation, coercion or command. To count as deliberative, any communication must be non-coercive. In addition, it ought to be able to induce reflection. Crucially, reflection requires effective listening, so deliberation is not just about talk.

Any participant in deliberation should strive to do two things. The first is to justify any self-interest or partial interest in terms of more general values. Sometimes, this is easy (eg when a representative of a small island state in climate change negotiations argues for the material interests of his/her state not to be destroyed as a result of rising sea levels and more ferocious storms as a matter of justice). Sometimes, it is harder, as when those who seek personal material gain have to argue in terms of how it would benefit some larger values (such as economic growth or generalised income security). The second relevant aspiration is what Gutmann and Thompson (1996) call reciprocity, which effectively means trying to communicate in terms that those who do not share one's frame of reference (be it national, religious or ideological) can accept. So, for example, in deliberations on divisive issues such as abortion or euthanasia, it is not enough for a speaker simply to assert that his or her religion requires a position to be taken. Rather, the speaker must go on to explain exactly why that is the case, and, in so doing, to try to make more sense to those who do not share the religion in question.

In its early days, some deliberative democrats flirted with the idea of consensus as an aspiration for collective decision processes. However, that aspiration to consensus (itself a term that has several different meanings, not usually recognised) has, for the most part, been abandoned by deliberative democrats. Instead, the task of deliberation can be seen as clarifying disagreement, or the mutual recognition of positions that are not shared. Deliberation can then coexist with a number of other procedures for reaching collective decisions, including voting. While it may be the case that deliberation concludes with workable agreements to which all participants consent, that is not the same as consensus in the stronger sense of agreement on preference orderings. A workable agreement may not, in fact, embody the first preference of any of the individuals or actors involved.

For deliberation to be styled as democratic, it must be inclusive of those affected by a collective decision; it must also be inclusive in the more subtle sense of enabling all those who are formally involved to have an effective voice, and to be listened to. Deliberation should also be consequential in having an effect on the content of the relevant collective decision. Deliberative democracy does not neglect the exercise of power, but it imposes stringent tests to determine when that exercise is legitimate (Mansbridge et al, 2010: 80–3).

Where, then, might we seek deliberation? Possibilities include: the existing institutions of government, such as legislatures, courts and administrative processes; governance networks; the informal processes of civil society; and designed forums. Given that most of these locations are not especially deliberative when left to their own devices, proponents of deliberative policy analysis have devoted sustained attention to the design and adoption of forums that would be better when it comes to embodying deliberative virtues. I will now take a look at the different kinds of forums that can be deployed, though I will argue later that it is important to look at how forums play out in larger systems of governance, for it is the deliberative virtues of the latter that are ultimately the main concern. Inattention to this systemic aspect means that analysis can go astray.

Deliberative forums

Designed deliberative forums now come in many varieties. Historically, those involving partisans with a history of activism on an issue were most popular (Dryzek, 1987). From the 1970s onward, such partisan forums came under many titles, such as policy dialogues, regulatory negotiation, environmental mediation, consensus building and dispute resolution. Despite the different names, the common idea is to take partisans out of the normal context of their strategic interaction and into a more deliberative setting. This setting usually features a facilitator or mediator, there to help ensure that interaction proceeds along deliberative lines. This can involve a set of guidelines that participants agree to in advance, such as no ad hominem arguments, no deception, everyone getting a chance to speak and no withholding of information. Such forums involve an effort to reach mutually acceptable outcomes. These outcomes should be better than simple compromises between the initial positions of the parties because they can involve a measure of creativity in finding ways to meet the key interests of all sides. Partisan forums may be deliberative, but sometimes they are not defensibly democratic because they are not inclusive of some larger citizenry. The fear is that well-defined and well-funded interests will produce agreements that suit one another but may hurt a larger public (especially if the public indirectly pays for what is proposed in the agreement) (Lowi, 1999).

More recently, deliberative practitioners have paid more attention to non-partisan forums composed of lay citizens with no history of interest or activism on an issue. These are otherwise known as minipublics (Grönlund et al, 2014). Some minipublics involve relatively small numbers (around 15–20): citizens' juries and consensus conferences are the most popular models here. These two models are actually very similar. Both involve convening a forum for an extended period of time (which can, for example, be over several weekends), a facilitator who oversees the interaction, providing the citizen-participants with relevant information and enabling them to hear from advocates from different sides and experts on the issue in question. The citizen-participants then deliberate among themselves and write a report containing their recommendations (the report can also identify disagreements).

Other minipublics involve larger numbers of citizens. The largest are those associated with the 21st Century Town Meeting model developed by the (now-defunct) America*Speaks* Foundation, which could involve thousands of people gathered in a large venue, divided into smaller groups and connected using information technology, and concluding with voting on an issue. While the sheer number of participants made possible by this model can impress politicians, most relatively large minipublics are more careful to ensure that the participants are representative (in statistical or demographic terms) of some larger population. The self-selection of participants for 21st Century Town Meetings means that there will normally be a substantial proportion of activists, as well as ordinary citizens. Deliberative polls and citizens' assemblies, in contrast, generally have about 150 participants, which is enough to sustain claims of statistical representativeness. Usually, they use stratified random sampling to select participants. (Smaller forums, such as citizens' juries or consensus conferences, can start with random sampling too, and then select from within the random sample to ensure participants with a variety of social characteristics.) The 150 participants may meet in plenary sessions where they hear from and can question advocates and experts, but their deliberation will be done in the small groups into which they are divided. In deliberative polls, the citizen-participants all complete a questionnaire (individually) at the end of the process. The idea in citizens' assemblies is a bit different: to craft a recommendation. The most well-known such assembly remains the British Columbia Citizens' Assembly, convened to recommend a new electoral system for the province.

Hybrid models that combine partisans and non-partisans are relatively rare. The most important is the 100-member Irish Constitutional Convention held during 2012–14, which was composed of two thirds lay citizens and one third politicians. This Convention was responsible for recommending the referendum on same-sex marriage in Ireland, which passed in 2015. Other constitutional and policy changes were recommended to the government, some of which were adopted, while others were rejected.

There are, then, a number of models of designed forums that can be deployed in deliberative policy analysis. Just how and to what effect they get deployed depends on how the role of that sort of analysis is conceptualised. So, I will now return to the five images of deliberative policy analysis I listed at the outset, and examine each in order to figure how best to make use of deliberative forums, and how to think about the role of deliberation in governance.

Deliberative policy analysis as an input into conventional policy analysis techniques

Deliberative monetary valuation has been pioneered in environmental economics as an alternative to more conventional sorts of cost–benefit analysis. Conventional cost–benefit analysis uses a variety of techniques to attach monetary values to costs and benefits that are not traded in any market, and so have no market price. Contingent valuation is important among these. Contingent valuation asks individuals what they would be willing to pay to, say, preserve a natural area or to have a particular source of pollution removed, or how much compensation they would require should the area be removed or a source of pollution established. Contingent valuation has been criticised for its reliance on ill-formed and poorly considered preferences. The idea of deliberative monetary valuation is to yield more considered and socially defensible measures of willingness to pay (or to be compensated). Instead of simply responding to survey questions, a deliberating group of those potentially affected by a decision can reflect upon their individual preferences. The group would normally be constituted by ordinary citizens (rather than partisans and activists, whose expressed valuations could be strategic). These considered individual preferences can then be inputted into the cost–benefit analysis. However, it is important to note that the sum of individual reflective monetary preferences can be very different from a considered group judgement about the appropriate price to put on an asset (Spash, 2007), and different again from a group decision about what policy choice should be made.

Conventional deliberative monetary valuation still imposes on the deliberating group the idea that value always can and should be expressed in monetary terms. It does not allow the deliberators to consider whether or not a monetary metric is appropriate. As Sandel (2013) points out, some things should not be treated as though they are for sale – at any price. Sandel's examples include children, friendship, queue jumping and life insurance that enables a company to benefit from the death of an employee. It is equally plausible to put unique landscapes, human communities or cultural creations in the same category. Deliberative monetary valuation also stops its participants short of considering the broader question of 'What is to be done?', a choice that can be informed by, but never fully determined by, the ratio of (tangible) costs to benefits. For all these reasons, deliberative monetary valuation fits uneasily with the broader commitments of deliberative democracy.

Deliberative policy analysis as conflict resolution

There is a strong affinity between public deliberation and conflict resolution, especially when it comes to the forms of communication that both prize, an affinity that is now recognised by conflict resolution professionals (Susskind, 2006). Of course, not all conflicts have a public policy dimension – but some do. In this light, deliberative principles can be applied to policy processes that involve partisans, especially in the kinds of forums listed earlier. Policy-related conflict resolution is especially popular in the US, where the large number of veto points in the political system, and substantial opportunities to take policy disputes into the legal system, often mean that competing interests can fight each other to a standstill, with considerable expenditure of time, money and energy on all sides. The idea of deliberative conflict resolution is to move beyond this kind of impasse. So, for example, Innes and Booher (2003) show how paralysing partisan conflict in California water management featuring environmentalists, local governments, irrigators and developers could be resolved in a deliberative forum.

While often productive in such terms, it may also be the case that deliberative conflict resolution does not find easy reception in policy processes – as it does not always take into account the authority of governments with a mandate over a particular policy area, which may have interests of their own. Perhaps more fundamentally, conflict resolution conceives of policy issues in terms of competing partial interests – which can mean that more general values or truly public interests are either downplayed or treated as just one kind of interest among others that are more partial and private. In this light, conflict resolution and deliberative principles can stand in some tension (Aragaki, 2009).

Deliberative policy analysis as public consultation

The more common forms of public consultation involve public hearings or requests for comments on draft policy documents, which tend to attract predictable respondents (the 'usual suspects') and predictable arguments. Deliberative public consultation can seek to improve matters. Even when it comes to the usual suspects, partisan forums can induce them to articulate their concerns in a way that can reach, and respond to, the frames of reference of those who do not share their positions. Non-partisan forums, by definition, involve recruiting those who have no history of activism on an issue, and no prior position. Thus, if nothing else, they provide a fresh representation of public opinion on an issue – which is why they may be attractive to policymakers tired of hearing the same old arguments from the same old activists. If the conclusions are to their liking, policymakers may be able to deploy them against the usual suspects – though there is, of course, no guarantee that any particular conclusions will be produced.

Fishkin (2009: 98) goes so far as to say that his kind of minipublic, the deliberative poll, provides a representation of what public opinion would be if all citizens had the opportunity to deliberate under good conditions. Critics point out that these 'good conditions' are highly artificial, and that only a tiny fraction of the population could ever participate in such a forum. Thus, at best, a citizen forum provides only one picture of public opinion, other methods such as surveys, referenda, election results or petitions provide other pictures (Parkinson, 2006). Defenders of minipublics would argue here that these other methods provide representations of unreflective preferences; the key quality of minipublics is that they are reflective.

It is easy to conclude that deliberative forms of public consultation are generally likely to be a big improvement over non–deliberative forms of public consultation (with only slight hesitation caused by the larger numbers of people that the latter may involve). However, a public consultation framing may mean that the full potential of deliberative processes is missed. This will be the case if such exercises are placed early in the policy process and seen as inputs to more consequential arenas (such as legislatures). To see why, we might ask what exactly minipublics, in particular, are good *for* when it comes to public deliberation. The short answer is that deliberation involves both justification and reflection; minipublics are relatively poor when it comes to justification, but relatively good when it comes to respect, civility and responsiveness to counter-arguments – the ingredients of reflection (Pedrini, 2014). Justification involves the making of claims either in support of or against a course of action. Reflection involves listening to and considering the claims, and an openness to changing one's mind if persuaded. Processes involving partisans – especially legislatures – generally involve sophisticated justification; however, in many ways, they are ritualised performances as legislators do not listen and reflect (though they may be more likely to do so in relatively low-visibility parliamentary committees, rather than on the floor of Parliament). Just as, for individuals, it may be hard to obtain the virtues of justification and reflection in a single personality type (Jennstål and Niemeyer, 2014), so it may be hard to obtain the virtues of justification and reflection in a single forum type. The solution may be to distinguish explicitly between chambers of justification and chambers of reflection.

The paradigm here is a jury trial, where the courtroom itself is the chamber of justification as advocates make and support claims for each side and try to undermine the other side. Reflection takes place in a separate jury room, from which the advocates are, of course, excluded. This division of labour across forums has major implications for how deliberative forums are placed in the policy process. Putting them early in the process – and thinking of them as public consultation inputs into larger processes of justification and policy decision – is a bit like asking the jury to deliberate before they hear the arguments of the advocates. It means that their potential will not be realised, and may help explain why inputs into processes from deliberative forums so often get lost in the subsequent cacophony of justification. (Though there are other reasons: actors who do not like the recommendations of deliberative processes may seek to undermine the legitimacy of the process; governments may set up such processes with the aim of generating support for predetermined positions and quickly drop the process when it appears not to comply; and there may sometimes simply be no channel through which a deliberative process could conceivably influence policy.)

Deliberative policy analysis as a unique source of inputs

Conceptualising deliberative processes as nothing more than forms of public consultation may, then, either see forums in the wrong place in a sequence or simply compete with the variety of other inputs into policy processes. Occasionally, though, deliberative forums are given a more central role. This occurs most prominently in connection with referenda. Here, the idea is that a citizen forum will hear from advocates on different sides on an issue (as well as relevant experts), and then reach considered recommendations for the larger body of citizens voting in the referendum. These recommendations can be in the form of a report recommending a particular alternative, or they can be in the form of an assessment of the arguments on both sides of the referendum question (with no necessary recommendation).

The British Columbia Citizens' Assembly mentioned earlier constitutes a prominent example of a minipublic that reached a single explicit recommendation. The Assembly, composed of 150 lay citizens, took place over several months; its members eventually concluded that an electoral system based on a single transferrable vote was preferable to the existing simple plurality system ('first-past-the post') operating in the province at the time (for details, see Warren and Pearse, 2008). This recommendation was put to a binding referendum. While 57% of those voting voted in favour of the Citizens' Assembly proposal, the extraordinarily high threshold requirement of 60% imposed (at the outset of the process) by the British Columbia government meant that the single transferrable vote system was not adopted. Surveys showed that those voting in favour did so not because they understood the intricacies of the proposed new system, but because they trusted the fact that the Assembly was composed of ordinary people like themselves.

A somewhat different way to link citizen deliberation with binding referenda has been developed in the State of Oregon. Like many US states, Oregon has a citizen-initiated referendum process. A measure can get onto the ballot with enough signatures from registered voters. If the measure passes, it becomes law (unless it is ruled unconstitutional). This means that every two years, Oregon voters get to decide on a large number of measures, which can range from property tax limitation to whether or not a nuclear power plant should be closed. Money plays a large role in the process as it can finance both signature-gathering and media campaigns prior to the vote. Reflective preferences are less in evidence as voters are overwhelmed by so many measures to vote on.

The Oregon Citizens' Initiative Review process was instituted in 2009 to provide a deliberative input into the referendum process. Essentially, a citizens' jury convenes and concludes with a one-page report on the measure in question, which is then included in a pamphlet that is sent to every registered voter in the state. The report does say how many jurors ended up both supporting and opposing the measure in question, but, more importantly, it contains what the jurors believe to be the best arguments both for and against the measure – the ones that can survive deliberative scrutiny. So far, only a minority of the measures proposed each election year have been subjected to this process (eg concerning the legalisation for medical use of marijuana or mandatory sentencing for particular criminal offences). Survey evidence suggests that those who read the report in the pamphlet are influenced by it (Knobloch et al, 2013).

The Oregon Citizens' Initiative Review is not a form of public consultation. Rather, the idea is that a deliberative citizens' jury reflects upon the claims that have already been made in the campaigns for and against a particular measure, and these reflections are inserted into the sequence immediately prior to the moment of decision in the referendum itself. So, unlike most public consultation, it occurs at the correct place in the sequence of policy making.

Deliberative policy analysis as a governance aspiration

The lesson from the Oregon Citizens' Initiative Review is that putting a deliberative process in the proper place in a decision sequence means that there can be a good (reflective) effect; however, even there, the citizens' jury and its report struggle against a host of non-deliberative factors. For a start, most voters do not bother to read the pamphlet that is sent to them, and they may still be swayed by partisan campaigns rather than the jury's reflections.

The deliberative systems approach that now dominates the theory of deliberative democracy highlights the limits of relying on any particular forum to fully meet the requisite deliberative virtues, no matter where it is placed in a decision sequence (Parkinson and Mansbridge, 2012). One of the key insights of this approach is that we should not impose the entire burden of achieving deliberative virtues on a single forum, be it a parliament, a constitutional court, a stakeholder dialogue or a minipublic. Instead, we should be more concerned with the deliberative qualities of a system as a whole. My earlier suggestion that we might want to seek moments of justification and moments of reflection in different, yet linked, institutions is consistent with this systemic view. However, the deliberative systems approach has larger ambitions.

Any system can be defined as a set of differentiated, yet linked, components that together can be interpreted in the light of some common purpose. For a deliberative system, the common purpose involves the generation of political legitimacy (which, in turn, depends on the achievement of a number of democratic values) and an effective, ethically defensible decision. The precise components of a deliberative system can vary, but they might include: everyday talk among friends, neighbours and colleagues; social movement activity and political activism; public consultations; civil society forums; minipublics; legislatures; nodes in governance networks; constitutional courts; international negotiations; and international organisations. These components can be formal or informal. A well-functioning deliberative system features integration and good communication flows across different sites (Hendriks, 2006).

In this light, deliberative policy analysis can most profitably describe, analyse, evaluate and perhaps even inform the design of deliberative systems. If it does not do so, but focuses instead on deliberative forums in isolation from the context provided by a system, then it is falling far short of the aspirations of deliberative democracy, which is about governance in its entirety – not small components of governance.

To date, most statements about deliberative systems have a programmatic or illustrative quality; comprehensive empirical analyses of particular deliberative systems are relatively rare. An early example, though, can be found in Parkinson's (2006) study of health-care policy in the UK. Parkinson shows how petitions, citizens' forums, bureaucratic processes and legislative debate can all be seen as contributing bits of legitimacy to policy making, though, individually and collectively, they fall far short of deliberative ideals. Dodge (2009) looks at the deliberative system for environmental policy (with a focus provided by the practices activists use in different locations). J. Boswell (2013b) shows how narratives on obesity policy get transformed as they traverse a deliberative system – and get exploited by powerful interests, to the democratic detriment of the system. Stevenson and Dryzek (2014) conduct a comprehensive analysis of the global governance of climate change in deliberative system terms. They map the system in terms of public spaces and empowered spaces, as well as the interconnections between them. Their study reveals a deliberative system in considerable disrepair as, for example, communications beyond enclaves of like-minded civil society actors (ranging from corporations to climate justice activists) are limited, the voice of civil society does not get heard effectively in more formal decision processes and emerging forms of networked governance are dominated by single (moderate) discourses. Stevenson and Dryzek conclude with a set of suggestions for improving the qualities of this particular deliberative system. These proposals include: improving communication across enclaves by extending invitations to forums held by (respectively) moderate and radical actors; and constructing accountability chains linking civil society to the formal United Nations negotiations to emerging centres of networked governance (which otherwise elude deliberative scrutiny). They do not ignore the part that could be played by designed deliberative forums such as transnational minipublics, but they stress the importance of looking at the systemic qualities to which any such innovations would contribute.

It is one of the core propositions of the deliberative systems approach that intrinsically non-deliberative actions and practices can have positive deliberative consequences at the system level. Examples would include ridicule that induces reflection on the part of those on the receiving end, or social movement activism that gets previously ignored dimensions of an issue onto the political agenda. The corollary is that intrinsically deliberative actions and practices can have systemically non-deliberative consequences. So, if a deliberative forum is established by a government to give the impression that it is doing something or cares about public opinion on an issue, with no intention of using the results, then that may detract from the deliberative capacity of the system as a whole. The same might be said if activists are induced into a conflict resolution exercise or dialogue with opponents – which proves to sap their energies but have no impact on policy.

The frequency with which designed deliberative forums fall short when it comes to being consequential suggests that it is important to always remember the systemic level of analysis. This has profound implications for the content of deliberative policy analysis. In the end, deliberative policy analysis cannot be just a set of techniques and tools for the design of forums and their use in more conventional policy analysis, in public consultation or in conflict resolution. Rather, deliberative policy analysis should analyse systems of governance in deliberative terms. Only in this way can deliberative policy analysis remain true to the core commitments of deliberative democracy, and contribute to more effective, as well as more legitimate, policy making.

Further reading

Fischer and Gottweis's (2012) *The argumentative turn revisited: Public policy as communicative practice* updates the argumentative turn in policy analysis and provides the context for deliberative policy analysis.

Hajer and Wagenaar's (2003) *Deliberative policy analysis* contains a classic set of essays on the need for deliberative policy analysis.

THIRTEEN

Co-design with citizens and stakeholders

Mark Evans and Nina Terrey

What is the magic? That someone bothered to listen. That we were able to plan for our future and make decisions about what works for us.

(Family member, 'Strengthening Services for Families' project, in Evans, 2013)

New methodologies for facilitating meaningful citizen engagement have become increasingly important in a world in which many of the responses to the critical public policy problems we face need to be co-created with citizens and stakeholders. This chapter focuses on the growing academic and practice-based interest in *co-design* and assesses its contribution to social progress. It argues that co-design has an essential role to play in building trust with citizens and stakeholders, eliciting knowledge of policy and delivery problems that public organisations do not possess, and monitoring and supporting the needs and aspirations of target groups over time. However, the success of co-design is all in the doing. Done badly, it can destroy trust systems; done well, it can help solve policy and delivery problems, stabilise turbulent lives and improve life chances.

The chapter aims to provide an understanding of the emergence and development of the co-design approach and associated methods, the principles underpinning it, and the ingredients of better practice. It will draw on both academic and practice-based understandings. Both of the authors of this chapter have long-standing experience working on co-design interventions in both developed and developing contexts. Certain of these interventions will be used to illustrate both the strengths and the weaknesses of the approach.

What is co-design?

As Box 13.1 illustrates, there is nothing new about the use of design thinking in the public sector. For example, the Design Council, formerly the Council of Industrial Design, was established by Winston Churchill's wartime coalition government in 1944 in Britain 'to champion great design that improves lives and makes things better'.[1] However, what does appear to be new is the multidisciplinary nature of its recent development. Co-design is now a hybrid concept that draws on:

- product design thinking, where design professionals seek to empower and guide users to solve design problems and refine existing products or invent new ones (see Buchanan, 2001; Heskett, 2002; Brown, 2009; Martin, 2009; Verganti, 2009);

- assumptions about what works in combating social exclusion in social policy, for example, the establishment of strong trust systems between citizen and case worker, the personalisation of provision, and the simplification of service interaction (see Evans, 2012, 2013; Fabian Society, 2010);

- normative social science that focuses on identifying and removing barriers to citizen participation in society, the economy or politics through various processes of empowerment, for example: the literatures on community-driven development (Barakat et al, 2012), political participation (Stoker, 2006a) or deliberative democracy (Dryzek, 2000); citizen-centred thinking in *public value management*, which argues that public intervention should be circumscribed by the need to achieve positive social and economic outcomes for the citizenry, but that, crucially, what is and what is not public value should be determined collectively through inclusive deliberation (see Stoker, 2006b; Alford, 2009; Mulgan, 2009); and other citizen-centred approaches to public sector reform (see Preston, 2004; Osborne and Brown, 2005; Parker and Heapy, 2006); and

- the practice-based literature on innovation, which stresses processes of co-design, co-production and co-creation (see Mulgan and Albury, 2003; Mulgan, 2007; Bason et al, 2009; Brown, 2009; Design Council, 2009; Bason, 2010).

Box 13.1: Selective list of governmental and non-governmental organisations devoted to design and innovation (all websites last accessed 8 April 2016)

- Ash Center for Democratic Governance and Innovation, Harvard University (US) – http://ash.harvard.edu/
- Australian Centre for Social Innovation – http://tacsi.org.au/
- Big Innovation Centre (UK) – www.biginnovationcentre.com
- Design Council (established in 1944) (UK) – www.designcouncil.org.uk
- DesignGov – http://design.gov.au/about/
- Design for Europe – www.designforeurope.eu
- Design Managers Australia – designmanagers.com.au
- Digital Transformation Office (Australia) – https://www.dto.gov.au/
- Helsinki Design Lab – helsinkidesignlab.org
- Human Experience Lab, Singapore
- Office for Design and Architecture, South Australia – odasa.sa.gov.au/
- Involve (UK) – www.involve.org.uk
- La 27e Region (France) – www.la27eregion.fr
- Danish Agency for Science, Technology and Innovation (Denmark) – ufm.dk/en
- MindLab (Denmark) – mind-lab.dk/en/
- Social Innovation and Entrepreneurship Research Centre (New Zealand) – sierc.massey.ac.nz
- Project H Design (US) – www.projecthdesign.org/
- Public Policy Lab (US) – publicpolicylab.org/
- Thinkplace (Australia and New Zealand) – thinkplaceglobal.com/
- Cabinet Office Policy Lab (UK) – https://openpolicy.blog.gov.uk/category/policy-lab/
- United Nations Research Institute for Disarmament Research (UNIDIR) – www.unidir.org/
- United Nations Development Programme Development Unit, Knowledge and Innovation – www.undp.org/content/undp/en/home/.../development.../innovation.html

These approaches have two core insights in common: that late modernity requires active citizenship; and that citizens have unique insights and expertise to bring to collective problem solving. Here, we find a happy marriage with design thinking, where it is generally recognised that the quality of design improves the more user interests are integrated into the design process (Brown, 2009). These insights have therefore galvanised innovation in service design, policy programming and governance practices, together with the proliferation of governmental and non-governmental organisations devoted to its application (see Box 13.1).

Co-design is therefore a methodology of research and professional reflection that supports inclusive problem solving and seeks solutions that will work for people. It places the citizen or stakeholder at the centre of a planned process of learning that focuses on the achievement of very specific outcomes. For example, our work with vulnerable families aims to build the capacity of the family to stabilise, recover and reintegrate into the community (see Evans, 2013).

The co-design process

Co-design thinking, then, is about understanding the lives of others (Buchanan, 2001; Leadbeater, 2004). It draws on ways of working that are commonplace in the design of objects and products, and suggests that those ways of working could be applied to wider system and process design. Co-design tends to involve three stages of learning; all of which are iterative and require engagement and re-engagement between researchers, practitioners and citizens. These include: (1) discovery and insight; (2) prototyping; and (3) evaluating and scaling co-design interventions.

Discovery and insight

> One of the most significant developments of system thinking is the recognition that human beings can never see or experience a system, yet we know that our lives are strongly influenced by systems and environments of our own making and by those that nature provides. By definition, a system is the totality of all that is contained, has been contained, and may yet be contained within it. We can never see or experience this totality. We can only experience our personal pathway through a system. (Buchanan, 2001: 12)

The first stage of learning involves establishing a shared representation of concerns and problems with the target group; it draws on evidence that is synthesised and tested for its robustness, but it also generates a broad range of perspectives on an issue as seen by different citizens. This requires creating a learning environment that allows citizens to tell their own stories rather than making assumptions about their preferences. It is based on the observation that citizens never experience the delivery system as a whole, just pathways through the system. We therefore seek to understand the problem through the eyes of the user. It does not require big numbers, unlike a statistically significant survey, but it does require spending quality time with a small number of participants, mapping their journeys, identifying obstacles and developing mitigating strategies.

This stage is about creating a space where participants can imagine and progress towards a future rather than becoming trapped in past models or ways of thinking. It uses a creative design dynamic to encourage new ways of thinking based on good practices. Some of the techniques that can be used include getting practitioners to experience the world from the perspective of others, getting citizens to draw or capture in non-written form their perceptions of a better future, and generally trying to encourage a freeing from past certainties and developing a space where creativity and learning, and taking risks, is encouraged. Beyond these process elements, this stage also involves a large-scale search for alternatives, options and innovations that appear to address the issue in focus.

Various methods and tools can be deployed to aid the process of discovery at this stage of learning. As Table 13.1 illustrates, this can include action learning, network and journey mapping tools, and reflexive practice. These learning methods are used to improve the quality of information about the citizen or stakeholder experience of the problem under study. This enables designers to build an evidence base on what does or does not work from the perspective of citizens and stakeholders.

Prototyping

The second phase of learning focuses on developing prototype interventions based on a joint commitment with key partners and developing appropriate rapid feedback research methods to support that dynamic. Here, the logic is of a design experiment (for a broader discussion, see Chapter Four of this book by Peter John). The experiment focuses on the design of an intervention as the core research problem. The techniques used at this stage will be contingent on the amount of time available to the project team. For example, the ideal-type experiment would allow for sufficient time to observe and manipulate the intervention over a period, usually in one location, until acceptable results emerge. The experiment would progress through a series of design–redesign cycles. There is feedback to the core participants, so as the intervention unfolds, the design adjusts to work in a particular context. Initially, the goal is success in a local

Table 13.1: Learning tools for co-design

Methods and tools	Purpose
Action learning	Recognises that solutions to problems can only be developed inside the context in which problems arise • *See connections between issues and events* • *Create a safe learning environment* • *Focus on the whole rather than the parts* • *Seek a holistic solution to the problem*
Network mapping	Observes that most interventions are delivered through network arrangements • *What actors/resources are critical to the delivery of progressive outcomes?* • *Who is not there?* • *Which actors/resources should be closer in or further away from problem solving* • *What does progress look like?* • *What are the key barriers to progress?*
Journey mapping	Understanding citizen/stakeholder journeys, challenges and aspirations • *What does the journey tell us about their story?* • *What has been the focus and what is missing?* • *What do you see as the barriers, risks and opportunities?*
Reflexive practice	Co-designing a plan to navigate the barriers: • *What changes are possible, desirable and sustainable?* • *Why are these changes relevant?* • *How can these changes be made?*

and particular setting, and that challenge is the focus of attention. The design experiment claims to provide an evidence base about 'what works' in the early stages of the development of an intervention; in addition, it may provide a staging post for a broader and more generalisable test in the future.

Evaluation and scaling

The third stage then reverts to a more traditional evaluation phase, where collaborative options analysis takes place on the basis of assessing pilot interventions through the use of randomised controlled trials or other robust forms of evaluation (see Figure 13.1).

In summary, then, with technical support, the group of citizens or stakeholders: scope and define the problem and identify the change objective to be produced; review the range of options to produce the change objective; choose the option to be pursued; design a prototype; and pilot, monitor, evaluate and refine. Figure 13.2 provides a graphic representation of how the learning process can be conceptualised. It

Figure 13.1: A classic randomised controlled trial

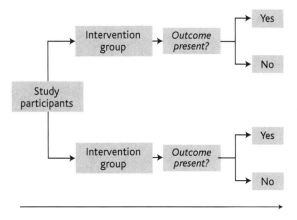

Figure 13.2: Learning through doing

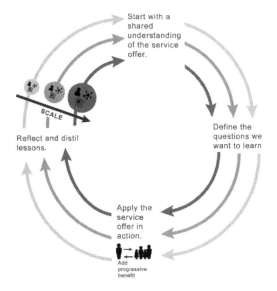

is important to note, however, that co-design is very much a process of 'muddling through the mess' as one stakeholder once put it to us. Craft rather than science; learning through doing.

Where can co-design make a real difference?

Various taxonomies have been devised in both academic and practice-based scholarship to match different engagement methods to different engagement purposes. These include Arnstein's (1969: 217) Eight Rungs on a ladder of citizen participation, developed in 1969, or the more recent spectrum of levels of participation developed by the International Association for Public Participation (IAP2) (see Figure 13.3), which better reflects the different purposes of participation.

Some practitioners do not see participation as having anything to do with politics or democracy, but see it simply as a more efficient and effective way of developing and implementing projects and programmes. Others see the entire process as fundamentally political, affecting the ways in which people have or take power in relation to the decisions that affect them, and changing the role of those affected from being 'targets' of policy change to joint designers of that change. Participation exercises can usually satisfy both, but the differences can affect the types of methods chosen. While such a taxonomy may be

Figure 13.3: The International Association for Public Participation spectrum of participation

Inform
Public participation goal: *To provide the public with balanced and objective information to assist them in understanding the problem, alternatives, opportunities and/or solutions*

Consult
Public participation goal: *To obtain public feedback on analysis, alternatives and/or decisions*

Involve
Public participation goal: *To work directly with the public throughout the process to ensure that public concerns and aspirations are consistently understood and considered*

Collaborate
Public participation goal: *To partner with the public in each aspect of the decision, including the development of alternatives and the identification of the preferred solution*

Empower
Public participation goal: *To place final decision-making in the hands of the public*

Source: https://www.iap2.org.au/resources/public-participation-spectrum

250

useful for determining what form of engagement may be necessary in different circumstances, policymakers also require a heuristic device to enable them to identify where co-design can be useful at different decision points in the policy process. Figure 13.4 provides a starting point to this discussion with reference to co-design.

Here, we understand good policy making as a process of learning that involves the absorption of target groups of citizens or stakeholders into different decision points in the policy process. It is noteworthy that decision points 1 (strategic direction), 2 (policy design), 3 (delivery) and 4 (learning) will inevitably involve greater decision-making competency for citizens and stakeholders than is traditionally the case if a co-design approach is used.

Figure 13.4: Learning and co-design

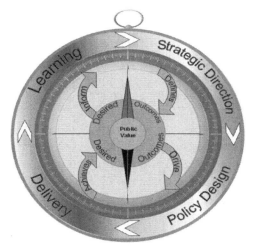

Case studies in co-design

This section provides some illustrative case studies of co-design in action at the three most prominent decision points where co-design is used by practitioners.

Co-design of delivery systems – 'Improving Services with Families'

> "This model implies that we are going to have to change some things to enable people to work in a different way." (Steering Group member)

'Improving Services with Families' (ISF) was a pilot project co-designed by the Community Services Directorate (CSD) in the Australian Capital Territory (ACT), ThinkPlace (a Canberra-based design consultancy) and a group of families experiencing multiple forms of exclusion. The project proceeded from the observation that a group of families in the ACT was experiencing a perpetual cycle of disadvantage. The policy issue at stake here was to improve outcomes for families that could not, or chose not, to access the support they required to meet their full range of needs. The CSD accepted that traditional service delivery methods did not support these citizens particularly well, and over recent years, looked to engage with new, innovative methods. As the Director of CSD put it: "[I] n this policy vacuum, a 'co-design' methodology with service users based on an action learning approach was more likely to be effective than a traditional policy making process". Design thinking provided an innovative methodology for building bridges between citizens experiencing multiple exclusions and their community.

ISF was an innovative project in at least six ways: (1) it was a place-based programme (via the family and public housing); (2) families were provided with personalised support through the provision of a lead worker who acted as a facilitating partner for the family; (3) it provided a choice of services for the family to access but they determined which services would work for them; (4) it used a communitarian approach – the family had rights but they also had an obligation to manage their own recovery processes; (5) the programme was delivered through a collaborative system of governance broadly representative of the community of practice for supporting families at risk in the ACT; and (6) the programme sought to build more detailed and sensitive family information profiles that could be shared by families, lead workers and appropriate agencies system-wide to both improve the quality of information and reduce the administrative burden.

Evaluation findings demonstrate that the fundamental benefit of the project to most project partners lay in the process of lesson-drawing across the partnership on the strengths and weaknesses of place-based service delivery using the lead worker model – learning through doing and professional reflection. ISF can be understood as a process of learning in which the means (place-based service delivery through the lead worker model) to an end (better well-being outcomes for vulnerable families) were subject to careful deliberation by informed and reflexive practitioners. In addition to the process of inter-organisational learning across the community of practice, the project also benefited from a common understanding of the problem, resource and information sharing, and the news skills that were transferred through the design process itself by ThinkPlace.

The ISF project also attracted high levels of participant satisfaction, with all participants getting what they wanted from the project; a remarkable outcome for this form of programming. The overall level of satisfaction that participants experienced with the project paints a strikingly different picture to that presented by participants prior to the intervention. The most frequently cited reasons for this reversal of fortunes are the role of the lead worker and the quality of the trusting relationships that they built with their families, the quality of mentoring and advocacy, and their role in facilitating access to particular services.

In terms of the process of project learning, the work of ThinkPlace was very well received in all respects – the efficacy of the tools and the outcomes achieved from their implementation, and the respectful and compassionate approach that ThinkPlace adopted in their interactions with participants. It is noteworthy that individual participants found the journey-mapping process emotionally difficult at times but ultimately rewarding. However, it is equally noteworthy that the children found the journey-mapping experience invaluable in helping them work through certain emotional problems.

Crucially, the ISF project provided a strong foundation to future community of practice initiatives in the ACT to combat various aspects of social exclusion regardless of the target group. In consequence of the successful pilot, the ACT government used co-design methods to establish a Human Services Blueprint – an innovative systems approach for social policy delivery in Canberra.

Co-design for community development – the case of Afghanistan's National Solidarity Programme

The Islamic Republic of Afghanistan's National Solidarity Programme (NSP) was created in 2003 by Dr Ashraf Ghani (the current President of Afghanistan) and Hanif Atmar (former Minister of Rural Rehabilitation and Development), and financed by a consortium of international donors coordinated by the World Bank. It was designed to reduce poverty by empowering communities through improved governance, as well as social, human and economic capital. The establishment of directly elected Community Development Councils (CDCs) lies at the heart of this strategy; putting communities in charge of their own development and providing them with technical support and resources to deliver co-designed projects that matter to them. The NSP adopts a community-driven development approach underpinned by co-design methods. The programme attempts to target the needs of rural communities by employing community-driven development, delivered through a collaborative partnership, encompassing central government, local and international non-governmental organisations (NGOs), and the communities – represented by purpose-built CDCs. Today, the NSP forms the central component of an architecture of national programmes managed by the Ministry of Rural Rehabilitation and Development (MRRD), designed both to help the Afghan people to rebuild their lives and nation, and to demonstrate that the Afghan government, with technical assistance, could develop the inclusive governance structures required to sustain a stable state.

As described in the founding document of the NSP, the goal of the programme is to reduce poverty through empowering communities to pursue two main objectives: (1) to lay the foundations for a strengthening of community-level governance; and (2) to support community-managed sub-projects comprising reconstruction and development that improve the access of rural communities to social and productive infrastructure and services. The implementation strategy of the NSP consists of four core elements: (1) facilitation at the community level to assist communities to establish inclusive community institutions (CDCs) through elections, reaching consensus on priorities and corresponding sub-project activities, co-designing sub-proposals that comply with NSP appraisal criteria, and implementing approved sub-projects; (2) a system of direct block grant transfers to support rehabilitation and development activities (sub-projects) planned and implemented by the elected CDCs; (3) a series of co-designed capacity-building activities to enhance the competence of members of CDCs (both men and women) in terms of financial management, procurement, technical skills and transparency; and (4) activities linking local institutions to government administration and aid agencies with available services and resources. The MRRD recognises that the quality of the implementation process of the NSP is essential for the long-term sustainability of community investments and for the overall success of the programme. As such, at the community level, the identification of priorities and the planning of sub-projects are based on principles of: co-design, participatory planning through inclusive community meetings and representative elected development councils; community contributions to capital costs and operation and maintenance; and project transparency and accountability to the community.

To help the MRRD achieve its targets, an Oversight Consultant (GTZ/IS) was contracted to oversee the overall management and supervision of the NSP. In addition, the MRRD contracted 22 NGOs (both national and international) and UNHABITAT to co-design and facilitate the delivery of the NSP in selected districts across all the provinces of Afghanistan. These NGOs are termed facilitating partners (FPs), and their role is to facilitate community participation in the planning, implementation and management of sub-projects financed by the NSP block grants and to ensure that these projects are genuinely co-designed with the community.

Evaluation data suggest that the NSP has been a great success. Although the NSP has struggled in meeting its economic recovery objective at the community level, its impact on community governance has been far-reaching. First, it has (re)built community governance by encouraging more accountable and inclusive forms of decision-making and representation through genuine processes of co-design with FPs. Second, it has enhanced the role of the government in planning and delivering recovery and development and strengthened capacities among some of the main ministries and their line departments. Third, it has led to increased dialogue between informal and formal institutions, thereby building the legitimacy of the fledgling state. As a fourth impact, in attempting to fill some of the critical gaps in the state structure at the sub-national level, the NSP has directly and indirectly created new coordinating bodies and has thus played a crucial role in joining up state infrastructure and changing attitudes (for further details, see Barakat et al, 2006).

Since its inception in September 2003, the programme has reached 22,500 rural communities, accounting for 10.5 million people – half Afghanistan's population – in 175 out of 364 rural districts across all 34 provinces in Afghanistan. Contrary to recent media reports, the evaluation identifies significant evidence of increased public faith in the system of government, improved community relations and the empowerment of CDCs. Fully 86% thought that it had brought greater unity and national solidarity, and 77% considered the government to be interested in their community, compared to 26% of those not involved in the NSP. As one respondent put it: "the NSP unites communities, bringing us together to solve our problems and plan for our future; for the first time, the government has shown that it cares about us, so we must now show our loyalty to our government".

Co-design for strategic learning – the case of the Australian Capital Territory government's 'Out of Home Care' system

In 2014, there was a growing awareness that the ACT's 'Out of Home Care' framework was not flexible either to the complex needs of children and young people in the care system, or to the increased demand for services. In particular, the inflexibility of the existing service model meant that the needs of children and young people in care, birth families and carers were not always met in a consistent and timely manner. Moreover, there was little evidence that the experience of service users was being utilised in policy development. 'Experiencing Care in the ACT' was designed to bridge the gap and inform the development of a five-year 'Out of Home Care' strategy. The project used a co-design approach to understand the experience of out of home care for service users. The project engaged citizens and stakeholders from all parts of the system, including indigenous and other culturally diverse users, service providers, and members of the Community Services Directorate, to understand how the broader out of home care service is experienced by users. ThinkPlace was commissioned to develop a research approach for listening to the experiences of birth families, young people who have been in out of home care, kinship carers and foster carers. The listening informed insights that have led to recommendations with implications for changes to policy, administration and organisational culture. Research questions were generated by a core design team in order to get an understanding of participants' experiences and to optimise the opportunity to generate rich narratives and journey maps. Some overarching themes that ThinkPlace sought to understand included: the user journey through care; what they understood about what was happening to them; how they felt; insights into whether they received the support they needed/wanted; their sense of belonging (particularly for young people); the identification of important relationships; and issues of self-agency (barriers and triggers).

The research interviews were conducted by ThinkPlace. The format of the interview was exploratory. A conversation was framed with clear boundaries and some pre-prepared questions. Within these parameters, the interview was allowed to unfold as an organic conversation. To a certain degree, the interviewer allowed the participant to lead the direction of the conversation, which meant that they were able to talk about what was most important to them. The interviews were audio-recorded and extensive notes were taken. The narratives have subsequently been rewritten, with names changed and identifying details omitted to protect the privacy of participants. The core design team collaborated in the analysis and synthesis of the narratives. From each narrative, macro-pathways were produced that represented the complex journeys experienced by each segment. The maps are divided into the phases of precare, entering care, ongoing care and leaving care, and represent the possible pathways that individuals and families can take through the care system. Detailed pathway maps were also created to describe the experience of one person's or family's story from each segment. Having analysed and compared all the narratives, the core design team summarised the needs and challenges for each group and synthesised these into four key insight areas. From these insight areas, the core design team developed 15 recommendations that have transformed the delivery of 'Out of Home Care' in the ACT.

Principles and conditions for co-design

Our case studies emphasise the importance of seven principles of co-design in action. First, it is important for the design process to have a clear policy intent – why is there a need for this policy, project or programme? What are the expected outcomes? What form of public value creation is intended? Co-design processes should be intentional and action-oriented.

Second, depending on the objective of learning, citizens and stakeholders should be placed at the centre of the process of learning and co-creation. It is therefore critical to select participants who have experience of the policy intent. This begs the question: who can provide insight into the lived everyday experience of the policy system? Whose voices have not been heard, first-hand? Who can offer perspectives that could transform existing paradigms and assumptions?

Third, co-design requires particular skills of observation, negotiation and empathy that are often in short supply in many public sectors. This raises a range of issues regarding capability and expertise to solve problems. What is the current experience like? What works? What is broken? What are the desires of the end users? What are the opportunities to design a change that meets the policy intent?

Fourth, there is often a need to adopt a multidisciplinary approach to the process of discovery that is often at odds with traditional ways of making policy through the usual suspects. How can decision-makers, front-line staff, key stakeholders and end users build a shared understanding of issues, opportunities and solutions at every stage?

Fifth, it is also important to rapidly prototype solutions, with end users engaging with creative questions, such as: what might the idea look like? How can the idea be physically created to 'play', to experiment? How many ways can the solution work? How can the concept be quickly tested, explored with end users, refined and redesigned?

Sixth, it is also fundamental to curate the knowledge created from each stage of learning, both in terms of establishing institutional memory and in terms of engaging in subsequent professional reflection and communication with potential funders. How can the story be told? What is the compelling narrative that will influence decision-makers? What are the critical success factors for delivering on the policy intent?

Finally, it is important to balance the desirable, the possible and the viable – how can we resolve the policy issue by addressing end user needs and make it work for government and others? How can the solution be financially viable and sustainable? How can we ensure the legitimacy of the intervention?

It is also evident that co-design appears to work best under certain starting conditions: where the policy setting is very complex and understanding the best policy option is unclear; where significant behavioural change is required from the target population; and where existing delivery systems simply do not work and an innovative or transformative solution is required. Moreover, acceptance of these starting conditions by policymakers leads to the recognition that business as usual will not work and innovative learning methods need to be deployed to address the problem. By implication, permission is required from policymakers to invest time in the inception of co-design projects, engage meaningfully with end users, address power imbalances in decision-making and suspend dominant problem-solving paradigms that are linear, logic-driven and past data-driven in order to be more exploratory and open to discovery.

Conclusion – capturing the political and bureaucratic imagination

The value of co-design to policymakers can be significant. It leads to sharper problem definition because of the inclusive character of policy formulation. It allows for the generation of evidence-based understanding of existing practice. Through action-learning approaches, this can lead to the generation of real-time data that can be integrated directly into decision processes. Co-design can identify multiple solutions to delivery problems that can be adapted into tailored interventions. These interventions tend to be afforded greater legitimacy because the end users have been involved throughout the process of policy development. In sum, co-design is an important approach for public policy because it allows for three important actions: the reframing of a complex policy setting; structured policy experimentation that generates rich evidence; and the sharing of the risks of policy failure with citizens and stakeholders. Through engaging end users early on, implementation issues can be integrated into policy design and help mitigate problems before they emerge. Co-design is a practical and applied approach which means that low residual prototypes can help both end users and policymakers see what will and will not work. For example, the Australian Commonwealth Government's Department of Human Services, responsible for making payments to unemployed people, conducted a co-design project with long-term unemployed young people and explored how an online service could replace the need for them to visit counters every week. In principal, the policy of shifting services online was right, and the department had developed a very basic interface. The co-design project involved working with young unemployed people to find out what online experiences worked best for them. The young people were given the opportunity to design their own interface based on what were understood as the critical functions and actions that they needed to demonstrate – such as keeping appointments to seek work, completing reports on interviews attended and tracking their payments (from multiple government agencies) and other household expenses, such as rent and other costs. The paper prototypes they generated were then compared with the departmental prototypes and it was discovered that the department had missed the core user requirement (to demonstrate self-management) and so they needed a more calendar- and notes-based approach, compared to lists of payments and other static information. This co-design work was integrated quickly into the department's online approach, saving them from a possible delivery failure and associated costs.

As noted at the outset, however, the success of co-design is all in the doing; hence, there is significant reliance on specific forms of capability in the method that are not always in plentiful supply in public bureaucracies. This includes a range of soft governance capabilities such as communication, facilitation, negotiation and adaptive capacity that tend to crystallise around qualities such as emotional intelligence and the ability to empathise and build trusting relationships. At the same time, there is a need for expertise in a range of innovative qualitative methods that emanate from both policy science and social psychology. Of course, this capability gap also provides the potential for partnership building with knowledge institutions (public and private) that possess the requisite skills.

Fundamentally, the key stumbling block to implementing co-design in practice lies not in the availability of underpinning capabilities, but in gaining the support of politicians and senior bureaucrats. Co-design challenges the established ways in which policy is made and services are delivered, monitored and evaluated. Most significantly, it questions dominant public sector cultures and values. Hence, the starting condition for co-design is a risk appetite in a context where short-term imperative is privileged over long-term developmental change.

Nonetheless, in our view, co-design can radically improve the quality of policy making and operational delivery. It can contribute to creating more active citizens, help manage complex problems in public service design and delivery, build new relationships and knowledge required for 21st-century governance, and develop individual skills, confidence and ambition. For these and other reasons, co-design has become an essential method for enhancing the quality of public policy making and delivery. The latest interventions to support vulnerable citizens have captured the political imagination because they are achieving better outcomes at a significantly lower cost (see Fabian Society, 2010; Evans, 2012, 2013), and they are seizing the bureaucratic imagination because they compel service providers to work beyond their traditional boundaries, join up through a systems approach and share skills, resources and risk. However, co-design does require strong political support, the appetite to try something new and the capacity to share power. Nonetheless, this is the stuff of effective future governance that places the citizen at the centre of a co-created process of policy learning.

Further reading
See the work of Richard Buchanan (1992, 2001) for the foundational thinking of much recent debate on the application of design to both the social sciences in general and public policy problems in particular. On the application of design thinking to service design, see Charles Leadbeater's (2003, 2004) work on personalisation through participation; for other public sector applications, see Richard Boland and Fred Collopy (2004). The Share, Engage and Educate (SEE) project's work on the evaluation of design is useful for analytical purposes.[2] On the relationship between design thinking and innovation, see Christian Bason (2010) and Geoff Mulgan (2009); on the management of innovation, see Stephen Osborne and Kerry Brown (2005). Finally, for leading applied thinking in public sector design, visit the Design Council (available at: www.designcouncil. org.uk), the Policy Lab (available at: https://openpolicy.blog.gov.uk/category/policy-lab/), MindLab (available at: http://mind-lab.dk/en/) and ThinkPlace (available at: http://www.thinkplaceglobal.com/).

Notes

1 See: www.designcouncil.org.uk

2 See: https://theseeproject.org/

Conclusion:
Connecting social science and policy

Gerry Stoker and Mark Evans

The primary purpose of this book has been to showcase a wide range of social science methods and how they could make a contribution to policy making. However, throughout the book, we have indicated that the connection between good evidence and policy making is far from automatic. In this concluding chapter, we return to the issues of how to connect social science and policy making.

Revisiting the barriers

There are four key barriers to bridging social science and policy (see Edwards, 2004, 2010; Lomas, 2005, 2007; Evans, 2007) that stand in the way of building meaningful knowledge networks between government and universities:

1. disconnection, mistrust and poor understanding between the worlds of ideas/research and action/practice;
2. a static view of academic research as a product, and system decision-making as an event, versus a dynamic view of both as social processes that need to be linked in ongoing exchange;
3. few skills or incentives in universities to do applied research; and
4. few skills or incentives in the system to use research.

Crucially, we see the problem as lying both with government and universities. For many decades now, there has been much discussion about how to obtain a better match between the kinds of research that governments want (*the demand side*) and the kinds of research that researchers undertake (*the supply side*). Indeed, there appears to be a significant disconnect between the two.

Peter Shergold (former Secretary of the Commonwealth Department of Prime Minister and Cabinet in Australia), in launching an Academy of Social Sciences book on *Ideas and influence* (Saunders and Walter, 2005), referred to the 'fragility of relationships' between public policy and the social sciences. He saw '[t]he relationships between social science and public policy, and between academic and public servant, are ones of the utmost importance', but he went on to say that 'They are not, I think, in particularly good shape' (cited in Saunders and Walter, 2005: 2). He elaborated little but could have gone on to mention, as others have, that academic research often deals with issues that are not central to policy and management debates, and can fail to take the reality of people's lives into account in setting research questions. Conversely, when research tries to be relevant, it can be seen as being driven by ideology dressed up as intellectual inquiry. Moreover, a frequent complaint is the lack of timeliness in academic research. Such are the frustrations of many policymakers (Edwards, 2010: 55).

The perspective of academic researchers has been well put by Saunders and Walter in the introduction to their book *Ideas and influence* (2005: 13): the lack of attention by policy practitioners to the subtleties and qualifications of their research findings and a fear that 'those driving policy are seeking to justify actions already decided by "cherry-picking" from among the available evidence with little regard for the robustness or validity of the material selected' (Saunders and Walter, 2005: 3). They go on to point out that 'those involved in policy development often have little idea of how or where existing research can contribute, or what is needed to help resolve outstanding issues' (Saunders and Walter, 2005: 13). To this observation could be added: an anti-intellectual approach sometimes formed within governments; a risk-averse attitude by public servants to findings that could embarrass the minister; the short time frames under which governments operate; and a lack of both respect for the independence of researchers and of incentives needed for researchers to produce policy-relevant material. In addition, of course, not all research is undertaken in order to influence policy, and when it does, this tends to be through what Carol Weiss (1982) has called 'the enlightenment effect'. Research may be used simply to raise awareness, though it may start to shape policy thinking through ideas, theories and concepts (Nutley et al, 2007: 2).

How to get to a better relationship

While few would disagree that there is a profound problem with the research–policy nexus, the complex nature of the relationship complicates the development of practical next steps. Moreover, what would the perfect evidence-based policy system look like when you have got it? We put this question to a workshop comprised of executive members of the Australian and New Zealand bureaucracies, and the findings are compelling (see Box 14.1). We have placed in *italics* those areas where social science researchers could contribute: postgraduate education on methods that matter for informing evidence-based policy making (one of the purposes of this book); research on long-term issues of national significance; research that monitors the field of action; research methods that support experimentation; collaborative forums to debate what the evidence tells us about what works; effective integration of policy and evidence through strategic partnerships; and enhancing the quality of collaboration through the creation of demand- and supply-side incentives to engage in knowledge networks between government and universities.

> ## Box 14.1: What would the perfect evidence-based policy system look like when you have got it?
>
> 1. *Where policy advisors have the capacity to act and the competences to understand the choices available to them.*
> 2. *A policy system that works beyond the electoral cycle and focuses on long-term issues of national significance.*
> 3. A system that utilises existing capacity.
> 4. *A system that is proactive to changes in the field of action.*
> 5. *Where there is room for experimentation.*
> 6. Where innovation is incentivised.
> 7. Where the capacity to speak truth to power exists.
> 8. Where there are clear accountabilities.
> 9. *Where policy and evidence are effectively integrated.*
> 10. Where information systems allow for the effective flow of information from the front line.
> 11. *Where evidence is freely debated and shared.*
> 12. *Where better practice is shared.*
> 13. *Where there is access to evidence and, by implication, strong productive working relationships with knowledge institutions.*
> 14. Where there is effective use of innovation intermediaries.
> 15. *Where there are demand- and supply-side incentives to engage in evidence-based policy making.*

Evidence and politics as reinforcing features of contemporary policy making

The first intervention is a cultural one that requires a shift in mindset. There is a tendency for many researchers to view politics as the enemy of evidence rather than as an integral tool for building efficient, effective and legitimate public policy. Politics demands that researchers demonstrate the public value of their findings. Researchers need to realise that they constitute one of many sources of policy advice at the behest of a policymaker, and given that policy is made in a contested arena, they need to understand that they are engaged in a war of ideas. This observation emphasises the importance of universities in general, and researchers in particular, developing the advocacy and brokering skills necessary for evidence to have impact.

Methods that matter for the policy profession

Governments need to ensure that their policy profession has the capability to use, commission or partner with knowledge institutions that deploy cutting-edge research methods to underpin evidence-informed policy making. The co-design of policy competences and policy science programmes would go some way towards achieving this aim and fostering trust systems between government and academia. Here, the Cameron government in the UK has introduced progressive change with the launch of the Policy Profession in 2013. Each central government department now has a head of policy who sits on a whole-of-government policy board headed by a senior permanent secretary. The purpose of the board is to identify 150 Whitehall policy professionals, and develop and foster a culture of high-quality advice delivered through enhanced strategic policy capability. A Masters of Public Policy has been co-designed with the London School of Economics to deliver on this purpose. It will be interesting to monitor its progress and evaluate whether it works or not!

Joining up research with decision-making

A tailored approach that is sensitive to the context for each policy problem is likely to be required if research is to be effectively harnessed; each issue may require different types of research output or engagement, depending on the stage in the development of policy. By implication, the research needed could be descriptive, analytical, diagnostic, theoretical or prescriptive (Solesbury, 2002: 94). In this context, there is one relatively recent and important insight that promises to bridge the perceived cultural gap between government decision-makers and researchers. A relatively recent synthesis of evidence shows that the traditional linear relationship between the separate processes of research and policy formulation is being seen as generally inferior to an interactive and ongoing relationship between policymakers and researchers covering both the production and take-up of knowledge. That is, research stands to be more effective when it is part of the decision-making process rather than a stand-alone activity (see Nutley et al, 2007; Waddell et al, 2007; Edwards, 2010), and engaging with researchers at an early stage in the research process 'is a key factor in helping to ensure that the research findings are subsequently taken up and exploited' (British Academy, 2008: 44).

Alongside this understanding has come greater emphasis by governments on tackling problems that traverse disciplines – requiring coordinated effort across government agencies – for example, ageing, climate change, social exclusion, terrorism and security. Moreover, many governments over the last decade have placed greater emphasis on the need for more 'evidence-based' or, more realistically, 'evidence-informed' policy making to help solve what appear to be increasingly complex public policy problems. What follows are a range of demand-side interventions through which academic researchers could enhance the strategic policy capability of public organisations.

Interactions throughout the policy process – the popularity of roundtables

Recent interviews with senior officials across Australasian jurisdictions pointed to a strong demand for facilitative or interactive research-related mechanisms that would assist practitioners address their current policy and management challenges. By far the most commonly favoured mechanism mentioned by senior officials was for knowledge institutions to facilitate roundtables or workshops involving both public servants and expert academics. This was especially so for emerging and 'wicked' issues, and also wherever there was an interest in practices in other jurisdictions and an interest in the 'how-to' questions, for example, jurisdictional comparisons of certain aspects of service delivery.

In this context, a recent UK Council for Science and Technology (CST) report on 'How academics and government can work together' addressed the ignorance of the benefits that interaction can deliver, and concluded that:

> A key problem appears to be the commissioning of academic work without academic input, meaning there is less understanding of the research, how to ask the right questions or how the response can be challenged and used. This can be especially important when addressing the big, cross-departmental questions where academics can have a vital role. (CST, 2008: 9)

There are essentially two broad roles that academics can play to assist in the policy process: by 'challenging, re-conceptualising and generally thinking innovatively about practitioner agendas'; and 'the more traditional role of the "expert" offering advice on how to do things' (Pollitt, 2006: 261). Some of the Westminster systems' most innovative policies have arisen from ideas and other input from academics (eg the Child Support Scheme, Family Tax Credit, Hardest to Reach programmes, Higher Education Contribution Scheme, Social Impact Bonds, etc).

The use of 'innovation intermediaries' and secondments

Senior officials who we interviewed about the potential research role of knowledge institutions also expressed considerable interest in using some form of 'knowledge broker' model to link the academic and government sectors. Four possible models were identified:

1. An academic working from a university who acts as an *intermediary* (such as under the Emerging Issues Program in New Zealand or the Australia New Zealand School of Government and the Institute for Governance and Policy Analysis at the University of Canberra).

2. A senior ex-public servant working within a university (*executive in residence*) who would have relevant government connections.

3. A *chief government social researcher* (as in the UK) or *chief social scientist* working from within government with similar functions as above.

4. An *academic in residence* attached to a central agency (a recent practice in the Australian Public Service Commission) or *senior practitioner in residence* attached to a university (a recent practice at the Institute for Governance and Policy Analysis at the University of Canberra).

Certain of these models require secondments in and out of government and knowledge institutions and are premised on the assumption that this will both enhance strategic policy capability and foster trust systems. An example is the arrangement that the Australian Treasury has with the Australian National University (ANU). The Child Support Scheme has its origins in the 1980s, when a senior public servant was given six months paid leave to work at the ANU to research some complex and politicised issues around child support reform, which led to a radical tax-based collection/enforcement proposal. Indeed, a paradigm shift in policy along those lines may not have been possible without prior deep research.

The options that we have reviewed so far have dealt with demand-side challenges that face policymakers in enhancing policy capabilities. There are also challenges facing policymakers in ensuring that researchers are able to participate and engage in policy processes.

Incentives to engage in applied research

A prominent issue in discussions with academic researchers interested in public policy processes is the lack of appropriate incentive structures to undertake this activity. In most countries, academic promotions and other rewards privilege publication in international, high-impact peer-reviewed journals. Winning grants from 'gold standard' research funding bodies (such as the Australian Research Council in Australia or the UK's Economic and Social Research Council) is another key esteem indicator for promotion. There is obviously a significant tension here between the way in which universities are funded by government to reward researchers through publications and competitive research grant capture, and governments wanting to encourage more policy-relevant research.

Government-funded research bodies are beginning to be much more proactive in encouraging processes and infrastructure to support linkage and exchange activities across the academic, government and private sectors, and across disciplinary boundaries. The Australian Research Council's Linkage Program and the Research Excellence Framework in the UK, for example, aim to create researcher incentives to assist government to achieve its policy agenda (British Academy, 2008: 36; CST, 2008: 21).

The use of action-based research programmes

Action-based research refers to the production of research that has 'explanatory', 'descriptive' and 'prescriptive' objectives. It differs from applied research in two respects: first, it includes practitioners in both the production and the analysis of research findings; and, second, it aims to produce research that can immediately be integrated within decision processes. Action-based research therefore involves forging teams of academics and practitioners in collaborative, applied research teams, as distinct from the tradition of separating research from practice (eg the creation of strategic policy hubs such as Data61 in Australia).

The previous observations imply a government commitment to a fundamentally different relationship between research and policy activities, with corresponding changes to cultures, structures and processes on both sides of the current 'divide'.

Endnote

If we are to increase the policy capability of government, we need to embed a culture of demand for evidence-informed policy making at all levels. The role of leaders, both political and permanent, in this process is crucial. They can emphasise the importance of evidence by shaping their demands for policy advice in more strategic terms through placing an emphasis on the medium to long term. If leaders do not show an appetite for long-term strategic thinking and the use of evidence, then policy advisors will simply not attempt to offer such thinking, preferring to offer a 'quick' win to cope with immediate budgetary concerns rather than achieving policy goals. At the same time, researchers need to recognise the importance of translating their research findings in a meaningful way for policymakers and exploiting the opportunities that politics provides for building more efficient, effective and legitimate public policy.

This book therefore argues for the integration of the world of thought and the world of action through 'enlightened' evidence-informed practice founded on strong principles of credible evidence, verifiable theory, the use of methods that matter and strategic communication – not just because it will improve our academic understanding of policy problems, but because social progress demands it.

References

Aaberge, R. and Colombino, U. (2014) 'Labour supply models', in C. O'Donoghue (ed) *Handbook of microsimulation modelling* (Bingley: Emerald).

Ackerman, F. (2008) 'Critique of cost–benefit analysis, and alternative approaches to decision-making. A report to Friends of the Earth England, Wales and Northern Ireland'. Available at: https://www.foe.co.uk/sites/default/files/downloads/policy_appraisal.pdf (accessed 25 January 2016).

Addonizio, E.M., Green, D.P. and Glaser, J.M. (2007) 'Putting the party back into politics: an experiment testing whether election day festivals increase voter turnout', *PS: Political Science & Politics*, 40(4), pp 721–7.

Adler, M. and Posner, E. (eds) (2001) *Cost–benefit analysis: Economic, philosophical, and legal perspectives* (Chicago, IL: University of Chicago Press).

ADRN (Administrative Data Research Network) (2016) 'Homepage'. Available at: https://adrn.ac.uk/ (accessed 4 January 2016).

Ahlquist, J.S. and Breunig, C. (2012) 'Model-based clustering and typologies in the social sciences', *Political Analysis*, 20(1), pp 92–112.

Alford, J. (2009) *Engaging public sector clients: From service delivery to co-production* (Basingstoke: Palgrave Macmillan).

Anderberg, M.R. (1973) *Cluster analysis for applications* (New York, NY: Academic Press).

Anderson, C. (2008) 'The end of theory: the data deluge makes the scientific method obsolete', *Wired*, 16(7).

Anderson, C. (2009) *Free! The future of a radical price* (New York: Hyperion).

Anduiza, E., Jensen, M.J. and Jorba, L. (eds) (2012) *Digital media and political engagement worldwide: A comparative study* (Cambridge: Cambridge University Press).

Angrist, J., Bettinger, E. and Kremer, M. (2006) 'Long-term educational consequences of secondary school vouchers: evidence from administrative records in Colombia', *The American Economic Review*, 96(3), pp 847–62.

Aragaki, H.N. (2009) 'Deliberative democracy as dispute resolution: conflict, interests, and reasons', *Ohio State Journal of Dispute Resolution*, 24(3), pp 406–78.

Armstrong, H. (2015) *Machines that learn in the wild: Machine learning capabilities, limitations and implications* (London: NESTA). Available at: http://bit.ly/1TDJSyo (accessed 5 January 2016).

Arnstein, S.R. (1969) 'A ladder of citizen participation', *Journal of the American Institute of Planners*, 35(4), pp 216–24.

Atkinson, M. (1984) *Our masters' voices: The language and body language of politics* (New York, NY: Psychology Press).

Ball, M. and Smith, G. (2011) 'Ethnomethodology and the visual: practices of looking, visualization, and embodied action', in E. Margolis and L. Pauwels (eds) *The Sage handbook of visual research methods* (London: Sage), pp 392–413.

Ball, M.S. and Smith, W.H.G. (eds) (1992) *Analyzing visual data* (vol 24) (London: Sage Publications).

Ball, S. and Gilligan, C. (2010) 'Visualising migration and social division: insights from social sciences and the visual arts', *FQS: Forum Qualitative Social Research*, 11(2). Available at: www.qualitative-research.net/index.php/fqs/article/view/1486/3002

Ballas, D., Rossiter, D., Thomas, B., Clarke, G. and Dorling, D. (2005) *Geography matters: Simulating the local impacts of national social policies* (York: Joseph Rowntree Foundation).

Banks, M. (2001) *Visual methods in social research* (London: Sage).

Banzi, R., Moja, L., Pistotti, V., Facchini, A. and Liberati, A. (2011) 'Conceptual frameworks and empirical approaches used to assess the impact of health research: an overview of reviews', *Health Research Policy and Systems*, 9(26). Available at: http://dx.doi.org/10.1186/1478-4505-9-26

Barakat, S., Evans, M. and Strand, A. (2006) *Mid-term evaluation report of the National Solidarity Programme, Afghanistan* (York: World Bank).

Barakat, S., Evans, M. and Zyck, S. (2012) 'Post-conflict legitimacy: an alternative paradigm for reconstruction and stabilization', *Policy Studies*, 33(5), pp 439–54.

Bardach, E. and Patashnik, E. (2016) *A Practical Guide for Policy Analysis* (5th edn) (Los Angeles, CA: Sage).

Barnett, J., Cooper, H. and Senior, V. (2007) 'Belief in public efficacy, trust, and attitudes toward modern genetic science', *Risk Analysis*, 27(4), pp 921–33.

Barret, D. (2004) '"Photo-documenting the needle exchange": Methods and ethics', *Visual Studies*, 19(2), pp 145–9.

Bason, C. (2010) *Leading public sector innovation: Co-creating for a better society* (Bristol: The Policy Press).

Bason, C., Knudsen, S. and Toft, S. (2009) *Sæt borgeren i spil: Sådan involverer du borgere ogvirksomheder i offentlig innovation* [*Put the citizen into play: How to involve citizens and businesses in public sector innovation*] (Copenhagen: Gyldendal Public).

Bastow, S., Dunleavy, P. and Tinkler, J. (2014) *The impact of the social sciences. How academics and their research make a difference* (London: Sage).

Bates, D.W., Saria, S., Ohno-Machado, L., Shah, A. and Escobar, G. (2014) 'Big data in health care: using analytics to identify and manage high-risk and high-cost patients', *Health Affairs*, 33(7), pp 1123–31.

BBC News (2016) 'Election polling errors blamed on "unrepresentative" samples', BBC News, 19 January. Available at: http://www.bbc.co.uk/news/uk-politics-35347948 (accessed 3 March 2016).

Beebeejaun, Y., Durose, C., Rees, J., Richardson, J. and Richardson, L. (2013) '"Beyond text": exploring ethos and method in co-producing research with communities', *Community Development Journal*, 49(1), pp 37–53.

Bélanger, F. and Crossler, R.E. (2011) 'Privacy in the digital age: a review of information privacy research in information systems', *Management Information Systems Quarterly*, 35(4), pp 1017–42.

Bell, P. (2000) *GREGWT and TABLE macros users guide* (Canberra: Australian Bureau of Statistics).

Bell, P. (2001) 'Content analysis of visual images', in T. van Leeuwen and C. Jewitt (eds) *Handbook of visual analysis* (London: Sage Publications), pp 10–34.

Benoit, K. and Laver, M. (2007) 'Estimating party policy positions: comparing expert surveys and hand-coded content analysis', *Electoral Studies*, 26(1), pp 90–107.

Bergs, J., Lambrechts, F., Simons, P., Vlayen, A., Marneffe, W., Hellings, J., Cleemput, I. and Vandijck, D. (2015) 'Barriers and facilitators related to the implementation of surgical safety checklists: a systematic review of the qualitative evidence', *BMJ Quality and Safety*. Available at: http://dx.doi.org/10.1136/bmjqs-2015-004021

Berg-Schlosser, D. and Cronqvist, L. (2005) 'Macro-quantitative vs. macro-qualitative methods in the social sciences an example from empirical democratic theory employing new software', *Historical Social Research*, 30(4), pp 154–75.

Best, A. and Holmes, B. (2010) 'Systems thinking, knowledge and action: towards better models and methods', *Evidence & Policy: A Journal of Research, Debate and Practice*, 6(2), pp 145–59.

Bevir, M. and Rhodes, R. (2006) *Governance stories* (London: Routledge).

Bholat, D. (2014) *Big data and central banks* (London: Bank of England, Centre for Central Banking Studies). Available at: www.bankofengland.co.uk/research/Documents/ccbs/bigdatawriteup.pdf

Bholat, D., Hansen, S., Santos, P. and Schonhardt-Bailey, C. (2015) 'Text mining for central banks: handbook', *Centre for Central Banking Studies* (33), pp 1–19. Available at: http://eprints.lse.ac.uk/62548/ (accessed 5 January 2016).

Birkin, M., Turner, A., Wu, B., Townend, P., Arshad, J. and Xu, J. (2009) 'MoSeS: a grid-enabled spatial decision support system', *Social Science Computer Review*, 27(4), pp 493–508.

BIS (Department of Business, Innovation and Skills) *Improving access for research and policy: The Government response to the report of the Administrative Data Taskforce* (London: BIS).

BIS (2015) *Growth vouchers programme: Phase one qualitative assessment report* (London: BIS).

Blackman, T. (2013) 'Rethinking policy-related research: charting a path using qualitative comparative analysis and complexity theory', *Contemporary Social Science*, 8(3), pp 333–45.

Blackman, T., Wistow, J. and Byrne, D. (2013) 'Using qualitative comparative analysis to understand complex policy problems', *Evaluation*, 19(2), pp 126–40.

Bloom, N., Garicano, L., Sadun, R. and Van Reenen, J. (2009) 'The distinct effects of information technology and communication technology on firm organization', NBER Working Paper, No 14975.

Blyth, M. (2013) *Austerity: The history of a dangerous idea* (Oxford: Oxford University Press).

Boero, R. and Squazzoni, F. (2005) 'Does empirical embeddedness matter? Methodological issues on agent-based models for analytical social science', *Journal of Artificial Societies and Social Simulation*, 8(4), pp 1–31.

Boland, R.J. and Collopy, F. (2004) *Managing as designing* (Stanford, CA: Stanford University Press).

Booth, H. (2006) 'Demographic forecasting: 1980 to 2005 in review', Working Papers in Demography No 100, ANU.

Boston, J. (2012) 'Reflections on "New political governance in Westminster systems"', *Governance*, 25(2), pp 201–7.

Boswell J (2013a) 'Why and how narratives matter in deliberative systems', *Political Studies*, 61(3), pp 620-36.

Boswell, J. (2013b) 'Between facts and fictions: narrative in public deliberation on obesity', PhD Thesis, Australian National University.

Bourguignon, F. and Spadaro, A. (2006) 'Microsimulation as a tool for evaluating redistribution policies', *The Journal of Economic Inequality*, 4(1), pp 77–106.

Bovaird, T. (2007) 'Beyond engagement and participation: user and community co-production of public services', *Public Administration Review*, (September/October), pp 846–60.

Boyd, D. and Crawford, K. (2012) 'Critical questions for big data provocations for a cultural, technological, and scholarly phenomenon', *Information, Communication and Society*, 15(5), pp 662–79.

Bradshaw, P. (2014) *Scraping for journalists* (Kindle edn) (London: Online Journalism Blog).

Brandes, U., Kenis, P., Raab, J., Schneider, V. and Wagner, D. (1999) 'The explorations into the visualisation of policy networks', *Journal of Theoretical Politics*, 11(1), pp 75–106.

Brewer, J.D. (2013) *The public value of the social sciences* (London: Bloomsbury).

British Academy (2008) 'Punching our weight: the humanities and social sciences in public policy making', British Academy report, September.

Brown, S.R. (1980) *Political subjectivity. Applications of Q method in political science* (New Haven, CT: Yale University Press).

Brown, T. (2009) *Change by design: How design thinking transforms organizations and inspires innovation* (New York, NY: HarperCollins).

Bruner, J. (2002) *Making stories: Law, literature and life* (New York, NY: Farrar, Straus & Giroux).

Brunton, J., Thomas, J. and Graziosi, S. (2017) 'Review management through information technology', in D. Gough, S. Oliver and J. Thomas (eds) *Introduction to systematic reviews* (2nd edn) (London: Sage).

Brzinsky-Fay, C. (2007) 'Lost in transition? Labour market entry sequences of school leavers in Europe', *European Sociological Review*, 23(4), pp 409–22.

Buchanan, R. (1992) 'Wicked problems in design thinking', *Design Issues*, 8(2), pp 5–21.

Buchanan, R. (2001) 'Design research and the new learning', *Design Issues*, 17(4), pp 3–23.

Bulmer, M., Coates, E. and Dominian, L. (2007) 'Evidence-based policy making', in H. Bochel and S. Duncan (eds) *Making policy in theory and practice* (Bristol: The Policy Press).

Burn-Murdoch, J. (2013) 'Why you should never trust a data visualisation'. Available at: www.theguardian.com/news/datablog/2013/jul/24/why-you-should-never-trust-a-data-visualisation (accessed January 2015).

Burton, P. (2006) 'Modernising the policy process. Making policy research more significant?', *Policy Studies*, 27(3), pp 173–95.

Cabinet Office (2013) 'G8 open data charter and technical annex'. Available at: http://bit.ly/1lRGFxq (accessed 5 January 2016).

Cairney, P. (2016) *The politics of evidence based policy making* (Basingstoke: Palgrave Macmillan).

Cartwright, N. and Hardie, J. (2012) *Evidence-based policy. A practical guide to doing it better* (Oxford: Oxford University Press).

Chalmers, I. and Glasziou, P. (2016) 'Systematic reviews and research waste', *Lancet*, 387 (10014), pp 122–3.

Charon, J.M. and Hall, P. (2009) *Symbolic interactionism: An introduction, an interpretation, an integration* (London: Pearson).

Charrad, M., Ghazzali, N., Boiteau, V. and Niknafs, A. (2014) NbClust: an R package for determining the relevant number of clusters in a data set.

Chhotray, V. and Stoker, G. (2009) *Governance theory and practice* (Basingstoke: Palgrave Macmillan).

Christakis, N. (2013) 'Let's shake up the social sciences', *New York Times Sunday Review*, 19 July. Available at: nyti.ms/1euewoY (accessed 6 January 2016).

Clarke, J. (2005) 'New Labour's citizens: activated, empowered, responsibilised, abandoned?', *Critical Social Policy*, 25(4), pp 447–63.

Coburn, J. (2005) *Street science: Community knowledge and environmental health justice* (Cambridge, MA: MIT Press).

Commonwealth Treasury (2015) *Intergenerational report* (Canberra: Commonwealth Treasury).

Constantiou, I.D. and Kallinikos, J. (2014) 'New games, new rules: big data and the changing context of strategy', *Journal of Information Technology*, 30(1), pp 44-57. Available at: http://bit.ly/1ZNdX28 (accessed 13 January 2015).

Cook, J.D. (2008) 'Five criticisms of significance testing', Blogpost, 15 November. Available at: http://bit.ly/1PzRYGH (accessed 5 January 2016).

Crawford, K. and Schultz, J. (2014) 'Big data and due process: toward a framework to redress predictive privacy harms', *Boston College Law Review*, 55(93). Available at: http://papers.ssrn.com/sol3/papers.cfm?abstract_id=2325784

CST (Council for Science and Technology) (2008) 'How academia and government can work together', October.

Cukier, K. and Mayer-Schonberger, V. (2013) *Big data: A revolution that will transform how we live, work and think* (London: Hodder).

Cullerton, K., Donnet, T., Lee, A. and Gallegos, D. (2015) 'Using political science to progress public health nutrition: a systematic review', *Public Health Nutrition*. Available at: http://dx.doi.org/10.1017/S1368980015002712

Davies, D., Bathurst, D. and Bathurst, R. (1990) *The telling image: The changing balance between pictures and words in a technological age* (Oxford: Clarendon Press).

Davies, D.L. and Bouldin, D.W. (1979) 'A cluster separation measure', *Pattern Analysis and Machine Intelligence, IEEE Transactions on*, (2), pp 224–7.

Davies, H.T.O., Nutley, S.M. and Smith, P.C. (eds) (2000) *What works? Evidence-based policy and practice in public services* (Bristol: The Policy Press).

Davies, H., Nutley, S. and Walter, I. (2008) 'Why "knowledge transfer" is misconceived for applied social research', *Journal of Health Services Research and Policy*, 13(3), pp 188–90.

Davies, L. et al (eds) (2013) *OPAL community environment report: Exploring nature together* (London: OPAL, Imperial College).

Davies, P., Walker, A.E. and Grimshaw, J.M. (2010) 'A systematic review of the use of theory in the design of guideline dissemination and implementation strategies and interpretation of the results of rigorous evaluation', *Implement Science*, 5(14). Available at: http://dx.doi.org/10.1186/1748-5908-5-14

De Jong, G.F., Faulkner, J.E. and Warland, R.H. (1976) 'Dimensions of religiosity reconsidered; evidence from a cross-cultural study', *Social Forces*, 54(4), pp 866–89.

Dekkers, G., Keegan, M. and O'Donoghue, C. (2014) *New pathways in microsimulation* (Vienna: Ashgate).

Desgraupes, B. (2013) 'Clustering indices. Package clusterCrit for R documentation'. Available at: https://cran.r-project.org/web/packages/clusterCrit/vignettes/clusterCrit.pdf

Design Council (2009) 'Public services by design'. Available at: www.designcouncil.org.uk (accessed 24 November 2015).

Devos, K. and Zackrisson, M. (2015) 'Tax compliance and the public disclosure of tax information: an Australia/Norway comparison', *eJournal of Tax Research*, 13(1), pp 108–29.

Dice, L.R. (1945) 'Measures of the amount of ecologic association between species', *Ecology*, 26(3), pp 297–302.

Dillon, W.R. and Goldstein, M. (1984) *Multivariate analysis: Methods and applications* (New York, NY: Wiley).

Ding, C. and He, X. (2004) 'K-means clustering via principal component analysis', paper presented at the proceedings of the twenty-first international conference on machine learning.

Dobernig, K., Lobinger, K. and Wetzstein, I. (2010) 'Covering conflict: differences in visual and verbal news coverage of the Gaza crisis 2009 in four weekly news media', *Journal of Visual Literacy*, 29(1), pp 88–105.

Dodge, J. (2009) 'Environmental justice and deliberative democracy: how social change organizations respond to power in the deliberative system', *Policy and Society*, 28(3), pp 225–39.

Dodge, J., Ospina, S. and Foldy, E. (2005) 'Integrating rigor and relevance in public administration scholarship: the contribution of narrative enquiry', *Public Administration Review*, 65(3), pp 286–300.

Dolowitz, D.P. and Marsh, D. (2000) 'Learning from abroad: the role of policy transfer in contemporary policy-making', *Governance*, 13(1), pp 5–23.

Donker-Kuijer, M., De Jong, M. and Lentz, L. (2010) 'Usable guidelines for usable websites? An analysis of five e-government heuristics', *Government Information Quarterly*, 27(3), pp 254–63.

Druckman, J.N. (2011) *Cambridge handbook of experimental political science* (Cambridge: Cambridge University Press).

Dryzek, J.S. (1987) 'Discursive designs: critical theory and political institutions', *American Journal of Political Science*, 31, pp 656–79.

Dryzek, J.S. (2000) *Deliberative democracy and beyond: Liberals, critics and contestations* (Oxford: Oxford University Press).

Dumbill, E. (2012) 'What is big data?', O'Reilly radar. Available at: http://oreil.ly/1O4CGK6 (accessed 10 May 2012).

Duncan, A. and Harris, M. (2002) 'Simulating the behavioural effects of welfare reforms among sole parents in Australia', *The Economic Record*, 78(242), pp 264–76.

Dunleavy, P., Margetts, H., Bastow, S. and Tinkler J. (2006) *Digital era governance: IT corporations, the state, and e-government* (Oxford: Oxford University Press).

Dunleavy, P., Bastow, S. and Tinkler, J. (2014) 'The contemporary social sciences are now converging strongly with STEM disciplines in the study of "human-dominated systems" and "human-influenced systems"', LSE Impact of the Social Sciences blog, 20 January. Available at: http://bit.ly/1mzJodJ (accessed 6 January 2016).

Dunn, J.C. (1974) 'Well-separated clusters and optimal fuzzy partitions', *Journal of Cybernetics*, 4(1), pp 95–104.

Dunning, T. (2012) *Natural experiments in the social sciences: A design-based approach* (Cambridge: Cambridge University Press).

Durose, C. and Richardson, L. (2016) *Designing public policy for co-production: Theory, practice and change* (Bristol: The Policy Press).

Durose, C., Richardson, L., Matthews, P., Rutherfoord, R., Vanderhoven, D. and Connelly, S. (2015) *Translation as performance: Understanding boundaries between academia and policy* (Birmingham: International Research Society for Public Management [IRSPM], University of Birmingham).

Edwards, K. and Clarke, G. (2009) 'The design and validation of a spatial microsimulation model of obesogenic environments for children in Leeds, UK: SimObesity', *Social Science and Medicine*, 69(7), pp 1127–34.

Edwards, M. (2004) *Social science and public policy; narrowing the divide*, Occasional Paper No 2 (Canberra: Academy of Social Sciences).

Edwards, M. (2010) 'The researcher–policy practitioner relationship: some evidence and suggestions', in G. Bammer (ed) *Bridging the 'know–do' gap* (Canberra: ANU e-press).

Eichbaum, C. and Shaw, R. (2007) 'Ministerial advisers, politicization and the retreat from Westminster: the case of New Zealand', *Public Administration*, 85(3), pp 609–40.

Eichbaum, C. and Shaw, R. (2008) 'Revisiting politicisation: political advisers and public servants in Westminster systems', *Governance*, 21(3), pp 337–65.

Eichbaum, C. and Shaw, R. (2011) 'Political staff in executive government: conceptualising and mapping roles within the core executive', *Australian Journal of Political Science*, 46(4), pp 583–600.

Ekblom, P. (2010) 'Crime prevention, security and community safety using the 5Is framework'. Available at: http://www.palgraveconnect.com/pc/doifinder/10.1057/9780230298996 (accessed 16 December 2015).

Elliott, J.H., Turner, T., Clavisi, O., Thomas, J., Higgins, J.P.T., Mavergames, C. and Gruen, R.L. (2014) 'Living systematic reviews: an emerging opportunity to narrow the evidence–practice gap', *PLoS Medicine*, 11(2): Available at: http://dx.doi.org/10.1371/journal.pmed.1001603

Escher, T., Margetts, H., Cox, I. and Petricek, V. (2006) 'Governing from the centre? Comparing the nodality of digital governments', paper to the annual meeting of the American Political Science Association, Philadelphia, 31 August–4 September. Available at: http://www.governmentontheweb.org/access_papers.asp#J (accessed 4 January 2016).

European Union (2016) 'Protection of personal data', Directorate-General, Justice. Available at: http://ec.europa.eu/justice/data-protection/ (accessed 5 January 2016).

Evans, M. (2007) 'The art of prescription: theory and practice in public administration research', *Public Policy and Administration*, 84(2), pp 128–52.

Evans, M. (2012) *Home to work an evaluation* (Canberra: DEEWR Innovations Fund). Available at: http://www.governanceinstitute.edu.au/research/publications/recent-reports

Evans, M. (2013) *Improving services with families: A perfect project in an imperfect system* (Canberra: ACTCSD). Available at: http://www.communityservices.act.gov.au/__data/assets/pdf_file/0011/566444/Strenthening-Families-ANZOG-Evaluation.pdf

Evans, M. and Edwards, M. (2011) *Getting evidence into policymaking*, ANZSIG Insights (Canberra: Institute for Governance and Policy Analysis).

Everitt, B.S., Landau, S., Leese, M. and Stahl, D. (2011) *Cluster analysis* (5th edn) (Chichester: Wiley).

Fabian Society (2010) *Hardest to reach? The politics of multiple needs and exclusions* (London: Fabian Society).

Fahmy, S. and Kim, D. (2008) 'Picturing the Iraq War: constructing the image of war in the British and US press', *International Communication Gazette*, 70(6), pp 443–62.

Farr, J., Hacker, J.S. and Kazee, N. (2006) 'The policy scientist of democracy: the discipline of Harold D Lasswell', *American Political Science Review*, 100(4), pp 579–87.

Feldman, M., Skoldberg, K., Brown, R. and Horner, D. (2004) 'Making sense of stories', *Journal of Public Administration Research and Theory*, 14(2), pp 147–70.

Ferguson, S.T. (2013) 'Using visual methods in social science research, in M. Walter (ed) *Social research methods* (2nd edn) (South Melbourne: Oxford University Press). Available at: https://www.academia.edu/9402854/Ferguson_S._T._2013_Using_Visual_Methods_in_Social_Science_Research_Second_Edition_in_M._Walter_ed_Social_Research_Methods_Oxford_University_Press_South_Melbourne (accessed June 2015).

Figari, F., Iacovou, M., Skew, A.J. and Sutherland, H. (2011) 'Approximations to the truth: comparing survey and microsimulation approaches to measuring income for social indicators', *Social Indicators Research*, 105(3), pp 387–407.

Filsinger, E.E., Faulkner, J.E. and Warland, R.H. (1979) 'Empirical taxonomy of religious individuals: an investigation among college students', *Sociology of Religion*, 40(2), pp 136–46.

Fischer, F. and Forester, J. (eds) (1993) *The argumentative turn in policy analysis and planning* (Durham, NC: Duke University Press).

Fischer, F. and Gottweis, H. (eds) (2012) *The argumentative turn revisited: Public policy as communicative practice* (Durham, NC: Duke University Press).

Fishkin, J. (2009) *When the people speak: Deliberative democracy and public consultation* (Oxford: Oxford University Press).

FitzGerald, P.C., Shlyakhtenko, A., Mir, A.A. and Vinson, C. (2004) 'Clustering of DNA sequences in human promoters', *Genome Research*, 14(8), pp 1562–74.

Fung, A. (2006) *Empowered participation: Reinventing urban democracy* (Princeton, NJ: Princeton University Press).

Gabbay, J. and Le May, A. (2004) 'Evidence based guidelines or collectively constructed "mindlines"? Ethnographic study of knowledge management in primary care', *British Medical Journal*, 329: 1013.

Gains, F. and Stoker, G. (2011) 'Special advisers and the transmission of ideas from the policy primeval soup', *Policy & Politics*, 39(4), pp 485–98.

Gammera, N., Cherrettb, T. and Gutteridgec, C. (2014) 'Disseminating real-time bus arrival information via QR code tagged bus stops: a case study of user take-up and reaction in Southampton, UK', *Journal of Transport Geography*, 34, pp 254–61.

Ganz, M. (2011) 'Public narrative: self, us and now'. Available at: http://marshallganz.usmblogs.com/files/2012/08/Public-Narrative-Worksheet-Fall-2013-.pdf

Gardner, A. and Lowndes, V. (2016) 'Negotiating austerity and local traditions', in M. Bevir and M. Rhodes (eds) *Rethinking governance* (London: Routledge).

Gates, K. (2011) *Our biometric future: Facial recognition technology and the culture of surveillance* (New York, NY: NYU Press).

Gatto, M.A. (2015) 'Making research useful: current challenges and good practices in data visualisation', Reuters Institute for the Study of Journalism with the support of the University of Oxford's ESRC Impact Acceleration Account in partnership with Nesta and the Alliance for Useful Evidence. Available at: https://reutersinstitute.politics.ox.ac.uk/publication/making-research-useful (accessed March 2016).

Gauchat, G. (2012) 'Politicization of science in the public sphere: a study of public trust in the United States, 1974 to 2010', *American Sociological Review*, 77(2), pp 167–87.

GDS (Government Data Service) (2014) 'Anomaly detection: a machine-learning approach', Government Data Service, blog, 15 August. Available at: http://bit.ly/1oVsmcp

George, A.L. (1993) *Bridging the gap: Theory and practice in foreign policy* (Washington, DC: United States Institute of Peace Press).

Gerber, A.S. and Green, D.P. (2012) *Field experiments: Design, analysis, and interpretation* (New Haven, CT: Yale University Press).

Gerring, J. (2001) *Social science methodology: A criterial framework* (Cambridge: Cambridge University Press).

Gilson, L. and Raphaely, N. (2008) 'The terrain of health policy analysis in low and middle income countries: a review of published literature 1994–2007', *Health Policy Plan*, 23(5), pp 294–307.

Ginsberg, J., Mohebbi, M., Patel, R., Brammer, L., Smolinski, M. and Brilliant, L. (2009) 'Detecting influenza epidemics using search engine query data', *Nature*, 457, pp 1012–14.

Gleick, J. (1987) *Chaos theory: Making a new science* (New York, NY: Viking).

Glennerster, R. and Takavarasha, K. (2013) *Running randomized evaluations. A practical guide* (Princeton, NJ: Princeton University Press).

Glynn, E.F. (2005) 'Correlation "distances" and hierarchical clustering', Stowers Institute for Medical Research.

Gommerman, L. and Monroe, M.C. (2012) *Lessons learned from evaluations of citizen science programs* (Gainseville, FL: University of Florida).

Goodson, L. and Phillimore, J. (2012) *Community research for participation: From theory to method* (Bristol: The Policy Press).

Gough, D. (2007) 'Weight of evidence: a framework for the appraisal of the quality and relevance of evidence', *Research Papers in Education*, 22(2), pp 213–28.

Gough, D. (2013) 'Meta-narrative and realist reviews: guidance, rules, publication standards and quality appraisal', *BMC Medicine*, 11(22).

Gough, D., Thomas, J. and Oliver, S. (2012) 'Clarifying differences between review designs and methods', *Systematic Reviews*, 1(28).

Gough, D., Oliver, S. and Thomas, J. (2017) *Introduction to systematic reviews* (2nd edn) (London: Sage).

Government Office for Science (2012) 'Foresight. Regulatory scrutiny of algorithmic trading systems: an assessment of the feasibility and potential economic impact', Economic Impact Assessment EIA16. Available at: http://bit.ly/1RgV5Yk (accessed 4 January 2016).

Grady, J. (2008) 'Visual research at the crossroads', *Forum Qualitative Sozialforschung/Forum: Qualitative Social Research*, 9(3), 38.

Graham, I.D., Logan, J., Harrison, M.B., Straus, S.E. and Tetroe, J. (2006) 'Lost in knowledge translation: time for a map?', *Journal of Continuing Education in the Health Professions*, 26(1), pp 13–24.

Green, D.P., McGrath, M.C. and Aronow, P.M. (2013) 'Field experiments and the study of voter turnout', *Journal of Elections, Public Opinion and Parties*, 23(1), pp 27–48.

Griggs, S., Norval, A. and Wagenaar, A. (eds) (2014) *Practices of freedom* (Cambridge: Cambridge University Press).

Grimshaw, A. and Ravetz, A. (eds) (2005) *Visualizing anthropology* (London: Intellect Books).

Grönlund, K., Bächtiger, A. and Setälä, M. (eds) (2014) *Deliberative mini-publics: Involving citizens in the democratic process* (Colchester: ECPR Press).

Guardian (2012) 'Riot rumours on social media left police on back foot', 2 July. Available at: http://bit.ly/1O9SRUt (accessed 5 January 2016).

Guardian (2016) 'The NSA files'. Available at: http://www.theguardian. com/us-news/the-nsa-files (accessed 5 January 2016).

Gutmann, A. and Thompson, D. (1996) *Democracy and disagreement* (Cambridge, MA: Harvard University Press).

Hajer, M.A. (1995) *The politics of environmental discourse* (Oxford: Oxford University Press).

Hajer, M.A. and Wagenaar, H. (eds) (2003) *Deliberative policy analysis* (Cambridge: Cambridge University Press).

Haklay, M. (2013) 'Citizen science and volunteered geographic information overview and typology of participation', in D.Z Sui, S. Elwood and M.F. Goodchild (eds) *Crowdsourcing geographic knowledge: Volunteered Geographic Information (VGI) in theory and practice* (Berlin: Springer), pp 105–22.

Hale, S., John, P., Margetts, H. and Yasseri, T. (2014) 'Investigating political participation and social information using big data and a natural experiment', paper to the 2014 annual meeting of the American Political Science Association, 28–31 August.

Halkidi, M., Vazirgiannis, M. and Batistakis, Y. (2000) 'Quality scheme assessment in the clustering process'. In: D.A. Zighed, J. Komorowski and J. Żytkow (eds), *Principles of Data Mining and Knowledge Discovery*. Proceedings of 4th European Conference, PKDD 2000 Lyon, France, 13–16 September (Berlin, Heidelberg: Springer), pp 265–76

Halkidi, M., Batistakis, Y. and Vazirgiannis, M. (2001) 'On clustering validation techniques', *Journal of Intelligent Information Systems*, 17(2), pp 107–45.

Hall, P. (1992) 'The movement from Keynesianism to monetarism', in S. Steinmo, K. Thelen and F. Longstreth (eds) *Structuring politics discourse* (Oxford: Oxford University Press), pp 90–113.

Halpern, D. (2015) *Inside the Nudge Unit: How small changes can make a big difference* (London: W.H. Allen).

Hampton, G. (2004) 'Enhancing public participation through narrative analysis', *Policy Sciences*, 37(3), pp 261–76.

Han, J., Kamber, M. and Pei, J. (2011) *Data mining: Concepts and techniques* (San Francisco: Elsevier).

Harden, A. and Thomas, J. (2010) 'Mixed methods and systematic reviews: examples and emerging issues', in A. Tashakkori and C. Teddie (eds) *Handbook of mixed methods in the social and behavioral sciences* (2nd edn) (London: Sage), pp 749–74.

Harding, A. and Polette, J. (1995) 'The price of means tested transfers: effective marginal tax rates in Australia in 1994', *Australian Economic Review*, 28(3), pp 100–6.

Harding, A., Vidyattama, Y. and Tanton, R. (2011) 'Demographic change and the needs-based planning of government services: projecting small area populations using spatial microsimulation', *Journal of Population Research*, 28(2), pp 203–24.

Hardy, A.L., Pearson, L.J., Davidson, P. and Kriwoken, L. (2014) *Social analysis of sustainable tourism development as a contributor to the economic development of Tasmania* (Hobart: University of Tasmania).

Harper, D. (2002) 'Talking about pictures: a case for photo elicitation', *Visual studies*, 17(1), pp 13–26.

Haslam, S., Reicher, S. and Platlow, M. (2010) *The new psychology of leadership: Identity, influence and power* (New York, NY: Psychology Press).

Hassin, R.R., Ferguson, M.J., Shidlovski, D. and Gross, T. (2007) 'Subliminal exposure to national flags affects political thought and behaviour', *Proceedings of the National Academy of Sciences*, 104(50), pp 19757–61.

Haynes, L., Green, D.P., Gallagher, R., John, P. and Torgerson, D. (2013) 'Collection of delinquent fines: a randomized trial to assess the effectiveness of alternative messages', *Journal of Policy Analysis and Management*, 32(4), pp 718–30.

Haynes, P. (2014) 'Combining the strengths of qualitative comparative analysis with cluster analysis for comparative public policy research: with reference to the policy of economic convergence in the Euro currency area', *International Journal of Public Administration*, 37(9), pp 581–90.

Heath, L., Tindale, R.S., Edwards, J., Posavac, E.J., Bryant, F.B., Henderson-King, E., Suarez-Balcazar, Y. and Myers, J. (eds) (1994) *Applications of heuristics and biases to social issues* (New York, NY: Springer).

Hendriks, C.M. (2006) 'Integrated deliberation: reconciling civil society's dual role in deliberative democracy', *Political Studies*, 54(3), pp 486–508.

Heskett, J. (2002) *Toothpicks & logos: Design in everyday life* (New York, NY, and Oxford: Oxford University Press).

Higgins, J.P.T. and Green, S. (eds) (2011) *Cochrane handbook for systematic reviews of interventions* (Chichester: Wiley-Blackwell).

Hogan, S. and Pink, S. (2012) 'Visualising interior worlds', in S. Pink (ed) *Advances in visual methodology* (London: Sage), pp 230–47.

Holcomb, P. and Grainger, J. (2006) 'On the time course of visual word recognition', *Journal of Cognitive Neuroscience*, 18. Available at: http://neomam.com/interactive/13reasons/#sthash.mTZ5FVAs.dpuf

Hood, C.C. and Margetts, H.Z. (2007) *The tools of government in the digital age* (2nd edn) (Basingstoke: Palgrave Macmillan).

Horn, R. (1998) *Visual language: Global communication for the 21st century* (Washington DC: MacroVU, Inc).

Hoschka, P. (1986) 'Requisite research on methods and tools for microanalytic simulation models', in G.H. Orcutt, J. Merz and H. Quinke (eds) *Microanalytic simulation models to support social and financial policy* (Amsterdam: North-Holland).

Houghton, J. (2011) 'Costs and benefits of data provision', Centre for Strategic Economic Studies, Victoria University. Available at: http://ands.org.au/__data/assets/pdf_file/0004/394285/houghton-cost-benefit-study.pdf

Howard, A. (2012) 'Connecting with communities: how local government is using social media to engage with citizens', ANZSOG Institute for Governance at the University of Canberra and Australian Centre of Excellence for Local Government.

Howlett, M. (2011) *Designing public policies* (London: Routledge).

Huang, A. (2008) 'Similarity measures for text document clustering', Proceedings of the Sixth New Zealand Computer Science Research Student Conference (NZCSRSC2008), Christchurch, New Zealand, pp 49–56.

Hubbard, G., Cook, A., Tester, S. and Downs, M. (2003) 'Social expression in institutional care settings: A multimedia research document', CD-Rom Published by Department of Applied Social Science, University of Stirling.

Huffington Post (2015) 'Tim Cook says Apple will resist the new UK spying law', 11 November. Available at: http://huff.to/1OLBXRE (accessed 5 January 2016).

Huffington Post (Australia) (2015) 'Obama asks for stricter laws on data hacking and privacy', 13 January. Available at: http://huff.to/1kNL1aF (accessed 6 January 2016).

Hug, S. (2013) 'Qualitative comparative analysis: how inductive use and measurement error lead to problematic inference', *Political Analysis*, 21(2), pp 252–65.

Humphreys, M., Sanchez de la Sierra, R. and Van der Windt, P. (2012) *Social and economic impacts of Tuungane final report on the effects of a community driven reconstruction program in Eastern Democratic Republic of Congo* (London: DfID).

Hurworth, R. (2004) 'Photo-interviewing', *Qualitative Research Journal*, 4(1), pp 73–9.

Immervoll, H., O'Donoghue, C. and Sutherland, H. (1999) 'An introduction to EUROMOD', EUROMOD Working Paper 0/99, Department of Applied Economics, University of Cambridge.

Innes, J.E. and Booher, D.E. (2003) 'Collaborative policymaking: governance through dialogue', in M.A. Hajer and H. Wagenaar (eds) *Deliberative policy analysis* (Cambridge: Cambridge University Press), pp 33–59.

Ioannidis, J.P.A. (2005) 'Why most published research findings are false', *PLoS Medicine*, 2(8), e124, pp 0696–0701. Available at: bit.ly/1zzrD71 (accessed 6 January 2016).

Jakulin, A., Buntine, W., La Pira, T.M. and Brasher, H. (2009) 'Analyzing the US senate in 2003: similarities, clusters, and blocs', *Political Analysis*, 17(3), pp 291–310.

Jamal, F., Bertotti, M., Lorenc, T. and Harden, A. (2013) 'Reviewing conceptualisations of community: reflections on a meta-narrative approach', *Qualitative Research*, 15(3), pp 1–20.

Jasanoff, S. (2009) 'The essential parallel between science and democracy', *Seed Magazine*, 17 February.

Jennstål, J. and Niemeyer, S. (2014) 'The deliberative citizen: exploring who is willing to deliberate, when and how through the lens of personality', Centre for Deliberative Democracy and Global Governance, University of Canberra, Working Paper No 1.

Jensen, M.J., Jorba, L. and Anduiza, E. (2012) 'Introduction', in E. Anduiza, M.J. Jensen and L. Jorba (eds) *In digital media and political engagement worldwide: A comparative study* (Cambridge: Cambridge University Press), pp 1–15.

Jervis, P. and Richards, S. (1997) 'Public management: raising our game', *Public Money and Management*, April–June, pp 9–16.

Joachim, D. (2003) 'What is intelligence chatter, anyway?', *Slate*, blog post, 12 September. Available at: http://slate.me/1kKz6Ku (accessed 5 January 2016).

John, P. (2014) 'Policy entrepreneurship in British government: the Behavioural Insights Team and the use of RCTs', *Public Policy and Administration*, 29(3), pp 257–67.

John, P. (2017) *Field trials in political science and public policy* (New York, NY: Routledge).

John, P., Cotterill, S., Moseley, A., Richardson, L., Smith, G., Stoker, G. and Wales, C. (2011) *Nudge, nudge, think, think: Experimenting with ways to change civic behaviour* (London: Bloomsbury Academic).

John, P., Cotterill, S., Richardson, L., Moseley, A., Stoker, G., Wales, C. and Smith, G. (2013) *Nudge, nudge, think, think: Experimenting with ways to change civic behaviour* (London: Bloomsbury Academic).

Jones, M. and McBeth, M. (2010) 'A narrative policy framework: clear enough to be wrong?', *Policy Studies Journal*, 38(2), pp 329–353.

Jones, M., Shanahan, E. and McBeth, M. (eds) (2014) *The science of stories: Applications of the narrative policy framework in public policy analysis* (Basingstoke: Palgrave Macmillan).

Kallinikos, J. (2006) *The consequences of information: Institutional implications of technological change* (Cheltenham: Edward Elgar Publishing).

Kallinikos, J., Aaltonen, A. and Marton, A. (2010) 'A theory of digital objects', *First Monday*, 15(6/7). Available at: http://pear.accc.uic.edu/ojs/index.php/fm/article/view/3033/2564

Kearney, R. (2001) *On stories* (London: Routledge).

Keegan, M. and Kelly, S. (2009) *APPSIM dynamic microsimulation modelling of social security and taxation*, Working Paper 2009/14 (Canberra: National Centre for Social and Economic Modelling).

Kitchin, R. (2014a) 'Big data should complement small data, not replace them', LSE Impact of Social Sciences blog, 27 June. Available at: http://blogs.lse.ac.uk/impactofsocialsciences/2014/06/27/series-philosophy-of-data-science-.rob-kitchin/ (accessed 8 January 2015).

Kitchin, R. (2014b) *The data revolution: Big data, open data, data infrastructures and their consequences* (London: Sage).

Knobloch, K.R., Gastil, J., Reedy, J. and Walsh, K.C. (2013) 'Did they deliberate? Applying an evaluative model of democratic deliberation to the Oregon Citizens' Initiative Review', *Journal of Applied Communication Research*, 41(2), pp 105–25.

Knott, J. and Wildavsky, A. (1980) 'If dissemination is the solution, what is the problem?', *Knowledge, Creation, Diffusion, Utilization*, 1(4), pp 537–78.

Knowles, C. and Sweetman, P. (2004) 'Introduction', in C. Knowles and P. Sweetman (eds) *Picturing the social landscape: Visual methods and the sociological imagination* (London: Routledge), pp 1–17.

Koch, K., McLean, J., Segev, R., Freed, M., Berry, M., Balasubramanian, V. and Sterling, P. (2006) 'How much the eye tells the brain', *Current Biology*, 16(14), pp 1428–34.

Kress, G.R. and Van Leeuwen, T. (1996) *Reading images: The grammar of visual design* (New York, NY: Psychology Press).

Krippendorff, K. and Bock, M.A. (eds) (2009) *The content analysis reader* (London: Sage).

Kyratsis, Y., Ahmad, R. and Holmes, A. (2012) 'Making sense of evidence in management decisions: the role of research-based knowledge on innovation adoption and implementation in healthcare. Study protocol', *Implement Science*, 7(22). Available at: http://dx.doi.org/10.1186/1748-5908-7-22

Lakoff, G. (2014) 'Set theory and fuzzy sets: their relationship to natural language: interview with George Lakoff conducted by Roxanna Ramzipoor', *Qualitative & Multi-Method Research*, 12(1), pp 9–14.

Land Registry (2016) Land Registry linked open data BETA site. Available at: http://landregistry.data.gov.uk/app/hpi/

Langer, L., Tripney, J. and Gough, D. (2016) *The science of using science knowledge* (London: Alliance for Useful Evidence).

Lapenta, F. (2011) 'Some theoretical and methodological views on photo-elicitation', in E. Margolis and L. Pauwels (eds) *The Sage handbook of visual research methods* (London: Sage Publications), pp 201–13.

Larcom, S., Rauch, R. and Willems, T. (2015) 'The upside of the London Tube strikes', Centrepiece LSE, Autumn, pp 12–14. Available at: http://cep.lse.ac.uk/pubs/download/cp455.pdf (accessed 4 January 2016).

Lasswell, H. (1949) *Power and personality* (New York, NY: WW Norton).

Laswell, H.D. (1951) 'The policy orientation', in D. Lerner and H.D. Laswell (eds) *The policy sciences* (Stanford, CA: Stanford University Press).

Laswell, H.D. (1971) *A pre-view of policy sciences* (New York, NY: American Elsevier).

Lavis, J.N. (2009) 'How can we support the use of systematic reviews in policymaking?', *PLoS Medicine*, 6(11), e1000141.

Lazer, D., Kennedy, R., King, G. and Vespignani, A. (2014) 'The parable of Google Flu: traps in big data analysis', *Science*, 343, pp 1203–5.

Leadbeater, C. (2003) *The man in the caravan and other stories* (London: abebooks).

Leadbeater, C. (2004) *Personalisation through participation: A new script for public services* (London: Demos).

Li, J. and O'Donoghue, C. (2013) 'A survey of dynamic microsimulation models: uses, model structure and methodology', *International Journal of Microsimulation*, 6(2), pp 3–55.

Liabo, K., Gough, D. and Harden, A. (2017) 'Developing justifiable evidence claims from reviews', in D. Gough, S. Oliver and J. Thomas (eds) *Introduction to systematic reviews* (2nd edn) (London: Sage)

Lindblom, C. (1959) 'The science of "muddling through"', *Public Administration Review*, 19(2), pp 79–88.

Lindblom, C. (1990) *Inquiry and change. The troubled attempt to understand and shape society* (New Haven, CT: Yale University Press).

Lindblom, C. and Cohen, D. (1979) *Useable knowledge* (New Haven, CT: Yale University Press).

Liverani, M., Hawkins, B. and Parkhurst, J.O. (2013) 'Political and institutional influences on the use of evidence in public health policy. A systematic review', *PLoS ONE*, 8(10), e77404.

Lomas, J. (2005) 'Using research to inform healthcare managers' and policy makers' questions: from summative to interpretive synthesis', *Healthcare Policy*, 1(1), pp 55–71.

Lomas, J. (2007) 'The in-between world of knowledge brokering', *BMJ*, 334, pp 129–32.

Lowi, T.J. (1999) 'Frontyard propaganda', *Boston Review.*

Lowndes, V. and Madziva, R. (2016) '"When I look at this van, it's not only a van": Symbolic objects in the policing of migration', *Critical Social Policy*. Available at: http://dx.doi.org/10.1177/0261018316643949

Lowndes, V. and Roberts, M. (2013) *Why institutions matter* (Basingstoke: Palgrave).

Lucas, S.R. and Szatrowski, A. (2014) 'Qualitative comparative analysis in critical perspective', *Sociological Methodology*, 44(1), pp 1–79.

Lymer, S. and Brown, L. (2012) 'Developing a dynamic microsimulation model of the Australian health system: a means to explore the impacts of obesity over the next 50 years', *Epidemiology Research International*, Article 132392.

Lymer, S., Brown, L., Payne, A. and Harding, A. (2006) 'Development of "healthmod" a model of the use and costs of medical services in Australia', paper presented to the 8th Nordic seminar on microsimulation models, Oslo, Norway.

Lymer, S., Brown, L., Harding, A. and Yap, M. (2009) 'Predicting the need for aged care services at the small area level: the CAREMOD spatial microsimulation model', *International Journal of Microsimulation*, 2(2), pp 27–42.

Majone, G. (1989) *Evidence, argument, and persuasion in the policy process* (New Haven, CT: Yale University Press).

Mannion, O., Lay-Yee, R., Wrapson, W., Davis, P. and Pearson, J. (2012) 'JAMSIM: a microsimulation modelling policy tool', *Journal of Artificial Societies and Social Simulation*, 15(1), p 8.

Mansbridge, J., Bohman, J., Chambers, S., Estlund, D., Føllesdal, A., Fung, A., LaFont, C., Manin, B. and Marti, J.L. (2010) 'The place of self-interest and the role of power in deliberative democracy', *Journal of Political Philosophy*, 18(1), pp 64–100.

Margetts, H. (2013) 'Data, data everywhere: open data versus big data in the quest for transparency', in N. Bowles and J. Hamilton (eds) *Transparency in politics and the media: Accountability and open government* (London: IB Tauris).

Margolis, E. and Pauwels, L. (eds) (2011) *The Sage handbook of visual research methods* (London: Sage).

Martin, R. (2009) *The design of business: Why design thinking is the next competitive advantage* (Cambridge: Harvard Business Press).

Maulik, U. and Bandyopadhyay, S. (2002) 'Performance evaluation of some clustering algorithms and validity indices', *Pattern Analysis and Machine Intelligence, IEEE Transactions on*, 24(12), pp 1650–4.

Mayer, F. (2014) *Narrative politics: Stories and collective action* (Oxford: Oxford University Press).

Maynard, B.R., McCrea, K.T., Pigott, T.D., Kelly, M.S. (2013) 'Indicated truancy interventions for chronic truant students. A Campbell Systematic Review', *Research on Social Work Practice*, 23(1), pp 5-21.

McBeth, M., Shanahan, E., Arnell, R. and Hathaway, P. (2007) 'The intersection of narrative policy analysis and policy change theory', *Policy Studies Journal*, 35(1), pp 87–108.

McGinnis, J.O. (2013) *Accelerating democracy: Transforming governance through technological change* (Princeton, NJ: Princeton University Press).

Merieb, E.N. and Hoehn, K. (2007) *Human anatomy and physiology* (7th edn), Pearson International Edition. Available at: http://neomam.com/interactive/13reasons/#sthash.mTZ5FVAs.dpuf

Merton, R.K. (1949) *Social theory and social structure: Toward the codification of theory and research* (Glencoe, IL: Free Press).

Michie, S., Johnston, M., West, R., Abraham, C., Hardeman, W. and Wood, C. (2014) 'Designing behavior change interventions: the behaviour change wheel and behavior change techniques', *Annals of Behavioral Medicine*, 47, S157.

Milat, A., Bauman, A. and Redman, S. (2015) 'A narrative review of research impact assessment models and methods', *Health Research Policy and Systems*, 13(18). Available at: http://dx.doi.org/10.1186/s12961-015-0003-1

Miller, G.J. (1998) *Handbook of research methods in public administration* (vol 134) (New York: CRC Press).

Mishler, E. (1995) 'Models of narrative analysis', *Journal of Narrative and Life History*, 5(2), pp 87–123.

Mohana, J., Twigg, L., Barnard, S. and Jones, K. (2005) 'Social capital, geography and health. A small area analysis for England', *Social Science and Medicine*, 60(6), pp 1267–83.

Moher, D., Liberati, A., Tetzlaff, J., Altman, D.G. and The PRISMA Group (2009) 'Preferred reporting items for systematic reviews and meta-analyses: the PRISMA statement', *PLoS Medicine*, 6(6), e1000097.

Moja, L., Kwag, K.H., Lytras, T., Bertizzolo, L., Brandt, L., Pecoraro, V., Rigon, G., Vaona, A., Ruggiero, F., Mangia, M., Iorio, A., Kunnamo, I. and Bonovas, S. (2014) 'Effectiveness of computerized decision support systems linked to electronic health records: a systematic review and meta-analysis', *American Journal of Public Health*, 104(12), pp e12–22.

Moore, G., Crosford, B., Adams, A., Cox, T. and Sharples, S. (2008) 'The photo-survey research methods: capturing life in the city', *Visual Studies*, 23(1), pp 50–62.

Morrison, R.J. (1990) 'Microsimulation as a policy input: experience at Health and Welfare Canada', in G.H. Lewis and R.C. Michel (eds) *Microsimulation techniques for tax and transfer analysis* (Washington, DC: Urban Institute Press).

Mulgan, G. (2007) *Ready or not? Taking innovation in the public sector seriously*, Provocation 03: April (London: Nesta).

Mulgan, G. (2009) *The art of public strategy* (Oxford: Oxford University Press).

Mulgan, G. and Albury, D. (2003) *Innovations in the public sector* (London: Cabinet Office).

NEF (New Economics Foundation) (2015) *Democracy: This missing link in the devolution debate* (London: New Economics Foundation).

Neomam Studios (2015) *13 reasons why infographics are successful*. Available at: http://neomam.com/interactive/13reasons/

Newcombe, T. (2014) 'How government can unlock economic benefits from open data'. Available at: http://bit.ly/16ttVrX (accessed 26 May 2015).

Newman, I. (2014) *Reclaiming local democracy* (Bristol: The Policy Press).

Newman, J. (2005) *Remaking governance: Peoples, politics and the public sphere* (Bristol: The Policy Press).

Noblit, G. and Hare, R.D. (1988) *Meta-ethnography: Synthesizing qualitative studies* (Newbury Park, NY: Sage Publications).

Nold, C. (ed) (2009) *Emotional cartography: technologies of the self* (London: Creative Commons).

Norton, A. (2004) 'Political science as a vocation', in I. Shapiro, R.M. Smith and T.E. Masoud (eds) *Problems and methods in the study of politics* (Cambridge: Cambridge University Press), pp 67–82.

Nutley, S., Walter, I. and Davies, H. (2007) *Using evidence. How research can inform public services* (Bristol: The Policy Press).

Nye, J.S. (2008) 'Bridging the gap between theory and policy', *Political Psychology*, 29(4), pp 593–603.

O'Donoghue, C. (2014) 'Handbook of microsimulation modelling', Emerald Contributions to Economic Analysis.

Offe, C. (2009) 'Governance an empty signifier?', *Constellations*, 16(4), pp 550–62.

Oliver, A. (2013) *Behavioural public policy* (Cambridge: Cambridge University Press).

Oliver, K., Innvar, S., Lorenc, T., Woodman, J. and Thomas, J. (2014) 'Systematic review of barriers to and facilitators of the use of evidence by policymakers', *BMC Health Services Research*, 14(2). Available at: http://dx.doi.org/10.1186/1472-6963-14-2

Oliver, S., Rees, R., Clarke-Jones, L., Milne, R., Oakley, A.R., Gabbay, J., Stein, K., Buchanan, P. and Gyte, G. (2008) 'A multidimensional conceptual framework for analysing public involvement in health services research', *Health Expectations*, 11(1), pp 72–84.

Oliver, S., Liabo, K., Stewart, R. and Rees, R. (2015) 'Public involvement in research: making sense of the diversity', *Journal of Health Services Research and Policy*, 20(1), pp 45–51.

O'Mara-Eves, A., Thomas, J., McNaught, J., Miwa, M. and Ananiadou, S. (2015) 'Using text mining for study identification in systematic reviews: a systematic review of current approaches', *Systematic Reviews*, 4(5). Available at: http://dx.doi.org/10.1186/2046-4053-4-5

O'Neill, S. and Nicholson-Cole, S. (2009) '"Fear won't do it": promoting positive engagement with climate change through visual and iconic representations', *Science Communication*, 30(3), pp 355–79.

Orcutt, G. (1957) 'A new type of socio-economic system', *The Review of Economics and Statistics*, 39(2), pp 116–23.

Orcutt, G., Greenberger, M., Korbel, J. and Rivlin, A. (1961) *Microanalysis of socioeconomic systems: A simulation study* (New York, NY: Harper and Row).

Orcutt, G., Caldwell, S., Wertheimer, R., Franklin, H.S., Hendricks, G., Peabody, G., Smith, J. and Zedlewski, S. (1976) *Policy exploration through microanalytic simulation* (Washington, DC: The Urban Institute).

Osborne, S. and Brown, K. (2005) *Managing change and innovation in public service organisations* (New York, NY: Routledge).

Ospina, S. and Dodge, J. (2005) 'It's about time: catching method up with meaning', *Public Administration Review*, 65(2), pp 143–57.

Ostrom, E. (1990) *Governing the commons: The evolution of institutions for collective action* (Cambridge: Cambridge University Press).

Ostrom, E. (1996) 'Cross the great divide: co-production, synergy and development', *World Development*, 24(6), pp 1073–87.

Paine, J. (2015) 'Set-theoretic comparative methods: less distinctive than claimed', *Comparative Political Studies*, published online.

Pang, B. and Lee, L. (2008) 'Opinion mining and sentiment analysis', *Foundations and Trends in Information Retrieval*, 2(1/2), pp 1–135. Available at: http://bit.ly/1WTK93u (accessed 5 January 2016).

Parker, S. and Heapy, J. (2006) *The journey to the interface: How public service design can connect users to reform* (London: Demos).

Parkinson, J. (2006) *Deliberating in the real world: Problems of legitimacy in deliberative democracy* (Oxford: Oxford University Press).

Parkinson, J. and Mansbridge, J. (eds) (2012) *Deliberative systems: Deliberative democracy at the large scale* (Cambridge: Cambridge University Press).

Pastek, J. and Krosnick, J. (2010) 'Optimizing survey questionnaire design in political science: insights from psychology', in J.E. Leighley (eds) *The Oxford handbook of American elections and political behavior* (Oxford: OUP), pp 27–50.

Pauwels, L. (2010) 'Visual sociology reframed: an analytical synthesis and discussion of visual methods in social and cultural research', *Sociological Methods and Research*, 38(4), pp 545–81.

Pauwels, L. (ed) (2011) *The Sage handbook of visual research methods* (London: Sage Publications).

Pawson, R. (2006) *Evidenced-based policy: A realist perspective* (London: Sage).

Pawson, R. and Tilley, N. (1997) *Realistic evaluation* (London: Sage).

Pearson, L.J. and Moon, K. (2014) 'A novel method for assessing integration activities in landscape management', *Landscape and Urban Planning*, 130(October), pp 201–5.

Pedrini, S. (2014) 'Deliberative capacity in the political and civic sphere', *Swiss Political Science Review*, 20(2), pp 263–86.

Pennings, P., Keman, H. and Kleinnijenhuis, J. (2006) *Doing research in political science: An introduction to comparative methods and statistics* (London: Sage).

Percival, R., Abello, A. and Vu, Q. (2007) 'STINMOD (Static Income Model)', in A. Harding and A. Gupta (eds) *Modelling our future: Population ageing, health and aged care* (Amsterdam: Elsevier B. V.).

Perry, W.L., McInnis, B., Price, C.C., Smith, S. and Hollywood, J.S. (2013) *Predictive policing: The role of crime forecasting in law enforcement operations* (Santa Monica, CA: Rand Corporation).

Peters, B.G., Pierre, J. and Stoker, G. (2010) 'The relevance of political science', in D. Marsh and G. Stoker (eds) *Theories and methods in political science* (Basingstoke: Palgrave Macmillan), pp 325–42.

Pierce, A. (2008) 'The Queen asks why no one saw the credit crunch coming', *The Telegraph*, 5 November. Available at: http://www.telegraph.co.uk/news/uknews/theroyalfamily/3386353/The-Queen-asks-why-no-one-saw-the-credit-crunch-coming.html (accessed 3 April 2016).

Pink, S. (2013) *Doing visual ethnography* (London: Sage).

Piven, F.F. (2004) 'The politics of policy science', in I. Shapiro, R.M. Smith and T.E. Masoud (eds) *Problems and methods in the study of political science* (Cambridge: Cambridge University Press), pp 83–105.

Police UK (2016) 'Automatic number plate recognition: how police forces and other law enforcement agencies use ANPR'. Available at: http://bit.ly/1S3a3AP (accessed 5 January 2016).

Pollard, A. and Court, J. (2005) *How civil society organisations use evidence to influence policy processes: A literature review*, ODI Working Paper 249 (London: ODI).

Pollitt, C. (2006) 'Academic advice to practitioners what is its nature, place and value within academia?', *Public Money and Management*, 26(4), pp 257–64.

Preston, A. (2004) 'Designing the Australian tax system', in R.J. Boland and F. Collopy (eds) *Managing as designing* (Stanford, CA: Stanford University Press).

Radziwill, N. (2015) 'Why the ban on p-values? Understanding sampling error is key to improving the quality of research', LSE Impact of the Social Sciences blog, 12 March. Available at: http://bit.ly/1Uvxm4i (accessed 5 January 2016).

Ragin, C.C. (1987) *The comparative method: Moving beyond qualitative and quantitative strategies* (Berkeley, CA: University of California Press).

Ragin, C.C. (2000) *Fuzzy-set social science* (Chicago, IL: University of Chicago Press).

Ragin, C.C. (2009) 'Qualitative comparative analysis using fuzzy sets (fsQCA)', in B. Rihoux and C.C. Ragin (eds) *Configurative comparative methods: Qualitative comparative analysis (QCA) and related techniques* (London: Sage).

Ragin, C.C. and Davey, S. (2014) *fs/QCA*, computer program (Version 2.5) (Irvine, CA: University of California).

Rand, W.M. (1971) 'Objective criteria for the evaluation of clustering methods', *Journal of the American Statistical Association*, 66(336), pp 846–50.

Rappaport, J. (1995) 'Empowerment meet narrative: listening to stories and creating settings', *American Journal of Community Psychology*, 23(5), pp 795–807.

Rendón, E., Abundez, I., Arizmendi, A. and Quiroz, E. (2011) 'Internal versus external cluster validation indexes', *International Journal of Computers and Communications*, 5(1), pp 27–34.

Rhodes, R.A.W. and Tiernan, A. (2014) *The gatekeepers. Lessons from Prime Ministers' chief of staff* (Carlton: Melbourne University Press).

Richardson, L. (2013) 'Putting the research boot on the policy-makers' foot: can participatory approaches change the relationship between policy-makers and evaluation?', *Social Policy and Administration*, 47(4), pp 483–500.

Richardson, L. (2014) 'Engaging the public in policy research: are community researchers the answer?', *Politics and Governance*, 2(1), pp 31–43.

Richardson, L. (2017, forthcoming) 'Participatory evaluation', in B. Greve (ed) *Handbook of social policy evaluation* (Cheltenham: Edward Elgar).

Rihoux, B. and Lobe, B. (2009) 'The case for qualitative comparative analysis (QCA): adding leverage for thick cross-case comparison', in D. Byrne and C.C. Ragin (eds) *The SAGE handbook of case-based methods* (London: SAGE).

Rihoux, B., Rezsöhazy, I. and Bol, D. (2011) 'Qualitative comparative analysis (QCA) in public policy analysis: an extensive review', *German Policy Studies*, 7(3), pp 9–82, 233–4.

Robertson, H. and Travaglia, J. (2015) 'Big data problems we face today can be traced to the social ordering practices of the 19th century', LSE Impact of the Social Sciences blog, 13 October. Available at: http://bit.ly/1k9Ec3w (accessed 6 January 2016).

Robillard, M. (2009) 'What makes APIs hard to learn? Answers from developers', *IEEE Software*, November/December, pp 27–34.

Robinson, M.J. (1976) 'Public affairs television and the growth of political malaise: the case of "the selling of the Pentagon"', *American Political Science Review*, 70(2), pp 409–32.

Roe, E. (1994) *Narrative Policy Analysis: Theory and Practice*, Duke University Press.

Rose, G. (2014) 'On the relation between "visual research methods" and contemporary visual culture', *The Sociological Review*, 62(1), pp 24–46.

Ross, H. (1970) 'An experimental study of the negative income tax', PhD thesis, Department of Economics, Massachusetts Institute of Technology, USA.

Rousseeuw, P.J. (1987) 'Silhouettes: a graphical aid to the interpretation and validation of cluster analysis', *Journal of Computational and Applied Mathematics*, 20(1), pp 53–65.

Rowe, J. (2011) 'Legal issues of using images in research', in E. Margolis and L. Pauwels (eds) *The SAGE handbook of visual research methods* (London: SAGE), pp 707–22.

Ruppert, T., Bernard, J. and Kohlhammer, J. (2013) 'Bridging knowledge gaps in policy analysis with information visualization', EGOV/ePart Ongoing Research, vol 221 of LNI, GI.

Ryan, M. (2014) 'Advancing comparison of democratic innovations: a medium-N fuzzy-set qualitative comparative analysis of participatory budgeting', PhD thesis, University of Southampton, UK.

Sabatier, P. (1988) 'An advocacy coalition framework of policy change and the role of policy-oriented learning therein', *Policy Sciences*, 21(2), pp 129–68.

Sabatier, P. (2007) *Theories of the policy process* (2nd edn) (Boulder, CO: Westview).

Sabatier, P.A. and Jenkins-Smith, H.C. (eds) (1993) *Policy change and learning: An advocacy coalition approach* (Boulder, CO: Westview Press).

Sabau, A.S. (2012) 'Survey of clustering based financial fraud detection research', *Informatica Economica*, 16(1), pp 110–22.

Sackmann, R. and Wingens, M. (2003) 'From transitions to trajectories. Sequence types', in Heinz, W.R. (ed.) *Social dynamics of the life course: Transitions, institutions, and interrelations* (New York, NY: Aldine de Gruyter), pp 93–115.

Saint-Arnaud, S. and Bernard, P. (2003) 'Convergence or resilience? A hierarchical cluster analysis of the welfare regimes in advanced countries', *Current Sociology*, 51(5), pp 499–527.

Saitta, S., Raphael, B. and Smith, I.F.C. (2007) 'A bounded index for cluster validity', in P. Perner (ed.), *Machine learning and data mining in pattern recognition*, Proceedings of 5th International Conference, MLDM 2007, Leipzig, Germany, 18-20 July. Berlin, Heidelberg: Springer, pp 174–87.

Sandel, M.J. (2013) *What money can't buy: The moral limits of markets* (New York, NY: Farrar, Straus and Giroux).

Sandelowski, M., Voils, C.J., Leeman, J. and Crandlee, J.L. (2012) 'Mapping the mixed methods–mixed research synthesis terrain', *Journal of Mixed Methods Research*, 6(4), pp 317–31.

Saunders, P. and Walter, J. (2005) *Ideas and influence* (Sydney: UNSW Press).

Savage, M. and Burrows, R. (2007) 'The coming crisis of empirical sociology', *Sociology*, 41(5), pp 885–99.

Savage, M., Devine, F., Cunningham, N., Taylor, M., Li, Y., Hjellbrekke, J., Le Roux, B., Friedman, S. and Miles, A. (2013) 'A new model of social class? Findings from the BBC's Great British Class Survey experiment', *Sociology*, 47(2), pp 219–50.

Sayre, S. (1994) 'Images of freedom and equality: a values analysis of Hungarian political commercials', *Journal of Advertising*, 23(1), pp 97–109.

Schneider, C.Q. and Rohlfing, I. (2013) 'Combining QCA and process tracing in set-theoretic multi-method research', *Sociological Methods & Research*, 42(4), pp 559–97.

Schneider, C.Q. and Wagemann, C. (2012) *Set-theoretic methods in the social sciences: A guide for qualitative comparative analysis (QCA) and fuzzy-sets* (Cambridge: Cambridge University Press).

Schofield, D. (1998) *Public expenditure on hospitals: Measuring the distributional impact*, NATSEM Discussion Paper 36 (Canberra: NATSEM).

Schofield, D., Cunich, M., Shrestha, R., Passey, M., Kelly, S., Tanton, R. and Veerman, L. (2014) 'The impact of chronic conditions of care recipients on the labour force participation of informal carers in Australia: which conditions are associated with higher rates of non-participation in the labour force?', *BMC Public Health*, 14(561).

Schrodt, P.A. and Gerner, D.J. (2000) 'Cluster-based early warning indicators for political change in the contemporary Levant', *American Political Science Review*, 94(04), pp 803-817.

Schucan Bird K. and Tripney, J. (2011) 'Systematic literature searching in policy relevant, inter-disciplinary reviews: an example from culture and sport', *Research Synthesis Methods*, 2(3), pp 163–73.

Semetko, H. and Scammell, M. (2012) *The SAGE handbook of political communication* (London: SAGE Publications). Available at: http://neomam.com/interactive/13reasons/#sthash.mTZ5FVAs.dpuf

Semetko, H.A. and Valkenburg, P.M. (2000) 'Framing European politics: a content analysis of press and television news', *Journal of Communication*, 50(2), pp 93–109.

Shanahan, E.A., Jones, M.D. and McBeth, M.K. (2011) 'Policy narratives and policy processes', *Policy Studies Journal*, 39(3), pp 535–61.

Shapiro, I. (2003) 'Problems, methods, and theories, or: what's wrong with political science and what to do about it', in I. Shapiro, R.M. Smith and T.E. Masoud (eds) *Problems and methods in the study of political science* (Cambridge: Cambridge University Press), pp 9–41.

Shapiro, I. (2007) *The flight from reality in the human sciences* (Princeton, NJ: Princeton University Press).

Shea, B.J., Grimshaw, J.M., Wells, G.A., Boers, M., Andersson, N., Hamel, C., Porter, A.C., Tugwell, P., Moher, D. and Bouter, L.M. (2007) 'Development of AMSTAR: a measurement tool to assess the methodological quality of systematic reviews', *BMC Medical Research Methodology*, 7(10), PMID: 17302989. Available at: http://dx.doi.org/10.1186/1471-2288-7-10

Siegler, M.G. (2010) 'Eric Schmidt: every 2 days we create as much information as we did up to 2003', *TechCrunch*. Available at: http://tcrn.ch/1h55bnj (accessed 8 January 2015).

Simon, H. (1947) *Administrative behavior* (New York, NY: Macmillan).

Simon, H. (1991) 'Bounded rationality and organizational learning', *Organization Science* 2(1), pp 125–34.

Sinsky, C.A., Beasley, J.W., Simmons, G.E. and Baron, R.J. (2014) 'Electronic health records: design, implementation, and policy for higher-value primary care EHRs for higher-value primary care', *Annals of Internal Medicine*, 160(10), pp 727–8.

Smith, G., Noble, M., Antilla, C., Gill, L., Zaida, A., Wright, G., Dibben, C. and Barnes, H. (2004) *The value of linked administrative records for longitudinal analysis*, report to the ESRC National Longitudinal Strategy Committee (London: Economic and Social Research Council).

Smith, K.L., Moriarty, S., Kenney, K. and Barbatsis, G. (eds) (2004) *Handbook of visual communication: Theory, methods, and media* (London: Routledge).

Snowden Surveillance Archive (2016) 'Snowden documents'. Available at: https://snowdenarchive.cjfe.org/greenstone/cgi-bin/library.cgi (accessed 5 January 2016).

Solesbury, W. (2002) 'The ascendancy of evidence', *Planning Theory and Practice*, 3(1), pp 90–6.

Sørensen, T.J. (1948) *A method of establishing groups of equal amplitude in plant sociology based on similarity of species content and its application to analyses of the vegetation on Danish commons* (København: I kommission hos E. Munksgaard).

Spash, C. (2007) 'Deliberative monetary valuation (DMV): issues in combining economic and political process to value environmental change', *Ecological Economics*, 63(4), pp 690–9.

Spencer, S. (2011) *Visual research methods in the social sciences: Awakening visions* (London: Routledge).

Stevenson, H. and Dryzek, J.S. (2014) *Democratizing global climate governance* (Cambridge: Cambridge University Press).

Stoker, G. (2006a) *Why politics matters: Making democracy work* (Basingstoke: Palgrave Macmillan).

Stoker, G. (2006b) 'Public value management: a new narrative for networked governance', *American Review of Public Administration*, 36(1), pp 41–57.

Stoker, G. (2010a) 'Blockages on the road to relevance: why has political science failed to deliver?', *European Political Science*, 9, pp S72–84.

Stoker, G. (2010b) 'Translating experiments into policy', *The Annals of the American Academy of Political and Social Science*, 628(March), pp 47–58.

Stoker, G. (2012) 'In defence of political science', *The Political Quarterly*, 83(4), pp 677–84.

Stoker, G. and Taylor-Gooby, P. (2013) 'How social science can contribute to public policy: the case for a "design arm"', in P. Taylor-Gooby (ed) *New paradigms in public policy* (Oxford: The British Academy/Oxford University Press), pp 239–48.

Stoker, G., Evans, M., Li, J. and Halupka, M. (2014) 'Judging democratic politics: exploring public opinion and reform preferences', paper presented at the European Consortium for Political Research, Glasgow, UK.

Stoker, G., Peters, B.G. and Pierre, J. (eds) (2015) *The relevance of political science* (London: Palgrave).

Stone, D. (2011) *The policy paradox* (3rd edn) (New York: WW Norton).

Stoudt, B.G. and Torre, M.E. (2014) 'The Morris Justice Project', in P. Brindle (ed) *Sage cases in methodology* (London: Sage).

Strauch, R.E. (1975) '"Squishy problems" and quantitative methods', *Policy Sciences*, 6, pp 174–84.

Sturgis, P. and Allum, N. (2004) 'Science in society: re-evaluating the deficit model of public attitudes', *Public Understanding of Science*, 13(1), pp 55–74.

Sunstein, C.R. and Thaler, R.H. (2009) *Nudge: Improving decisions about health, wealth and happiness* (London: Penguin).

Susskind, L. (2006) 'Can public policy dispute resolution meet the challenges set by deliberative democracy?', *Dispute Resolution Magazine*, winter, pp 5–6.

Symon, G. and Cassell, C. (eds) (2012) *Qualitative organizational research: Core methods and current challenges* (London: Sage).

Taagepera, R. (2008) *Making social sciences more scientific: The need for logical models* (Oxford: Oxford University Press).

Tan, P.N., Steinbach, M. and Kumar, V. (2006) 'Data mining cluster analysis: basic concepts and algorithms', in *Introduction to Data Mining*. Essex: Pearson, pp. 487–567 (Chapter 8).

Tanton, R. (2011) 'Spatial microsimulation as a method for estimating different poverty rates in Australia', *Population, Space and Place*, 17(3), pp 222–35.

Tanton, R. (2014) 'A review of spatial microsimulation methods', *International Journal of Microsimulation*, 7(1), pp 4–25.

Tanton, R. and Edwards, K.L. (2013) *Spatial microsimulation: A reference guide for users* (Netherlands: Springer).

Tanton, R., Vidyattama, Y., McNamara, J., Vu, Q.N. and Harding, A. (2009) 'Old, single and poor: using microsimulation and microdata to analyse poverty and the impact of policy change among older Australians', *Economic Papers: A Journal of Applied Economics and Policy*, 28(2), pp 102–20.

Tanton, R., Vidyattama, Y., Nepal, B. and McNamara, J. (2011) 'Small area estimation using a reweighting algorithm', *Journal of the Royal Statistical Society: Series A (Statistics in Society)*, 174(4), pp 931–51.

Thiem, A. and Duşa, A. (2013a) 'QCA: a package for qualitative comparative analysis', *The R Journal*, 5(1), pp 87–97.

Thiem, A. and Dusa, A. (2013b) *Qualitative comparative analysis with R: A user's guide* (London: Springer).

Thiem, A., Baumgartner, M. and Bol, D. (2015) 'Still lost in translation! A correction of three misunderstandings between configurational comparativists and regressional analysts', *Comparative Political Studies*, published online, March.

Thomas, J. and Harden, A. (2008) 'Methods for the thematic synthesis of qualitative research in systematic reviews', *BMC Medical Research Methodology*, 8(45). Available at: http://dx.doi.org/10.1186/1471-2288-8-45

Thomas, J., O'Mara-Eves, A. and Brunton, G. (2014) 'Using qualitative comparative analysis (QCA) in systematic reviews of complex interventions: a worked example', *Systematic Reviews*, 3(67). Available at: http://dx.doi.org/10.1186/2046-4053-3-67

Thomas, J., O'Mara-Eves, A., Harden, A. and Newman, M. (2017) 'Synthesis methods for developing and exploring theory. Frameworks or themes', in D. Gough, S. Oliver and J. Thomas (eds) *Introduction to systematic reviews* (2nd edn) (London: Sage).

Tiernan, A. (2007) *Power without responsibility: Ministerial staffers in Australian governments from Whitlam to Howard* (Sydney: University of New South Wales Press).

Torgerson, D.J. and Torgerson, C. (2008) *Designing randomised trials in health, education and the social sciences: An introduction* (Basingstoke: Palgrave).

Treasury (2011) *The magenta book: Guidance for evaluation* (London: HMSO).

Uimonen, P. (2013) 'Visual identity in Facebook', *Visual Studies*, 28(2), pp 122–35.

Van Dijck, J. (2008) 'Digital photography: communication, identity, memory', *Visual Communication*, 7(1), pp 57–76.

Van Eerd, D., Cole, D., Keown, K., Irvin, E., Kramer, D., Brenneman, G.J., Kohn, M.K., Mahood, Q., Slack, T., Amick III, B.C., Phipps, D., Garcia, J. and Morassaei, S. (2011) *Report on knowledge transfer and exchange practices: A systematic review of the quality and types of instruments used to assess KTE implementation and impact* (Toronto: Institute for Work & Health).

Van Imhoff, E. and Post, W. (1998) 'Microsimulation methods for population projection', *Population, English Selection*, 10(1), pp 97–138.

Van Leeuwen, T. and Jewitt, C. (eds) (2001) *The handbook of visual analysis* (London: Sage).

Van Oostendorp, H., Preece, J. and Arnold, A.G. (1999) 'Designing multimedia for human needs and capabilities', *Interacting with Computers*, 12(1), pp 1–5.

Varian, H.R. (2014) 'Big data: new tricks for econometrics', *Journal of Economic Perspectives*, 28(2), pp 3–28.

Verganti, R. (2009) *Design-driven innovation: Changing the rules of competition by radically innovating what things mean* (Boston, MA: Harvard Business Press).

Vidyattama, Y., Rao, M. and Tanton, R. (2014) 'Modelling the impact of declining Australian terms of trade on the spatial distribution of income', *International Journal of Microsimulation*, 7(1), pp 100–126.

Von Hippel, E. (2006) *Democratizing innovation* (Cambridge, MA: The MIT Press).

Wachter, K., Hammel, E. and Laslett, P. (1978) *Statistical studies of historical social structure* (Waltham, MA: Academic Press).

Waddell, C., Shepherd, C.A., Lavis, J.N., Lomas, J., Abelson, J., and Bird-Gayson, T. (2007) 'Balancing rigour and relevance: researchers' contributions to children's mental health policy in Canada', *Evidence and Policy*, 3(2), pp 181–95.

Wagenaar, H. (2011) *Meaning in action: Interpretation and dialogue in policy analysis* (New York, NY: ME Sharpe).

Wagner, A. (2006) 'The rules of the road, a universal visual semiotics', *International Journal for the Semiotics of Law*, 19(3), pp 311–24.

Walt, S. (2005) 'The relationship between theory and policy in International Relations', *Annual Review of Political Science*, 8, pp 23–48.

Warren, M.E. and Pearse, H. (eds) (2008) *Designing deliberative democracy: the British Columbia Citizens' Assembly* (Cambridge: Cambridge University Press).

Wasserstein, R.L. and Lazar, N.A. (2016) 'The ASA's statement on p-values: context, process and purpose', *American Statistician*, March. Available at: http://amstat.tandfonline.com/doi/pdf/10.1080/0003 1305.2016.1154108

Weiss, C. (1979) 'The many meanings of research utilization', *Public Administration Review*, 39(5), pp 426–31.

Weiss, C. (1982) 'Policy research in the context of diffuse decision-making', *Policy Studies Review Annual*, 6, pp 12–36.

Weiss, C. (1998) *Evaluation* (2nd edn) (Upper Saddle River, NJ: Prentice-Hall).

Welch, V., Petticrew, M., Tugwell, P., Moher, D., O'Neill, J., Waters, E. and White, H. (2012) 'PRISMA-equity 2012 extension: reporting guidelines for systematic reviews with a focus on health equity', *PLoS Medicine*, 9(10), e1001333.

White, J.D. (1999) *Taking language seriously: The narrative foundations of public administration* (Washington DC: Georgetown University Press).

Wikipedia (2016a) 'Application program interfaces'. Available at: https://en.wikipedia.org/wiki/Application_programming_interface (accessed 15 February 2016).

Wikipedia (2016b) 'List of cognitive biases'. Available at: https://en.wikipedia.org/wiki/List_of_cognitive_biases (accessed 5 January 2016).

Wiles, R., Prosser, J., Bagnoli, A., Clark, A., Davies, K., Holland, S. and Renold, E. (2008) 'Visual ethics: ethical issues in visual research', National Centre for Research Methods Review Paper 011. Available at: http://eprints.ncrm.ac.uk/421/ (accessed June 2015).

Wiles, R., Clark, A. and Prosser, J. (2011) 'Visual research ethics at the crossroads', in E. Margolis and L. Pauwels (eds) *The SAGE handbook of visual research methods* (London: SAGE), pp 685–706.

Williamson, B. (2014) 'The death of the theorist and the emergence of data and algorithms in digital social research', LSE Impact of the Social Sciences blog, 10 February. Available at: bit.ly/1dfOvMR (accessed 6 January 2016).

Williamson, B. (2016) 'Digital education governance: data visualization, predictive analytics, and "real-time" policy instruments', *Journal of Education Policy*, 31(2), pp 123–41.

Wills, B., Berthelot, J., Nobrega, K., Flanagan, W. and Evans, W. (2001) 'Canada's Population Health Model (POHEM)', *European Journal of Cancer*, 37(14), pp 1797–804.

Wolfson, M., Madjd-Sadjadi, Z. and James, P. (2004) 'Identifying national types: a cluster analysis of politics, economics, and conflict', *Journal of Peace Research*, 41(5), pp 607–23.

Wong, G., Greenhalgh, T., Westhorp, G. and Pawson, R. (2014) 'Development of methodological guidance, publication standards and training materials for realist and meta-narrative reviews: the RAMESES (Realist And Meta-narrative Evidence Syntheses Evolving Standards) project', *Health Services and Delivery Research*, 2(30). Available at: www.ncbi.nlm.nih.gov/pubmedhealth/PMH0080879/pdf/PubMedHealth_PMH0080879.pdf

Wooding, S., Nason, E., Klautzer, L., Rubin, J., Hanney, S. and Grant, J. (2007) 'Policy and practice impacts of research funded by the Economic and Social Research Council. A case study of the Future of Work programme, approach and analysis', RAND Corporation.

Wynne, B.E. (2004) 'May the sheep safely graze? A reflexive view of the expert–lay knowledge divide', in S. Lash, B. Szerszynski and B. Wynne (eds) *Risk, environment and modernity: Towards a new ecology* (London: Sage), pp 45–80.

Yanow, D. (2000) *Conducting interpretive policy analysis* (Thousand Oaks, CA: Sage).

Zaidi, A., Harding, A. and Williamson, P. (2009) *New frontiers in microsimulation modelling* (Vienna: Ashgate).

Zedlewski, S. (1990) 'The development of the dynamic simulation of income model (DYNASIM)', in G. Lewis and S. Michel (eds) *Microsimulation techniques for tax and transfer analysis* (Washington, DC: Urban Institute Press), pp 109–36.

Index

A

a priori approach 46, 47, 49, 54, 57, 58
A/B testing 78
ABS (Australian Bureau of
  Statistics) 189, 191, 194
accessibility of data
  citizen social science 220
  latent 33, 34
  text records 154
  visual approaches 123, 135, 136
accountability 55, 214, 240, 254
Ackerman, F. 7
Action Research Collective see ARC
action-based research 269, 270
adaptive trial design 76
administrative data and big data 148,
  149–53
ADRN (Administrative Data Research
  Network) 149
agenda-setting 18, 61
agent-based models 188
aggregation of data
  cluster analysis 181
  microsimulation 187, 188, 189, 191,
    195, 196, 199, 201
  systematic reviews 46–7, 49, 57, 58
AmericaSpeaks Foundation 232
AMSTAR systematic review appraisal
  tool 62
Anderberg, M.R. 170
Anderson, Chris 162
Anglican Church 220
anonymity
  and big data 144, 151, 153, 155, 160,
    165
  and citizen social science 210
  and visual approaches 136
ANPR (Automatic Number Plate
  Recognition) 155
ANU (Australian National
  University) 268
API (Application Programming
  Interface) 152, 153

ARC (Action Research Collective) 118
Arnstein, S.R. 250
Atkinson, M. 128, 129
Atmar, Hanif 253
ATO (Australian Tax Office) 155, 156
Audubon Bird Count 208, 209
austerity 17, 81, 111, 112, 113–14
Australia, Federal Budget 199–200
Australian Bureau of Statistics see ABS
Australian Department of Human
  Services 259
Australian National University see ANU
Australian Tax Office see ATO
Automatic Number Plate Recognition
  see ANPR

B

Bardach, E. and Patashnik, E. 29, 30,
  34, 35
Bastow, S. et al (2014) 2, 3, 164, 165
Behavioural Insights Team, UK see BIT
behavioural public policy 69, 76,
  159–60, 188–91, 197, 258
Berger, Jim 157
'best practice' research 5
Bevir, Mark and Rhodes, Rod 108,
  109, 112, 120
bias 92–4, 159
bibliographic databases 50
big data 143–67
  analysis 33, 38, 39
  and citizen privacy 165
  and competition 164
  control approach 157, 158
  as cost free 147
  definition of 145–8
  digital residues 153, 154–5, 156
  disease incidence 163
  and expertise 146, 147
  importance of theory 161–3
  improved organisation and
    regulation 148
  'machine-learning' techniques 160

new methods and approaches 156–60
and nodality 147
and organisational infrastructure 146
and policymaking 163–6
and projects by big companies 166
and RCTs 81
and sources of administrative
  data 146, 148, 149–53
'toolkit' of government 146
and variables 156, 156–8
BIS (Department for Business
  Innovation and Skills), UK 148,
  149
BIT (Behavioural Insights Team),
  UK 76, 81, 159
'black box' approach 57
Blyth, Mark 111
Boolean reduction 86, 91–2
Boswell, J. 103, 104, 239
British Academy 267
British Columbia Citizens'
  Assembly 233, 237
Brzinsky-Fay, C. 181, 182
BSA (British Social Attitudes
  survey) 214
Buchanan, R. 246

C

Canberra, University of 130, 189, 268
Cartwright, N. and Hardie, J. 5
causal mechanisms 74, 79
causality 25, 158
causation 70, 79, 99, 157
CCTV cameras 155
CDC (Centre for Disease Control),
  US 163
CDCs (Community Development
  Councils), Afghanistan 253, 254,
  255
CDR (community-driven
  reconstruction) 75
CGE (Computable General
  Equilibrium) model 188
Charrad, M. et al (2014) 178, 179
childcare policy 188, 190, 194, 198,
  202
Christakis, Nicholas 161
citizen 'hactivists' 215
citizen science 37, 38, 39, 208, 209
citizen social science 207–27
  big and open data 215
  case studies 217, 218–21
  data collection 214, 215–16, 217
  impacts of 213, 214

level and type of involvement 212–17
  and policy leverage 214
  quality of research 213
  and social change 221, 222–4, 225
  uses of 209, 210, 211, 225–6
Clarke, John 110
cluster analysis 33, 169–85
  benchmarking 178
  cluster algorithms 172, 175, 176, 177
  clustering methods 175–7
  correlation distance 174
  cosine distance 174, 175
  data selection 173
  definition of 170
  Euclidean distance 173, 174
  hierarchical 172, 175, 176, 177fig
  inductive approach 169, 170, 171
  K-means algorithm 176, 177
  Manhattan distance 173, 174
  measures of distance 173
  Minkowski distance 173, 174
  partitional 172, 176, 177
  policy transfer 182
  procedures 172, 173–9
  and QCA 182
  replicability of 170
  strengths and limitations 182–3
  and theory of change 40
  uses of 179, 180–1, 182
  validity indices 177, 178–9
co-design approach 243–61
  discovery and insight 246, 247, 248t
  evaluation and scaling 248, 249
  'Improving Services with Families',
    Australia 251, 252–3
  learning environment 246, 249fig,
    251fig
  National Solidarity Programme,
    Afghanistan 253, 254–5
  'Out of Home Care' system,
    Australia 255, 256, 257
  principles and conditions 257–8
  prototyping 247, 248
  uses of 249, 250–1
cognitive biases 159
collectivism 112, 113
'community commissioning' 113
Community Development Councils,
  Afghanistan see CDCs
Community Services Directorate see
  CSD
community-driven development 253,
  254–5
Computable General Equilibrium
  model see CGE

community-driven reconstruction *see* CDR
confidentiality 136, 161, 165
configuration of data 46, 47, 57, 58
connections, social science and policy 264–70
'construction' barriers 17, 18
constructivism 9
content analysis 132, 133t, 134
contingent valuation 233
Cook, J.D. 156
co-production 31, 32, 38–9
correlational logic 86
cost–benefit analysis 7, 8, 34, 36, 37, 233, 234
Council for Science and Technology, UK *see* CST
court fines, payment of 76, 158, 159, 160
Crime Reduction Toolkit 55
crises 22
'crisp' dichotomies 95
crowd-sourced data 215, 216
CSD (Community Services Directorate), Australia 252
CST (Council for Science and Technology), UK 267

D

D-index 179
data, definition of 105
Davies–Bouldin index 179
Davies, H.T.O. et al (2000) 63
'decision fatigue' 110
'decisionism' 103
deliberative policy analysis 35, 36, 229–41
  and 'argumentative turn' 229
  and citizen involvement 39
  as conflict resolution 234, 235
  consensus 230
  and conventional policy analysis 233, 234
  deliberative forums 231, 232–3, 235, 236, 237, 239–40
  as governance aspiration 238, 239–40
  as inclusive and consequential 231
  minipublics 232, 235, 236, 237
  monetary evaluation 233, 234
  as public consultation 235–6, 237
  and reciprocity 230
  and reflection 236
  stratified random sampling 232
  time required 39

as unique source of inputs 237–8
demand 60t
Department for Business Innovation and Skills, UK *see* BIS
Desgraupes, B. 178, 179
Design Council, UK 244
development aid and passivity 75
devolution 87–8, 116, 117–18, 219
digital artefacts 146
Dillon, W.R. and Goldstein, M. 170
Dobernig, K. et al (2010) 126, 127, 128
Dodge, J. 239
Dodge, J. et al (2005) 111, 112
Dunn index 179
Durose, C. and Richardson, L. 32, 38, 39
Dynasim 196, 197

E

Economic and Social Research Council *see* ESRC
Education Endowment Foundation 55
'effectiveness' evidence 5
Eight Rungs on ladder of citizen participation 250
Ekblom, P. 31
'England's Dreaming' project 116, 117
Enterprise Nation 74
'environmental' barriers 17, 18t, 19
Escher, T. et al (2006) 153
ESRC (Economic and Social Research Council) 64
ethnography 46, 108, 109, 129
Euromod 187
evidence, definition of 105
evidence, existing 32, 33
Evidence and Policy (journal) 63
evidence-based policymaking 4, 5, 6, 15–27
  barriers to 17–22, 263–4
  limits 16–19
extended 'tools of government' framework *see* NATOE

F

Facebook 154, 155
Fahmy, S. and Kim, D. 126
Family Mosaic 217, 218–19
Farr, J. et al (2006) 24
Feldman, M. et al (2004) 104, 109
Filsinger, E.E. et al (1979) 180, 181
Fishkin, J. 235

'5i' framework 31
'found' images 136, 137
framework synthesis 57
fsQCA (fuzzy-set variety of QCA) 95–6, 97fig
funding 269
Future of Work programme, ESRC 64

G

G7 group of countries 151
Ganz, Marshall 114, 115, 116
Gardner, Alison 112
Gatto, M.A. 123
GCHQ, UK 163
Gelman, Andrew 156, 157
Ghani, Dr Ashraf 253
GMPAG (Greater Manchester Poverty Action Group) 219, 220–1
Google 163
Gosset, William 157
Government Data Service 163
GRADE health evaluation 56
Graham, I.D. et al (2006) 64
Greater Manchester 117, 118, 219, 220–1
Greater Manchester Poverty Action Group see GMPAG
growth vouchers 73, 74, 75
Gutmann, A. and Thompson, D. 230

H

'Hawthorne effects' 159
Haynes, P. 182
healthcare
  big data 149, 160, 163
  citizen social science 210
  deliberative policy analysis 239
  GRADE 56
  microsimulation 196, 197, 198
  narrative 111, 116
  QCAs 99
  RCTs 69, 81
  systematic reviews 62
Her Majesty's Revenue and Customs, UK 164
HMCTS (Her Majesty's Courts and Tribunals Service) 76
Hood, C.C. and Margetts, H.Z. 146
Horn, Robert E. 124
Howlett, M. 31
Human Services Blueprint 253
human-created systems 2, 3
human-dominated systems 2, 3

human-influenced systems 2, 3

I

IAP2 (International Association for Public Participation) 250
Ideas and influence (Saunders and Walter) 263, 264
'identity leadership' 110
'impact agenda' 65
impact, 5i framework 32
The impact of the social sciences (Bastow et al) 164, 165
implementation, 5i framework 31
implementation science 60t, 64, 65
incentive structures 16, 22–3, 264, 265, 269
inclusion criteria 49–50, 51, 53, 58
'influence diagrams' 130, 131fig, 134
information, definition of 105
informed consent 136, 137, 217
Innes, J.E. and Booher, D.E. 234, 235
innovation, pressure for 94
'institutional' barriers 17, 18t, 19
intelligence, 5i framework 31
interaction 60t
intermediaries 268, 269
International Association for Public Participation see IAP2
interpretive policy analysis 108
intervention, 5i framework 31
intervention, timing of 19, 20
involvement, 5i framework 31
Ioannidis, John 157
Irish Constitutional Convention 233

J

Jensen, M.J. et al (2012) 146

K

Kearney, Richard 109, 110
Kinsey Institute 210
Kitchin, Rob 145
Knott, J. and Wildavsky, A. 64
knowledge base, development of 59, 60t, 61
'knowledge broker' model 268, 269
knowledge-to-action cycle 43

L

Lakoff, G. 96
Land Registry, UK 152
Lasswell, Herbert 62, 106

Laswell, Harold 94, 100
latent data 33, 34
Lindblom, Charles 4, 6, 9, 106
Lindblom, Charles and Cohen, D. 10
literature review 45
living reviews, updating of data 58
local government traditions 112, 113–14
London School of Economics 266
Lowndes, V. and Roberts, M. 111

M

machine learning 151t, 153, 160, 162, 163, 164
Macmillan, Harold 22
The Magenta Book (Treasury) 81
Majone, Giandomenico 105, 110, 120
Maulik–Bandyopadhyay index 179
Mayer, Fritz 105
McBeth, M. et al (2007) 104
Merton, R.K. 62
meta-ethnography 46, 54, 57
meta-narrative reviews 62
method, selection of 29–40
  co-production 38, 39
  current knowledge 32, 33
  latent data 33, 34
  target of intervention 37–8
  time constraints 39
microsimulation modelling 187–203
  demographic models 197
  distributional results 188
  dynamic models 191
  and healthcare 197, 198
  limitations of 200, 201
  procedure 193–6
  spatial microsimulation 191, 192fig, 193, 198
  tax/transfer policies 187–96
  uses of 196, 197–8
  value of 198
  'what if' scenarios 198, 201
minipublics 232, 235, 236, 237
Mishler, E. 110
mixed-methods and components reviews 57
MRRD (Ministry of Rural Rehabilitation and Development), Afghanistan 254
multivariate analysis 156
'municipal enterprise' 113
'municipal socialism' 113

Murray-Darling Basin Futures Collaborative Research Network (University of Canberra) 130

N

N data sets 96, 97, 98, 99, 156–8
narratives 103–21
 and agency 110
 contesting 117–18, 119, 120
 definition of 104
 in healthcare 111
 generating 114, 115–16, 117, 120
 heuristics 106–7
 hybrid 113
 and identities 109, 110
 importance of 109–11
 as knowledge 112, 113–14
 limitations of 119, 120
 as meaning 112, 114, 115–16, 117
 as metaphor 112, 117–18, 119
 mobilising 112, 113–14, 120
 and policy analysis 108, 111
 and policy stability 110, 111
 and power relations 117
 'public narrative' approach 114, 115, 116
 research on 107, 108–9
 and theory of change 40
 and value 109, 111
National Centre for Social and Economic Modelling *see* NATSEM
National Health Service *see* NHS
National Information Infrastructure project 151
National Institute for Health and Care Excellence 56
NATOE (extended 'tools of government') framework 147t
NATSEM (National Centre for Social and Economic Modelling) 189, 199–200, 201
natural systems 2, 3
networks and policymaking 21
New Economics Foundation 116
'new public administration' 107, 108
Newman, Janet 110
NHS (National Health Service), UK 111, 163
Norway 165
nudges 69, 159
Nutley, S. et al (2007) 5, 8
Nye, J.S. 22, 23

O

Obama, Barack 114
observational data 58, 216, 223
Offe, C. 109
official registry of research 72
O'Neill, S. and Nicholson-Cole, S. 127
online advice 73, 74
'open data' policies 151–3
openness to new research 34–5
Orcutt, Guy 187, 188, 197
Oregon, referenda 237–8
Oregon Citizens' Initiative Review 238
Ospina, S. and Dodge, J. 109
Ostrom, Elinor 216
outliers 93–4, 176
output-oriented studies 63
overdetermination 99

P

Parkinson, J. 239
'paternalistic libertarianism' 159
Pauwels, L. 124, 125
PB (participatory budgeting)
     programmes 84–92
Pearson correlation coefficient 174
perception data 216, 217
photo elicitation 128
Piven, F.F. 25
pluralism 6–9, 31, 32
POHEM (Population Health Model),
     Canada 197, 198
policy legitimacy 36, 37
Policy Profession, UK 266
'policy-based evidence-making' 16,
     18, 103
political indifference to evidence 18
Pollitt, C. 268
Population Health Model, Canada see
     POHEM
positivism 8, 9, 108
post-positivism 108
power interdependencies 35
'predictive policing,' and big data 162
primary research 45, 46, 49, 52, 56,
     57, 61
PRISMA statement 62
problem-oriented approach 26
process-oriented studies 64
propositional logic 86
public opinion surveys 37
public value management 244

Q

Q-methodology sort 128, 129fig
QCA (qualitative comparative
     analysis) 83–101
  analysis of variation 87–8
  appropriate use of 95–9, 100
  biases 92–4
  data matrices 86, 87–9
  fuzzy-set 95–6, 97fig
  limitations 99, 100
  mechanisms 99
  multicollinearity 88
  Ns 96, 97, 98, 99
  regular data matrix 86
  software packages 101
  as time efficient 39
  truth table 88–90
  use of 33, 84, 85–6
qualitative research 46, 61
quantitative research 46, 47
quasi-experimental methods 71

R

Ragin, Charles 33, 97
Rappaport, Julian 119
randomised control trials (RCTs) 69–
     82
  analysis and writing up 73
  applications of 77–80
  basics of 71–3
  commercial use 78
  and co-design approach 249fig
  control group 78
  data collection and management 72
  embedded randomness 79, 81
  ethical guidelines 79
  examples of use of 73, 74–7
  external validity of 79
  Family Mosaic 218
  meta-analysis 79
  multiple arms and stages 70, 71
  online and big data 158
  outcome variables 72–3
  quality appraisal 54
  software 71, 72
  and specific groups 38
  and theory of change 40
  time required 39
  use of 33, 36, 58
realist approaches 55, 57, 58, 62
reciprocity 230
referenda 233, 237–8

regression analysis 47, 73, 86, 94, 98, 156, 169
relevance 23, 24–6
Religiosity Scale 180, 181
representative sample survey 37
respondent-generated imagery 129, 130, 131fig, 132
retrofitting evidence 16, 72
risk aversion 16, 93, 94
Robertson, H. and Travaglia, J. 166
Robillard, M. 153
roundtables 267, 268

S

Sabatier, Paul 109
Sackmann, R. and Wingens, M. 182
Saint-Arnaud, S. and Bernard, P. 181
sampling 8, 37, 223, 232
Sandel, M.J. 234
SAS statistical package 193
Saunders, P. and Walter, J. 263, 264
Savage, M. and Burrows, R. 161, 162
Schneider, C.Q. and Wagemann, C. 91
science, technology, engineering and mathematics see STEM subjects
score function (SF) 179
SD index 179
selection criteria 50, 51
Semetko, H.A. and Valkenburg, P.M. 181
semiotics 132, 133t, 134
Shapiro, I. 26
Shergold, Peter 263, 264
silhouette-statistic 179
Simon, Herbert 106
social sciences, relevance of 2, 3–6
Socrates 121
SOCSIM 197
spatial microsimulation modelling 191, 192fig, 193, 198
special political advisors, influence of 18
specialisation, academic 22, 23
standardised lists of questions 49
statistical analysis 47
statistical meta-analysis 47
STEM subjects (science, technology, engineering and mathematics) 161, 166
Stevenson, H. and Dryzek, J.S. 239, 240
STINMOD tax/transfer system, Australia 188, 189–95, 198, 199–200, 202

Stoker, G. and Taylor-Gooby, P. 27
Stoker, G. et al (2014) 180
Stone, Deborah 104, 105
Sunstein, C.R. and Thaler, R.H. 159
sustainability 36, 254
symbolic interactionism 132, 133t, 134
synthesis 52–5, 57, 58, 66, 256, 257
systematic reviews of research 43–67
  and cause and effect 36
  clarification of relevance of studies 49
  coding of studies 52, 53
  communication 55
  development of research question 48, 49
  dimensions of difference and developments 56–8, 59
  identification of studies 49, 50
  and knowledge-to-action cycle 43
  mapping of research literature 51–2
  nature of 45–7
  need for 44, 45
  practice of 47–56
  quality 53, 54
  recommendations and guidance 55, 56
  relevance 53, 54
  reporting standards 62
  and research production and use 59–65
  selection criteria of studies 50, 51
  synthesis of primary studies 54
  as time efficient 39
  time constraints 56

T

Tanton, R. 188
target of research 37–8
technical concerns 36, 37, 60t
text analysis 154–5
thematic synthesis 57
theory of change 40
Thiem, A. et al (2015) 86, 91
ThinkPlace 252, 253, 256
Thrasymachus 158
time constraints 21, 39, 56
topic specialism 44
Transport for London 144, 152, 164
trust and policymaking 21
  and co-production 39
'the truth' 6, 7
truth table 88–90

Tube strike, London 143–4
Tuungane, community development,
    East Congo 75–6
21st Century Town Meeting 232
24/7 media cycles 18
Twitter 154

U

underdetermination 99
unemployment 259
unintended consequences 21, 35
'useable knowledge' 10

V

values and policymaking 21
Varian, Hal 157, 160
verstehen (understanding) 106
visual approaches 123–40
  analytical issues 132–6
  artefacts 129–32, 134, 136, 137
  body language 128, 129
  challenges to 137–9
  consent, anonymity and
    confidentiality 136–7
  context 124, 125
  data analysis and interpretation 134,
    135fig
  data collection 134, 135fig
  ethical issues 136–7
  and new technology 123
  objective/subjective information 127
  strengths of 137–9
  uses of 140
  visual information 123–4
  visual methods 125, 126–31, 132
  writing and reporting 135
voice analysis 155, 156
voter turnout 76, 77

W

Wagenaar, Henk 110
Walt, S. 22, 25
Web-based surveys 37
Web-based toolkits 55
Weber, Max, concept of *verstehen*
    (understanding) 106
Web-scraping 153
Weiss, Carol 19, 63, 264
What Works Centre for Crime
    Reduction 55
White Rock Trust 221, 222–4, 225
Williamson, B. 136

Wolfson, M. et al (2004). 181
Wooding, S. et al (2007) 64
World Bank 253

Z

Ziliak, Stephen and McCloskey,
    Deirdra 157